SELECTION AND DECISION IN JUDICIAL PROCESS AROUND THE WORLD

T0373799

This book empirically explores whether and under what conditions the judicial process is efficient. Three specific issues are addressed: first, disputants self-select into litigation. Do they tend to bring cases with merit? Second, filed cases differ in their social import. Do courts select more important cases to devote more resource to? Third, courts establish precedents, affect resource allocation in the cases at hand, and influence future behaviours of transacting parties. Do courts, like Judge Posner asserts, tend to make decisions that enhance allocative efficiency and reduce transaction costs? Positive answers to the above questions attest to the efficiency of the judicial process. What drive efficient or inefficient outcomes are the selections and decisions by litigants, litigators, and judges. Their earlier selections and decisions affect later ones. Eleven chapters in this book, authored by leading empirical legal scholars in the world, deal with these issues in the US, Europe, and Asia.

YUN-CHIEN CHANG is a Research Professor at Institutum Iurisprudentiae, Academia Sinica, Taipei, Taiwan, and serves as the Director of its Empirical Legal Studies Center. He was a visiting professor at New York University, University of Chicago, University of St. Gallen, University of Haifa, Hebrew University of Jerusalem, and Erasmus University Rotterdam. Professor Chang has authored and co-authored more than ninety journal articles and book chapters. His English articles have appeared in leading journals in the world, such as the *University of Chicago Law Review*; the *Journal of Legal Studies*; the *Journal of Legal Analysis*; the *Journal of Law, Economics, and Organization*; the *Journal of Empirical Legal Studies*; *International Review of Law and Economics*; European Journal of Law and Economics among others.

SELECTION AND DECISION IN JUDICIAL PROCESS AROUND THE WORLD

Empirical Inquiries

Edited by

YUN-CHIEN CHANG

Institutum Iurisprudentiae, Academia Sinica, Taiwan

CAMBRIDGE
UNIVERSITY PRESS

CAMBRIDGE
UNIVERSITY PRESS

University Printing House, Cambridge CB2 8BS, United Kingdom

One Liberty Plaza, 20th Floor, New York, NY 10006, USA

477 Williamstown Road, Port Melbourne, VIC 3207, Australia

314-321, 3rd Floor, Plot 3, Splendor Forum, Jasola District Centre, New Delhi - 110025, India

103 Penang Road, #05-06/07, Visioncrest Commercial, Singapore 238467

Cambridge University Press is part of the University of Cambridge.

It furthers the University's mission by disseminating knowledge in the pursuit of education, learning and research at the highest international levels of excellence.

www.cambridge.org
Information on this title: www.cambridge.org/9781009305785
DOI: 10.1017/9781108694469

© Cambridge University Press 2020

First published 2020
First paperback edition 2022

A catalogue record for this publication is available from the British Library

Library of Congress Cataloging in Publication data
Names: Zhang, Yongjian, 1978– editor.
Title: Selection and decision in judicial process around the world : empirical inquires /
[edited by] Yun-chien Chang.
Description: New York : Cambridge University Press, 2019. | Includes bibliographical
references and index.
Identifiers: LCCN 2019035803 (print) | LCCN 2019035804 (ebook) |
ISBN 9781108474870 (hardback) | ISBN 9781108694469 (epub)
Subjects: LCSH: Judicial process. | Judgments. | Semiotics (Law) | Law–Methodology.
Classification: LCC K213 .S457 2019 (print) | LCC K213 (ebook) | DDC 347/.05–dc23
LC record available at https://lccn.loc.gov/2019035803
LC ebook record available at https://lccn.loc.gov/2019035804

ISBN 978-1-108-47487-0 Hardback
ISBN 978-1-009-30578-5 Paperback

Dedicated to the memory of Ted Eisenberg (1947–2014), mentor, colleague, coauthor, and friend

Everyone who was doing or entering empirical legal studies in the first golden decade (2004–2013; *JELS* was founded by Ted and others in 2004) of this approach was affected by Ted in some ways. One may take a course or workshop from Ted in the United States, Europe, or Asia. One may submit to *JELS* and receive emails from Ted. One may attend the poster sessions at CELS and encounter Ted in front of his poster. I am lucky enough to have my paths crossed with Ted's in all of the aforementioned ways and many other ways – we had conversations in the highest building in Israel, in his offices at Cornell and NYU (where he visited when I was a JSD student there), in local restaurants in Taipei, on a Hawaii beach, and elsewhere. Ted published my first-ever article in English and converted me to Stata. Both of my grandfathers died when I was little, so Ted is not only the grandfather of ELS but also a grandfather figure to me. Ted, I hope that you are still alive to see how my colleagues and I have tried to promote ELS in Asia and give us guidance.

CONTENTS

LIST OF FIGURES

LIST OF TABLES

LIST OF CONTRIBUTORS

RONEN AVRAHAM Professor of Law, Tel Aviv Faculty of Law and Lecturer, the University of Texas at Austin

YUN-CHIEN CHANG Research Professor, Academia Sinica

ALMA COHEN Associate Professor, Eitan Berglas School of Economics, Tel Aviv University

CHRISTOPH ENGEL Director, Max Planck Institute for Research on Collective Goods

MICHAEL FRAKES Professor of Law, Duke Law School

MICHAEL HEISE William G. McRoberts Professor in the Empirical Study of Law, Cornell Law School

WILLIAM HUBBARD Professor of Law, the University of Chicago Law School

ERIC LANGLAIS Professor of Economics, Université Paris Nanterre

FLORENCIA MAROTTA-WURGLER Professor of Law, NYU School of Law

MANABU MATSUNAKA Professor of Law, Nagoya University

ALESSANDRO MELCARNE Assistant Professor of Economics, Université Paris Nanterre

HATSURU MORITA Professor of Law, Tohoku University

ANTHONY NIBLETT Associate Professor and Canada Research Chair in Law, Economics, & Innovation, University of Toronto Faculty of Law

J.J. PRESCOTT Henry King Ransom Professor of Law, University of Michigan

GIOVANNI RAMELLO Professor of Economics, Università del Piemonte

ALEXANDER SANCHEZ Franklin County Municipal Court

ITY SHURTZ Lecturer, Ben-Gurion University Department of Economics

MELISSA WASSERMANN Professor of Law, University of Texas at Austin Law School

ACKNOWLEDGMENTS

This volume grows out of the symposium held in the first CELSA (Conference on Empirical Legal Studies in Asia) at Academia Sinica in Taipei, Taiwan, in June 2017. As the editor of this volume and organizer of the first CELSA, I invited all chapter contributors to present their drafts in the conference and exchange ideas. I thank all of them for traveling all the way to Taiwan and contributing their original works in this book.

I also thank the board of SELS (Society for Empirical Legal Studies) for their faith in me. It is important to bring the CELS brand to Asia, where empirical legal studies are on the rise, so that the emerging young scholars have a chance to get together and present their works alongside the more established scholars from Europe and the United States.

All of the chapters in the book (except the Introduction) have been sent to two anonymous referees for review. All authors have revised the chapters according to referee comments. The Editorial Board of *Academia Sinica Law Journal* makes the final decision to accept these book chapters. I thank the two Editors-in-Chief (qua Director of Institutum Iurisprudentiae, Academia Sinica), Tzu-Yi Lin and Chien-Liang Lee, and the Executive Editor Jimmy Chia-Shin Hsu for their generous support. Kai-Ping Chang, Ming-Hsi Chu, and Hsin-Yi Yeh provided invaluable editorial assistance.

This is my third edited volume published with Cambridge University Press. Each volume has a different focus. I thank Joe Ng, the commissioning editor, for his time and efforts during publication process. I am also grateful for the anonymous referees of the book proposal and all the chapters for the helpful suggestions. The photograph used in the book cover was taken by me in New York City when I visited NYU School of Law as a Global Professor in 2019 Spring. I thank the editorial team for making the cover design possible.

~

Introduction

YUN-CHIEN CHANG

This book empirically explores whether and under what conditions the judicial process is efficient. Three specific issues are addressed: First, disputants self-select into litigation. Priest and Klein (1984) famously point out that litigated disputes are not representative of all disputes (but compare Helland, Klerman, and Lee 2018). This book looks into one aspect of this question: *Do litigants tend to bring cases with merit?*

Second, courts establish precedents, affect resource allocation in the cases at hand, and influence future behaviors of transacting parties. *Do courts, as Judge Posner (1973a) asserts, tend to make decisions that enhance allocative efficiency and reduce transaction costs?* Put differently, does judge-made common law tend to become more efficient over time, while legislator-made statutes do not? This is one of the oldest and longest debates in law and economics (Depoorter and Rubin 2017; Garoupa and Ligüerre 2011; Mahoney 2001; Parisi 2004; Priest 1977; Rubin 1977; 1982; Zywicki 2003; Zywicki and Stringham 2010). Insufficient attention has been paid, however, to whether judge-made law in civil-law countries tends to be (or become) efficient. Private laws in civil-law countries are codified and civil-law judges usually shy away from making policies.[1] While whether judges decide cases efficiently[2] and whether private law is efficient are an intertwined question in the United States, they are distinct questions in civil-law countries. For instance, in

---

[1] Civil-law judges generally consider themselves faithful servants of lawmakers. That is, they interpret laws but do not make laws. This dichotomy, of course, is more stylized than realistic. There are always gaps in statutory text, leaving civil-law judges spacious room for interpreting their civil codes.

[2] How can researchers measure whether judges decide cases efficiently? I propose that court rulings in each case are measured against an ideal ruling favored by economic theories. If judges choose a different interpretation or make a different decision, their decisions will be labeled as inconsistent with efficiency. When such evaluations are conducted systematically, across jurisdictions, and over time, empirical evidence regarding whether judicial rulings are substantively efficient can be accumulated.

Chang (2016), I note that the revision of the property parts of the Civil Code in Taiwan generally moves toward efficiency but there are still doctrines that become less efficient. My evaluation there is purely based on the doctrines laid out by the Taiwan Civil Code. Judges often have room to interpret the doctrines in a more (or less) efficient way. This book explores judicial interpretations of statutes to examine whether and under what conditions judge-made law tends to be efficient.

Whether courts rule efficiently can be observed from two angles: one substantive, one procedural. A substantively efficient ruling or precedent, for instance, allocates resources to the right party (Chang and Lin 2017), and creates wealth-maximizing ex ante incentives for future parties.[3] By contrast, a procedurally efficient ruling or precedent minimizes the sum of two costs: direct costs and error costs. Direct costs are attorneys' fees and other litigation expenses, whereas error costs are inefficient behavior that results from inaccurate adjudication (Klerman 2015; Posner 1973b). Procedural and substantive efficiency sometimes overlap: a clearly efficiency-enhancing rule induces more settlement, thus saving attorney fees and other litigation expenses. Oftentimes, however, there is a trade-off between the two (cf. Demsetz 2011; Fennell 2013). Intuitively, it takes more effort to reach an accurate and efficient decision (cf. Kaplow 1994; Shavell and Kaplow 1996). A fast decision may create substantive inefficiency.

The second inquiry of this book, laid out above, falls along the line of substantive efficiency. The third inquiry of this book looks into one aspect of procedural efficiency: *Do courts select more important cases to devote more resource to?* Filed cases differ in their social import. Cases that affect more people and more stakes create more error costs if court adjudications are incorrect.

Positive answers to the above questions attest to the efficiency of the judicial process. What drives efficient or inefficient outcomes is selections and decisions by litigants, litigators, and judges. Their earlier selections and decisions affect later ones. For instance, if many meritless cases are brought, courts are forced to allocate less time on cases with merits, no matter how effective courts are in picking important cases. The less time judges have in any given case, the less likely it is that judges will make substantively efficient rulings.

---

[3] As Farnsworth (2016) points out, "judges may display a tacit understanding of efficiency as a value in their decisions without thinking about the term."

There are eleven chapters in this volume, and each of the three issues is explored by several chapters. Chapters 1 and 7 deal with the first issue. Chapter 1 finds that patents with more questionable validity are more likely to be the subject to litigation. Chapter 7 explores the implication of the high win rates for non-adverse appeals – that is, appeals brought by parties who win in trial courts.

Chapters 4, 6, 8, 9, and 10 focus on the second issue. Chapter 4 explores whether the lower tax courts in Canada have followed the footsteps of the Federal Court of Appeal when the latter changed the substance of a well-known doctrine. Using empirical studies of court cases in Taiwan, Chapter 6 tests the hypothesis that judges tend to avoid ex post inefficiency but not ex ante inefficiency. Chapter 8 observes that in consumer contract law, a few federal appellate or district cases dominate in terms of out-of-jurisdiction citations. Precedential cascades and superstar effects explain the phenomenon. Convergence in private law doctrines, however, may or may not produce the most efficient doctrines. Chapter 9 analyzes whether judge-made insurance discrimination law is efficient. Chapter 10 looks into the European Court of Human Rights and examines whether this Court, in setting the amount of compensation, takes into account whether the state in question usually complies with the norm – it does! The finding has strong implications for optimal deterrence theories and practice.

Chapters 2, 3, 5, and 11 deal with the third issue. Chapter 2 explores the positive impact of a court-assisted online dispute resolution system in closing easy disputes in the US Chapter 3 finds that 40 percent of the Taiwanese court caseload is debt-collection cases, and they usually end with default judgments that were rendered shortly after filing. Chapter 5 finds that Japanese courts prioritize speedy judgments. Chapter 11 looks into the German Constitutional Court, which has mandatory jurisdiction. Nonetheless, this chapter finds that the Court has found ways to filter out unimportant cases so as to devote their time to important ones.

The eleven chapters are not ordered in terms of issue similarity. Rather, they are ordered along the temporal dimension of a dispute. Chapter 1 focuses on patent validity when it is decided by an administrative agency. Chapter 2 keeps an eye on the effect of technology platforms on filing and resolving small disputes. Chapter 3 deals with case resolution and settlement in courts of the first instance. Chapter 4 explores to what extent higher court decisions affect lower courts. Chapter 5 summarizes the overall decision-making pattern in the Japanese courts. Chapter 6 uses three case studies on district court decisions to formulate a judicial behavioral theory. Chapter 7 enters into appeals. Chapter 8 compares citations among the highest courts, appellate courts, and district courts. Chapter 9 gauges the effect of decisions by higher court decisions in each US state. Chapter 10 explores a regional high court: the European Court of Human Rights. Finally, Chapter 11 looks into German Constitutional Court.

Diversity in legal fields and jurisdictions in this book is by design, not by accident. As mentioned above, while Judge Posner's original thesis focused on the common law system, later commentators extend the debate to the civil law system as well. Other related canonical articles, such as Priest and Klein (1984), have an explicit or implicit US focus. To deal with these classic issues after several decades, a broader focus is warranted and more interesting. In this volume, authors cover traditional common laws as well as statutory laws to better tease out whether the judicial system operates efficiently. More explicitly, data used in this book concern judicial systems in the United States, Canada, Germany, Japan, and Taiwan, as well as the European Court of Human Rights. The substantive issues are drawn from patent law, property law, tort law, contract law, civil procedural law, constitutional law, insurance law, tax law, corporate law, and human rights law.

References

Chang, Yun-chien. 2016. The Evolution of Property Law in Taiwan: An Unconventional Interest Group Story. Pp. 212–44 in *Private Law in China and Taiwan: Economic and Legal Anaylses*, edited by Yun-chien Chang, Wei Shen and Wen Yeu Wang. Cambridge: Cambridge University Press.

Chang, Yun-chien, and Chang-ching Lin. 2017. Do Parties Negotiate After Trespass Litigation: An Empirical Study of Coasean Bargaining. https://ssrn.com/abstract=2805063 (accessed July 8, 2019).

Demsetz, Harold. 2011. The Problem of Social Cost: What Problem? A Critique of the Reasoning of A.C. Pigou and R.H. Coase. *Review of Law & Economics* 7: 1–13.

Depoorter, Ben, and Paul Rubin. 2017. Judge-Made Law and the Common Law Process. Pp. 129–42 in *The Oxford Handbook of Law and Economics: Volume 3: Public Law and Legal Institutions*, edited by Francesco Parisi. Oxford: Oxford University Press.

Farnsworth, Ward. 2016. The Empirical Accuracy and Judicial Use of the Coase Theorem (vel non). Pp. 346–57 in *The Elgar Companion to Ronald H. Coase*, edited by Claude Menard and Elodie Bertrand. Northampton, MA: Edward Elgar.

Fennell, Lee Anne. 2013. The Problem of Resource Access. *Harvard Law Review* 126(6): 1471–531.

Garoupa, Nuno, and Carlos Gómez Ligüerre. 2011. The Syndrome of the Efficiency of the Common Law. *Boston University International Law Journal* 29: 287–335.

Helland, Eric, Daniel Klerman, and Yoon-Ho Alex Lee. 2018. Maybe There's No Bias in the Selection of Disputes for Litigation. *Journal of Institutional and Theoretical Economics* 174(1): 143–70.

Kaplow, Louis. 1994. The Value of Accuracy in Adjudication: An Economic Analysis. *Journal of Legal Studies* 23(1): 307–401.

Klerman, Daniel. 2015. The Economics of Civil Procedure. *Annual Review of Law & Social Science* 11: 353–71.

Mahoney, Paul G. 2001. The Common Law and Economic Growth: Hayek Might Be Right. *Journal of Legal Studies* 30: 503–25.

Parisi, Francesco. 2004. The Efficiency of the Common Law Hypothesis. Pp. 195–98 in *Encyclopedia of Public Choice*, edited by Charles K. Rowley and Friedrich Schneider.

Posner, Richard A. 1973a. *Economic Analysis of Law*. Boston, MA: Little, Brown.
1973b. An Economic Approach to Legal Procedure and Judicial Administration. *The Journal of Legal Studies* 2: 399–458.

Priest, George L. 1977. The Common Law Process and the Selection of Efficient Rules. *The Journal of Legal Studies* 6: 65–82.

Priest, George L., and Benjamin Klein. 1984. The Selection of Disputes for Litigation. *The Journal of Legal Studies* 13(1): 1–56.

Rubin, Paul H. 1977. Why Is the Common Law Efficient? *The Journal of Legal Studies* 6(1): 51–63.
1982. Common Law and Statute Law. *Journal of Legal Studies* 11: 205–24.

Shavell, Steven, and Louis Kaplow. 1996. Accuracy in the Assessment of Damages. *Journal of Law and Economics* 39: 191–210.

Zywicki, Todd J. 2003. The Rise and Fall of Efficiency in the Common Law: A Supply-Side Analysis. *Northwestern University Law Review* 97: 1551–634.

Zywicki, Todd J., and Edward Peter Stringham. 2010. Common Law and Economic Efficiency, available at http://ssrn.com/abstract_id=1673968 (accessed July 8, 2019).

Do Patent Law Suits Target Invalid Patents?

MICHAEL D. FRAKES AND MELISSA F. WASSERMAN

1.1 Introduction

Though there are many facets to the notion of efficiency within the litigation system, a core component to this discussion is the degree to which the system is capable of separating meritorious from non-meritorious claims and appropriately targeting legal recourse to the meritorious disputes. Of course, this sorting function need not happen entirely at trial. In fact, efficiencies may arise when some degree of screening is undertaken earlier on in the dispute process. In this chapter, we will focus on screening that takes place when deciding to file cases in the first place. Do litigants randomly pick from among a set of *potential* disputes when deciding to file, or do they pull more heavily from the legally meritorious end of the distribution among this set? What one means by the legal merits of a suit certainly differs across contexts, and it will be an especially touchy term in the patent context that we explore, as we will discuss at length below. Nonetheless, in these opening remarks, we simply raise the general question over the degree to which litigants' suit-filing decisions already begin to "weed out" some of the types of disputes to which the litigation system itself is expected to deny protection.

Our overarching methodological approach toward answering this question is rather simple and intuitive. When we compare one potential dispute with a second that is otherwise equal but that carries a higher likelihood of legal merit, do we observe a higher likelihood of a lawsuit being filed among this latter, more meritorious option? The challenge of course comes in constructing this counterfactual and in creating exogenous variation in potential claim meritocracy.

To confront this challenge, we turn our eyes to the US patent system. The goals of the patent litigation system are multifold and include enforcing legally valid patents against infringers as well as identifying legally invalid patents and returning them back to the public domain

(Lemley 2001). The importance of this latter aim is even stronger the lesser we screen along patent validity lines during the patent examination stage. Focusing specifically on this latter validity-screening aim, the litigation system could achieve certain efficiencies should it be able to target some of these invalidation efforts at the initiation of a suit, rather than reserving all of those validity-screening efforts for trial itself. In this chapter we attempt to shed empirical light on whether such efficiencies indeed arise. In other words, considering the patent litigation system's partial objective of invalidating patents that fail to meet the patentability requirements and rejecting an invalidation argument in the case of those patents that indeed merit patentability, we attempt to test for empirical evidence suggesting that screening along these patentable/unpatentable lines happens at the time of suit-filing itself.

To explore targeting of litigation efforts in this manner, our analysis will actually turn heavily on a discussion of the US Patent and Trademark Office (Patent Office). This focus on the administrative side of the patent system may be perhaps surprising at first blush given that our ultimate goal is to illuminate the degree to which the litigation system screens cases. However, there are several features of the administrative process of examining patent applications that enhance our ability to construct the necessary counterfactual for this litigation exercise. These features include: (1) random assignment of applications to different examiners,[1] (2) heterogeneity among examiners in their fundamental approaches toward applying the patentability standards, and (3) the availability of data on inventors who, together with their US patent applications, likewise seek patent protection at the European Patent Office and the Japan Patent Office, two offices with roughly similar patentability standards but that invest notably greater resources per application in applying those standards. As we will explain in greater detail in Section 1.3, these features will allow us to compare lawsuit rates among different sets of issued patents that vary – in arguably random ways – in their underlying

---

[1] Frakes and Wasserman (2017) and Lemley and Sampat (2012) interviewed a number of examiners to confirm that applications are randomly assigned within Art Units. A recent paper, however, by Righi and Simcoe (2017) documents evidence of within-Art-Unit assignments based on sub-technology specializations. However, Righi and Simcoe's analysis finds no evidence to suggest that applications are sorted across examiners based on the importance or claim breadth of the applications. As such, heterogeneity across examiners in the underlying legal validity of patents that they issue can nonetheless be attributed to examiner behavior as opposed to the assignment process at the Patent Office.

rates of legal validity. Do we then observe a higher probability of legal challenge in the face of a patent that carries a higher probability of legal invalidity? All told, the Patent Office context affords us the ability to generate exogenous sources of variation in patent validity that will allow us to explore this question. This is the good news.

The bad news with our use of the patent system to explore whether litigants screen on the base of legal merit at the time of the suit filing is that the merits of a typical patent lawsuit often exist along two dimensions: the validity/invalidity of the underlying patent and the infringement/non-infringement of the patent in question. Our methodological approach is designed to capture exogenous variation in only the validity/invalidity of the underlying patent. This is problematic in that plaintiffs arguably do not make decisions about these two aspects to the case independent of each other; on the contrary, they may make strategic choices that trade these dimensions off each other (Ford 2013). Consider a plaintiff initiating an infringement suit. Undoubtedly, a primary consideration in filing such a suit is the plaintiff's belief as to whether the potential defendant is infringing the patent in question. The likelihood the potential defendant is infringing is intimately tied to the likelihood the underlying patent is valid. A plaintiff may bolster her case for infringement by arguing for broad claim scope. By arguing for broad claim scope, however, she may weaken her case that her patent is valid. Alternatively, the plaintiff may bolster her case that her patent is valid by arguing for narrow claim scope; though by doing so, she may weaken her case for infringement. Thus, the plaintiff initiating an infringement suit often makes strategic trade-offs between validity and infringement, confounding any attempt to exploit exogenous variation along the patent validity dimension alone to speak to the targeting efficiency of the plaintiff's overall filing decision.

At first blush, one might think that by turning to an evaluation of declaratory judgment actions by non-patentee plaintiffs (seeking only to invalidate another's patent) we may be able to avoid these challenges and focus on lawsuits with a single, clean dimension of legal merit. Unfortunately, matters are perhaps not so simple in that declaratory judgment actions are very frequently filed in the face of an imminent infringement action. Arguably, with one side wishing to seek litigation to validate and enforce a patent and the other side wishing to seek litigation to invalidate a patent, patent lawsuits complicate the ability to model the decision-making process of a given party initiating litigation.

For these and related reasons, we do not attempt in this chapter to assess the case-screening efficiency of the individual decisions made by the litigants themselves. Rather, we abstract away from the individual level and evaluate the screening efficiency of the patent litigation system as a whole, where this system is the product of the joint decision-making of the plaintiffs and defendants in patent litigation (whether in an infringement action or a declaratory judgment action). Again, if a goal of this system is to help invalidate weak patents that were not previously screened out by the Patent Office, we may at least ask the more general question of whether the patent litigation system targets these invalidation efforts on more questionable patents, rather than expending considerable resources on challenging the validity of legally sound patents. To assess whether these system-level efficiencies are being attained, we test for higher rates of litigation among a set of patents with weaker underlying legal validity relative to a set of patents with stronger markers of validity. We indeed find evidence suggestive of system-level triage of this nature, with patents with more questionable validity attracting greater legal scrutiny. As such, from the validity-challenging perspective, the US patent system appears to perform some degree of sorting at the time of case filing itself, targeting its general litigation resources at more legally invalid patents. We acknowledge that this analysis does not speak directly to the degree of efficient screening along the infringement margin.

Conditional on the level of litigation actually occurring in the patent space, this finding may be encouraging from an economic efficiency perspective. We stress, however, that the system may nonetheless be globally inefficient insofar as we may be relying too much on litigation in the first place to evaluate and screen invalid patents. As with many other areas of regulation, the possibility for patent invalidity determinations exists along both ex-ante and ex-post lines. That is, we are faced with the classic dilemma: should we reserve this function for the courts (ex-post) or should we address it in advance (ex-ante) at the agency level – in this case, by rejections from patent examiners at the US Patent and Trademark Office. In a recent paper, we set forth evidence suggesting that the United States might get better bang-for-the-buck on the margin by investing more in ex-ante patent examination (Frakes and Wasserman 2017).

While the degree of screening that occurs with the initial case filing decision may be interesting in its own right, our choice to focus on the lawsuit filing stage also carries with it certain methodological advantages over analyses aiming to assess the screening performance of judges and juries. Any evaluation of sorting efficiencies of trials will be hampered by well-known selection problems stemming from, among other things, the fact that the vast majority of cases will have settled prior to the conclusion of trial itself. Those cases that see litigation through to its conclusion may not be representative of all actual cases and controversies. By maintaining a broader base of disputes within our sample, our investigation into case targeting at the case-filing stage faces fewer selection concerns of this nature.[2]

We, of course, acknowledge that our study is not immune to selection biases stemming from considerations of settlement. After all, active patent disputes and discussions between parties often arise before a case is filed. Patentees who suspect a third party is infringing their patent often contact the alleged infringer before filing a suit (Lemley et al. 2017). As a result, a patent dispute may settle even before a suit is filed. Which suits settle and which do not may also turn on factors relating in some manner to the underlying legal merits (Kessler et al. 1996; Priest and Klein 1984). While settlement dynamics are beyond the scope of this book chapter, we mention pre-filing settlement only to make the point that it may be difficult to draw strong inferences about efficient screening by individual litigants when it comes to the even earlier decision of initiating some dispute in the first place. Again, however, we proceed largely by abstracting away from the individual litigants and instead exploring efficiency considerations at a broader litigation system level. And, from this perspective, our focus starts with the suit filing itself. Moreover, from this perspective, settlement considerations of this nature do not necessarily challenge the basic question we are attempting to answer: do invalid patents attract costly lawsuits to a higher degree relative to valid patents?

The rest of this chapter proceeds as follows. In Section 1.2, we review the relevant literature. In Section 1.3, we set forth the methodology by which we will capture exogenous variation in underlying patent validity. In Section 1.4, we present the results of this screening exercise and in Section 1.5, we conclude.

---

[2] There is no question that patents subject to litigation are a highly select group that are not representative of patents more generally issued by the Patent Office. Our analysis seeks to determine whether patent litigation suits are targeting patents of more questionable validity and thus necessarily acknowledges that patents that are the subject of litigation are different-in-kind from the average patent issued by the Patent Office.

1.2   Literature Review

1.2.1   Patent Literature

Our study builds on several others that have investigated the characteristics of patents that are most strongly associated with the incidence of patent litigation. For instance, Allison et al. (2004) find that litigated patents have more claims, derive more frequently from continuation applications, and are more likely to be cited, among other characteristics that are indicative of valuable patents. While these characteristics may be predictive of litigation, they seem more likely to be correlated with the private economic value to the patent holder than the validity of the underlying patent. Thus Allison et al. arguably does not directly speak to the degree to which patent law suits sort along the validity dimension to patent law. Harhoff and Reitzig (2004) offer a similar analysis for the case of EPO post-grant opposition proceedings. Both of these studies do find an association between litigation/opposition likelihoods and the size of patent "families" – the number of patent offices where the innovation in question has received a patent. This patent family analysis is close to the EPO/JPO benchmarking approach we set forth below, though it is not necessarily tailored in the way that we suggest to create a proxy for patent validity.[3]

Closest to the present analysis is arguably our prior work (Frakes and Wasserman 2017), in which we explored the impact on examination practices of decreasing the amount of time extended to examiners to review applications. Given that examiners are legally expected to allow applications should they not have the time or ability to find and articulate bases of rejections, we theorized that binding time constraints may leave examiners in a position where they must grant more patents and where those marginal patent grants are of marginally more questionable validity. To execute that analysis, we identified time allocation decreases by tracking individual examiners throughout the course of certain promotions that carry with them heightened workload expectations. We found that examination time decreases were associated with (1) higher grant rates and (2) the issuance of lower quality patents on the margin. This provided us an opportunity to compare litigation rates for patents that should not have been issued but that were issued with patents that were

---

[3] For related studies, see also Chien (2011) and Lanjouw and Schankerman (2001).

rightfully issued. We found that the former (invalid) patents were more likely to wind up in litigation.

The analysis in Frakes and Wasserman (2017) focus on a particular characteristic of the patent examination process – time allocations – that contributes to greater examiner leniency and that provides a methodological basis by which to test whether an exogenous increase in the likelihood that an issued patent is invalid leads to a higher likelihood of litigation for that issued patent. In the present chapter, we simply aim to generalize that prior analysis beyond the context of that single feature of the examination process and to more generally explore how the issuance of invalid patents resulting from lenient examiners will lead to higher litigation rates.[4]

Likewise related to the present study is Feng and Jaravel (2016). They employ a similar methodology – drawing on random assignment and examiner heterogeneity – to explore the characteristics of examiners whose patents wind up being purchased by non-practicing entities (NPEs) (in an effort to mediate the debate over the benevolent or malevolent nature of NPE). As part of the many estimates they derive in this effort, they do show a positive relationship between an examiner's overall grant rate and the likelihood of litigation. However, as their paper was not aiming to explore the screening analysis motivating our own investigation, they do not fully develop those particular findings. For instance, Feng and Jaravel do not consider the particular instrumental variables approach set forth below to derive an unbiased effect of patent validity on the likelihood of litigation.

1.2.2   Litigation Literature Generally

Our research into the targeting efficiency of the filing of patent lawsuits is also related to a larger literature on whether civil lawsuits in general target meritorious claims at the filing stage. While we do not attempt to conduct a full review of these studies in this background, we do wish to make note of similar studies in the context of one area of civil litigation that has received considerable attention by the empirical legal studies community, especially regarding questions of this nature: medical malpractice litigation. In a fascinating and influential publication in the *New England Journal of Medicine*, David Studdert and colleagues (2006)

---

[4] Tu (2014) similarly found evidence that senior examiners issue patents that are more likely to wind up in litigation.

tasked trained physician experts with reviewing over 1,400 closed medical malpractice claims to determine, among other things, if those claims involved verifiable medical injuries and physician errors. They found that 3 percent of closed claims involved no injuries while roughly 37 percent involved no errors, with the implication being that plaintiffs filing medical malpractice suits are more likely than not to focus their efforts on situations in which they have a strong claim for recourse.

Of course, it is not surprising that some meaningful amount of non-meritorious claims are filed to the extent that one key role of the litigation system is to help uncover facts that may not have otherwise been revealed (especially in the medical context where concerns have often been raised that medical providers enter a mode of silence after iatrogenic injuries arise). At the same time, it is also not surprising that malpractice plaintiffs and their attorneys are, even at the stage of filing, focusing their efforts on claims in which they can make out successful malpractice arguments. After all, malpractice plaintiffs' attorneys are customarily compensated on a contingency fee basis, leaving them inclined to be selective in the few cases that they choose to accept. For a thorough review of relevant studies, see Hyman and Silver (2006).

1.3 Background, Methodology, and Data

1.3.1 Background

Every patent application filed with the US Patent and Trademark Office ("Patent Office") contains a specification, which describes the invention, and a set of claims that defines the metes and bounds of the legal rights the applicant is seeking. After arriving at the Patent Office, the application is routed to an Art Unit, an administrative unit within the Patent Office consisting of a group of eight to fifteen patent examiners who review applications in the same technological field. Upon arrival at the Art Unit, the Supervisory Patent Examiner (SPE) of that Art Unit randomly assigns the application to a specific examiner.[5] The assigned

---

[5] SPEs may sometimes make non-random assignments, but in those instances, they do not do so based on any characteristic related to the legal validity of the application but instead on the backlog of applications among the examiners in the Art Unit (Lemley and Sampat, 2012). In a prior piece (Frakes and Wasserman 2017), we conducted a series of telephone interviews with former SPEs to confirm these details of patent examination assignment. Our interviews further substantiated that SPEs do not make any substantive evaluation of an application before assigning it to a particular examiner.

examiner then assesses the patentability of the invention based on the criteria outlined in the Patent Act – e.g., the examiner assesses whether the claimed invention does not involve statutory subject matter, whether the invention is not useful or that the application fails to satisfy the disclosure requirements, whether the invention is obvious or whether the invention lacks novelty.

Though the patent examination process is relatively structured, examiners are granted considerable discretion on how they approach the process (Cockburn et al. 2003). Not surprisingly, in the face of this discretion, examiners have been shown to exhibit a strong degree of heterogeneity in practices, especially in their application of the patentability standards and the ultimate degree to which they allow applications.[6]

1.3.2   Methodology

The essence of our empirical approach is to embrace both the heterogeneity in permissiveness across examiners and the fact that applications are randomly assigned to examiners. Together, these two features of the US patent examination system create an exogenous source of variation in examiner leniency, which in turn opens up the possibility for an exogenous source of variation in the underlying legal validity of patents. In other words, by comparing a patent issued by a high grant-rate/permissive examiner with a patent issued by a low grant-rate/restrictive examiner, we have the ability to compare certain litigation outcomes for a patent that, with a higher likelihood, should not have been issued in the first place but that was nonetheless issued with the litigation outcomes for a patent on stronger legal grounds. To approach this comparison more comprehensively and to assess whether the litigation system targets invalid patents, we consider a sample of patents issued by the Patent Office and estimate the degree to which the likelihood of a given patent ultimately being challenged in court is associated with the mean grant rate of the examiner assigned to the given application, where this overall grant rate is calculated leaving out the influence of the given application. More specifically, we estimate:

$$Asserted_{it} = \alpha + \lambda_{k,t} + \beta_1 Examiner\_Grant\_Rate_{et} + [\beta_2 X_{it}] + \varepsilon_{it}$$

---

[6] Studies documenting examiner heterogeneity include Cockburn et al. (2003), Frakes and Wasserman (2017), Lemley and Sampat (2012), Lichtman (2004), and Mann (2014).

where t denotes the year in which the patent was granted by the Patent Office, k denotes the Art Unit in which the application was reviewed, and e denotes the examiner.[7] Art-unit-by-year fixed effects are captured by $\lambda_{k,t}$ and are necessary to ensure that the leave-one-out grant-rate is truly random considering that application assignments are randomized at a point in time within art units (Feng and Jaravel 2016). With this inclusion, $E(\varepsilon_{it}|\lambda_{k,t}) = 0$, in which event β_1 captures an unbiased association between an examiner's granting propensity and the likelihood that any patent that she issues will end up in litigation.[8] In other words, with art-unit-by-year fixed effects, the examiner's leave one-out grant rate can be taken as exogenous to any unobserved characteristic of the patent that might otherwise explain its likelihood of being the subject of litigation. This specification is essentially the reduced form of an instrumental variables (IV) regression of the incidence of a patent being asserted in litigation on the underlying legal validity of that patent, where the patent's validity is instrumented by the leave-one-out grant-rate of the associated examiner.[9] Below, we will actually estimate that IV specification. We present the reduced form, however, as our primary analysis given that the full IV specification can only be estimated on a restricted subsample of patents that are part of triadic patent "families" (with only 268,430 applicable patents in the relevant analytical sample), whereas the reduced form specification can be estimated over our whole sample of issued patents (with 981,765 patents in the relevant analytical sample).

A key assumption of this approach is that examiners with higher grant rates will indeed issue, on average, more legally invalid patents. Despite the reasonableness of this assumption in light of the random assignment of applications to examiners, we attempt to validate it by developing a metric indicative of patent validity and estimating the relationship between this validity metric and the leave-one-out examiner grant rate.

---

[7] To account for autocorrelation in unobservables within Art Units over time, we cluster the standard errors at the Art-Unit level.

[8] In some specification checks, we also include various application-level characteristics as controls, X_{it}.

[9] In this spirit, this design is similar to recent studies using random assignment and examiner heterogeneity in grant rates to assess the impact of patent rights on various outcomes, such as follow-on innovation (Sampat and Williams 2015), receipt of venture capital and other outcomes by start-up companies (Farre-Mensa et al. 2017), and inventor mobility (Melero et al. 2017).

For these purposes, we follow Frakes and Wasserman (2017) and Lemley and Sampat (2012) and exploit the fact that US applicants often file for patent protection in the European Patent Office (EPO) and the Japan Patent Office (JPO), two foreign offices with roughly similar patentability requirements but that invest substantially more per application in the examination process relative to the US Patent Office. With this in mind, when considering a set of patents issued by the US Patent Office, we may flag those of more questionable validity by determining whether they are rejected by the EPO and/or JPO. To use the strongest validity benchmark, our analysis below will attempt to flag valid patents issued by the United States by looking at those allowed by both of these foreign patent offices. Accordingly, to execute this validation exercise, we estimate specifications similar to Equation (1) above, but restricting the sample to those issued patents in which the relevant US applicant likewise sought protection at the EPO and JPO and using the incidence of allowances at these foreign offices as the dependent variable.

As already previewed, having validated the mapping of higher examiner grant rates onto the spectrum of underlying legal validity of issued patents, we also turn to an IV specification where we estimate the relationship between an issued patent being asserted at some point in litigation and our constructed validity measure – the incidence of the patent likewise being granted at both the EPO and JPO. We instrument this validity measure with the leave-one-out grant rate of the examiner (discussed above). The IV specification arguably provides us with a set of results that are more easily interpreted than the reduced form specification discussed above. Put simply, the estimated impact of patent validity on litigation likelihoods is more immediately helpful for policy discussions than the estimated impact of examiner grant rates on litigation likelihoods. Of course, we acknowledge that this IV implementation can only be estimated on a more restricted sample (of patents that are part of triadic patent families).

We acknowledge one limitation of this approach at the outset. We are effectively identifying the impact of examiner leniency on the incidence of litigation only among the subgroup of patents whose allowance was affected by that leniency (Farre-Mensa et al. 2017). Patents with the strongest degree of legal validity and the weakest degree of legal validity would likely be treated the same by all examiners and are thus not likely to be sensitive to examiner leniency fluctuations. Our approach will not capture the difference in litigation rates between these two groups and we caution that our analysis should not be generalized as such. On the contrary, our identification strategy relies upon the subgroup of patents wherein the leniency of an examiner matters – those patents with arguably questionable validity.

1.3.3   Data

To conduct this analysis, we rely on the analytical dataset that we constructed in a previous analysis (Frakes and Wasserman 2017). At its core, this data consists of individual application level records from the Patent Office's Patent Application Information Retrieval (PAIR) database. Specifically, we collected microlevel application data on approximately 1.4 million utility patent applications that were filed on or after March 2001 and that reached a final disposition – i.e., excluding ongoing applications – by July 2012. The data contain a number of characteristics and outcomes associated with the application, including, importantly, the name of the associated patent examiner. Our analysis primarily focuses on the set of the patents that issue from these applications (981,765 patents). To each patent, we merge various information from other sources, including information on whether or not the patent at issue was ultimately asserted in litigation, information that we obtain from the Lex Machina database.

Finally, in an alternative sample, we further restrict this dataset to those patents whose underlying inventions were also the subject of applications at both the European Patent Office (EPO) and the Japan Patent Office (JPO). Among this restricted dataset, we collect information on whether a US issued patent was likewise allowed by both the EPO and JPO. We obtained this information using the Triadic Patent Family database maintained by the Organization for Economic Co-operation and Development. Below, we refer to this subsample as the Triadic Patent Family patents.

We present summary statistics of the key analytical variables in this data set in Table 1.1 The mean examiner grant-rate is roughly 0.69, with a standard deviation of roughly 0.23. Patents themselves are asserted in litigation very infrequently, with an incidence of only 0.005 (with a mean number of times asserted equal to 0.011). Finally, turning to our validity benchmark metric, roughly 0.44 of those patents issued in the United States are likewise allowed at the EPO and JPO (among those that file at all three offices).

Table 1.1 *Summary statistics*

Examiner leave-one-out grant rate	0.697
	(0.234)
Number of times asserted in litigation	0.011
	(0.432)
Incidence of patent asserted in litigation	0.005
	(0.069)
Incidence of any litigation assertion, excluding frequently litigated patents	0.005
	(0.067)
Incidence of any litigation assertion, excluding any patent litigated more than once	0.003
	(0.053)
Incidence of allowance at both EPO and JPO	0.446
	(0.497)

Note: Statistics are from the collection of applications in the Patent Office's PAIR database that reached a final disposition and that were published in the PAIR records between March 2001 and July 2012. Statistics bearing on EPO and JPO allowance rates are from the subset of patents that were granted out of this initial set of applications and whose applicant's likewise sought patent protection at the EPO and JPO.

1.4   Results

In Columns 1–4 of Table 1.2, we present our key results regarding the link between litigation frequency and examiner leniency. We find that applications reviewed by more lenient examiners are more likely to wind up in litigation. The results imply that applications reviewed by examiners with a leave-one-out grant rate of 1 relative to a grant rate of 0 are roughly 0.6 percentage points – or about 120 percent – more likely to wind up in litigation. Interpreted differently, this suggests that a one-standard deviation increase in the grant rate of the application's associated examiner corresponds with about a 28 percent increase in the likelihood of winding up litigation. When focusing on the number of times an application is asserted in litigation as the relevant dependent variable, the results suggest that an increase from 0 to 1 in the associated examiner's grant rate corresponds with a 0.024 – or a roughly 218 percent – increase in the mean number of times a patent will be

Table 1.2 *Relationship between examiner grant-rate and the frequency of patent assertion in court*

	(1)	(2)	(3)	(4)	(5)	(6)
	Incidence of Any Litigation Assertion		Number of Times Asserted in Litigation		Incidence of Allowance at Both EPO and JPO (among Triadic Patent Families)	
Leave-one-out examiner grant-rate	0.006***	0.006***	0.024***	0.025***	−0.050***	−0.051***
	(0.001)	(0.001)	(0.004)	(0.004)	(0.011)	(0.012)
Application covariates?	NO	YES	NO	YES	NO	YES
N	981763	821209	981763	821209	270721	223806

Note: + significant at 10%; * significant at 5%; ** significant at 1%; *** significant at 0.1%. Standard errors are reported in parentheses and are clustered to correct for autocorrelation within Art Units. Application covariates (where indicated) include the entity size of the applicant and an indicator variable representing the incidence of foreign priority. The sample in Columns 5 and 6 is further restricted to those applications that actually culminated in a patent grant and whose underlying inventors also sought patent protection at the JPO and EPO. All regressions include art-unit-by-year fixed effects.

asserted at court. In other terms, this suggests that a one-standard-deviation increase in the associated examiner's grant rate corresponds with a roughly 50 percent increase in the number of times a patent is asserted in litigation. Moving forward, we focus on the binary approach and simply explore the determinants of any litigation assertion.[10] Further, we note that the various findings from Table 1.2 are nearly identical when controlling for the entity size of the patentee (large or small, as such terms are used by the Patent Office to determine fee levels) and for the foreign priority status of the initial application.

These results demonstrate a large sensitivity in the likelihood of patent litigation to the inherent leniency of the associated examiner. While this is highly suggestive of a sensitivity in litigation likelihood to the underlying legal validity of an issued patent, that relationship is not immediately clear from Columns 1–4 alone. To validate the use of examiner leniency as a proxy for underlying validity – albeit on a restricted subsample of the Triadic Patent Family patents – we next associate the leave-one-out grant rate of the assigned examiner with the likelihood that a parent within this subsample was likewise allowed at both the EPO and JPO. In Columns 5 and 6 of Table 1.2, we find a negative relationship between the leniency of the examiner reviewing a given application that culminates in a Triadic Patent Family patent and the likelihood that the patent in question is allowed at both the EPO and JPO. In particular, the results imply that a one-standard-deviation increase in the examiner's leave-one-out grant rate is associated with about a 2.7 percent decrease in the likelihood that the patent is allowed at both of the benchmark patent offices.

In Table 1.3, we replicate this analysis (focusing only on those specifications with application controls for the sake of brevity) but using an alternative construction of an examiner leniency measure. Instead of simply using an examiner's unadjusted grant rate (other than removing the influence of the given application), we use the examiner's estimated

---

[10] Our interests are more in asking whether a case is asserted at all. Litigants may follow various strategies in approaching patent cases and deciding whether to consolidate defendants in given cases or file separate suits. Focusing on the binary approach allows us to abstract away from any such litigant behavior. Nonetheless, the results to follow generalize to specifications that embrace the volume of litigation per patent. We acknowledge that this volume analysis may be affected by the joinder provisions of the America Invents Act of 2011; however, the effective date for those provisions is after the time period of our analytical sample.

Table 1.3 *Relationship between examiner grant-rate and the frequency of patent assertion in court, alternative construction of examiner leniency*

	(1)	(2)
	Incidence of any litigation assertion	Incidence of allowance at both EPO and JPO (among Triadic Patent Families)
Examiner fixed effect	0.005***	−0.086***
	(0.001)	(0.017)
N	973743	268430

Note: + significant at 10%; * significant at 5%; ** significant at 1%, *** significant at 0.1%. Standard errors are reported in parentheses and are clustered to correct for autocorrelation within Art Units. The sample in Column 2 is further restricted to those applications that actually culminated in a patent grant and whose underlying inventors also sought patent protection at the JPO and EPO. All regressions include art-unit-by-year fixed effects.

fixed effect from an application-level regression of the incidence of a patent being granted on a series of examiner fixed effects along with various measures capturing characteristics of the application and of the examiner, including the examiner's pay-grade level and experience level. Since grade and experience levels have been shown to strongly correlate with grant rates (Frakes and Wasserman 2017; Lemley and Sampat 2012), this approach attempts to abstract away from variations in examiners across such dimensions and develop a metric indicative of an examiner's more inherent grant rate. We note, however, that it is not immediately clear that the failure to do so – i.e., failure to risk adjust in this manner – will generate a bias in any particular direction. As demonstrated by Table 1.3, the results are nearly unchanged when using the estimated examiner effects instead of the mean grant rates as the underlying examiner leniency measure.

The results in Table 1.2 can effectively be seen as the reduced form and the first stage of an instrumental variables approach in which we estimate the impact of underlying patent validity on the likelihood of litigation while instrumenting the patent's validity with a metric of examiner leniency. In Table 1.4, we present the IV results themselves. This has the advantage of providing a more accessible interpretation of the above

Table 1.4 *Relationship between patent validity and the incidence of litigation*

	(1)	(2)	(3)
Validity indicator (incidence of patent likewise being granted at both the EPO and JPO)	0.003*** (0.001)	−0.150*** (0.050)	−0.048+ (0.028)
Instrument validity indicator with leave-one-out examiner grant rate?	NO	YES	YES
Construction of examiner leniency measure	Leave-one-out grant rate	Leave-one-out grant rate	Examiner fixed effect
N	223806	223806	223372

Note: + significant at 10%; * significant at 5%; ** significant at 1%, *** significant at 0.1%. Standard errors are reported in parentheses and are clustered to correct for autocorrelation within Art Units. All regressions include art-unit-by-year fixed effects and application-level controls for the entity size of the applicant and an indicator variable representing the incidence of foreign priority. The sample is restricted to those applications that actually culminated in a patent grant and whose underlying inventors also sought patent protection at the JPO and EPO.

reduced-form findings – i.e., it associates litigation likelihood with an actual measure of legal merit. However, the IV specification carries a couple of caveats. First, the above reduced form results were estimated over the full issued patents sample, whereas this IV approach is limited to those that are part of Triadic Patent Families (with only 268,430 patents in the restricted sample, compared with nearly a million in the reduced form). Second, the accuracy of this interpretation depends on the appropriateness of EPO/JPO benchmarking as a proxy for patent validity. With these concerns in mind, in Table 1.4, we present IV estimates (in addition to OLS results in column 1). Instrumenting the incidence of allowance at both the EPO and the JPO – an indicator for validity – with the associated examiner's leave-one-out grant rate, we find that valid patents are 4–15 percentage points less likely to be asserted in litigation relative to invalid patents. In light of the mean litigation assertion rate among Triadic Patent Families, these findings suggest that invalid patents are a staggering 5–18 times more likely to be asserted than valid patents, depending on the construction of the examiner leniency measure. Even taking the more conservative value in this range, this finding suggests a strong degree of targeting of litigation on invalid patents.[11]

As a final empirical exercise we attempt to separate the degree of sorting for patents held by operating companies and by NPEs. Though, as above, we are abstracting away from an evaluation of the efficiency of case selection by individual litigants, we seek to separately assess the degree of sorting along operating company/NPE lines in light of the often discussed differences in litigation strategies between these two groups, the former sometimes being blamed for asserting weak/invalid patents in the hopes of extracting nuisance settlements (Cotropia et al. 2014; Feng and Jaravel 2016). With these latter claims in mind, one may be concerned that our results – strong association between weak patents and litigation likelihood – are merely being driven by nuisance behaviors of NPEs. Of course, that NPE-driven story may nonetheless be consistent with a story in which the patent litigation system targets invalid patents, a story that may have implications for the efficiency of the validity screening function of the system. In any event, we seek to assess whether the targeting evidence that we document also appears when focusing on operating companies.

A key challenge in this final exercise is that we do not have data on which patents are and are not held by NPEs.[12] As a result, we draw on Allison et al. (2011), which presented evidence suggesting that the vast majority of those patents that were only asserted once in litigation are held by operating companies, whereas the majority of those patents that were asserted 8 or more times in litigation are held by NPEs. To be clear, our use of Allison's et al. (2011) finding that patents asserted 8 or more times are predominantly owned by NPEs provides a proxy, albeit an imperfect one, of NPE ownership and our results should be interpreted with this caveat in mind. In Table 1.5, we replicate the analysis from Table 1.2 and 1.4 across three separate specifications: (1) as above, including all patents regardless of the number of times asserted in litigation, (2) excluding patents that were asserted 8 or more times in litigation, and (3) excluding any patent asserted more than once in

---

[11] We note that the above results are robust to more nonlinear and nonparametric treatment of the examiner leniency measures, including logs of either measure or dummy variables representing above-median levels of the respective measures.

[12] We are currently in the process of obtaining this data.

Table 1.5 *Impact of examiner leniency and patent validity on litigation likelihood, including and excluding patents litigated more than once*

	(1)	(2)	(3)
	Incidence of any litigation assertion, including frequently litigated patents	Incidence of any litigation assertion, excluding frequently litigated patents	Incidence of any litigation assertion, excluding any patent litigated more than once
Panel A. Impact of leave-one-out grant rate on litigation likelihood			
Leave-one-out examiner grant-rate	0.006***	0.006***	0.004***
	(0.001)	(0.001)	(0.001)
N	821209	820965	818980
Panel B. Impact of patent validity on litigation likelihood, instrumenting validity with leave-one-out grant rate			
Validity indicator (incidence of patent likewise being granted at both the EPO and JPO)	−0.150***	−0.129***	−0.093***
	(0.050)	(0.046)	(0.034)
N	223806	224697	229998

Note: + significant at 10%; * significant at 5%; ** significant at 1%; *** significant at 0.1%. Standard errors are reported in parentheses and are clustered to correct for autocorrelation within Art Units. All regressions include art-unit-by-year fixed effects and application-level controls for the entity size of the applicant and an indicator variable representing the incidence of foreign priority. The sample is restricted in Panel B to those applications that actually culminated in a patent grant and whose underlying inventors also sought patent protection at the JPO and EPO. Frequently litigated patents are those asserted eight or more times (Allison et al. 2011).

litigation. This final specification will explore the effect of examiner leniency on the likelihood of a patent being litigated, but where litigation events are predominantly drawn from operating companies. As demonstrated by Table 1.5, the results do not change meaningfully with this alternative specification, which is consistent with the conclusion that the findings above are not predominantly driven by NPE litigation behavior. Nevertheless, better data, such as data on which patents are and are not held by NPEs, is necessary before any strong conclusions as to whether our findings are driven by NPE litigation behavior can be made.

1.5 Discussion and Conclusion

In this chapter, we have set forth evidence suggesting that a patent's underlying invalidity has a strong positive association with its likelihood of being asserted in litigation (and, thus, that that a patent's underlying validity has a strong negative association with its likelihood of being asserted in litigation). Insofar as one of the chief social aims of the patent litigation system is to help weed out valid from invalid patents, this analysis suggests a degree of rationality and efficiency in this endeavor. Of course, even if valid and invalid patents were asserted at equal rates, the system could nonetheless properly execute this weeding-out function at trial. Nonetheless, to the extent this screening function begins to occur at the case filing stage, certain efficiency gains may be obtained. All of this being said, our results only speak to one element of a much larger discussion regarding efficiency of the litigation system.

To begin, as stated in the introduction, our analysis only relates to targeting of cases along the invalidity margin. It could very well be the case that case screening operates poorly along the infringement dimension. Second, and relatedly, it is difficult to take from this analysis anything about the efficiency of the decision-making of individual litigants. Rather, we have approached this investigation from a more abstract direction and have asked whether the system as a whole – as the product of some individual decision-making and interaction among litigants – is targeting invalid patents.

Third, this analysis perhaps speaks to the efficiency of the litigation system conditional on the amount of litigation actually chosen – that is, are the current litigation resources at least targeting invalid patents to a relatively stronger degree than they are targeting valid patents? It could of course be that the patent system is nonetheless litigating to an inefficiently high degree. To consider this possibility, for the sake of analytical traction, stay within the mindset of a system focused solely on serving the function of sorting valid from invalid patents (i.e., leaving infringement aside). It may indeed serve society's interest to return invalid patents to the public domain. For instance, maintaining monopoly power for the owner of an invention that is obvious would be imposing deadweight losses on society with no commensurate benefits (considering that the invention would have likely emerged anyway). However, there are two institutions that may serve this function: the courts or the Patent and Trademark Office. As such, we are faced with the age-old question of ex-ante regulation versus ex-post adjudication.

Mark Lemley (2001) has argued that it is perhaps more efficient to reserve this function for the courts. Though litigation is expensive, its incidence may be rare enough that better bang-for-the-buck could be obtained by investing to a lighter degree in patent examination, even if that means the issuance of more invalid patents. Lemley's analysis, however, is missing a salient empirical input to the exercise. Though he does perform some back-of-the-envelope calculations using data on certain parameters, one key finding that is critically missing from his analysis is an estimate of the amount of litigation – and thus litigation expenses – that may actually be prevented by investing more resources – mainly, examination time – in the Patent Office. In a recent analysis (Frakes and Wasserman 2017), the present authors have attempted to confront this oversight. Taking advantage of the fact that examination time allocations decrease upon certain promotions, we estimated examiner fixed effects specifications so as to track individual examiners across certain events that left them with less and less time to review applications (while attempting to separate these promotion effects from general experience effects). We found evidence that examiners began to grant more patents when their time allocations tightened and that the additional patents being issued on the margin were of more questionable validity. Moreover, we found that as examiners received less time, the patents that they issued were ultimately adjudicated at higher rates. Performing a back-of-the-envelope calculating stemming from this analysis, we found that the savings in litigation costs that could come from giving examiners more time on the margin exceeded the additional administrative expenses associated with that additional time. From the perspective of ensuring that patent protection only be afforded to legally valid patents, these findings imply that we may indeed be relying too much on litigation itself, despite whatever efficiency we may experience in achieving this sorting conditional on litigation.

Our prior analysis used data that largely took place prior to the America Invents Act and hence prior to the new post-grant adjudicatory proceedings, which provided a robust pathway for third parties to challenge the validity of issued patents, that emanated from that Act. Future research should attempt to ascertain whether we are achieving the optimal mix of screening across three stages: patent examination, post-grant adjudicatory proceeding, and litigation. Early empirical work suggests that vast majority of patents being challenged in these new post-grant adjudicatory proceedings are concomitantly being litigated in federal district courts, suggesting that we are not currently approaching the optimal mix of screening across these three stages (Vishnubhakat et al. 2016). In summary, our empirical finding that patent lawsuits in district courts target invalid patents to a greater extent than they target valid patents provide insight into one dimension of the efficiency of the patent litigation system. Much work remains to understand the extent to which the patent litigation system is efficient across a full spectrum of considerations.

References

Allison, John, Mark Lemley, Kimberley Moore, and R. Derek Trunkey. 2004. Valuable Patents. *Georgetown Law Journal* 92: 435–79.

Allison, John, Mark Lemley, and Joshua Walker. 2011. Patent Quality and Settlement among Repeat Patent Litigants. *Georgetown Law Review* 99: 677–712.

Chien, Colleen. 2011. Predicting Patent Litigation. *Texas Law Review* 90: 283–329.

Cockburn, Ian, Samuel Korum, and Scott Stern. 2003. Are All Patent Examiners Equal? Examiners, Patent Characteristics, and Litigation Outcomes, in *Patents in Knowledge-Based Economy,* edited by Wesley M. Cohen and Stephen A. Merril. Washington, DC: National Academies Press.

Cotropia, Christopher, Jay Kesan, and David Schwartz. 2014. Unpacking Patent Assertion Entities. *Minnesota Law Review* 99: 649–703.

Farre-Mensa, Joan, Deepak Hegde, and Alexander Ljungqvist. 2017. What Is a Patent Worth? Evidence from the U.S. Patent "Lottery." NBER Working Paper 23268.

Feng, Josh, and Xavier Jaravel. 2016. Who Feeds the Trolls? Patent Trolls and the Patent Examination Process. Working Paper. Harvard University, Cambridge, MA.

Ford, Roger Allan. 2013. Patent Invalidity versus Noninfringement. *Cornell Law Review* 99: 71–128.

Frakes, Michael D., and Melissa F. Wasserman. 2017. Is the Time Allocated to Review Patent Applications Inducing Examiners to Grant Invalid Patents?: Evidence from Micro-Level Application Data. *Review of Economics and Statistics* 99: 550–63.

Harhoff, Dietmar, and Markus Reitzig. 2004. Determinants of Opposition against EPO Patent Grants – The Case of Biotechnology and Pharmaceuticals. *International Journal of Industrial Organization* 22: 443–80.

Hyman, David, and Charles Silver. 2006. Medical Malpractice Litigation and Tort Reform: It's the Incentives, Stupid. *Vanderbilt Law Review* 59: 1085–136.

Kessler, Daniel, Thomas Meites, and Geoffrey Miller. 1996. Explaining Deviations from the Fifty-Percent Rule: A Multimodal Approach to the Selection of Cases for Litigation. *Journal of Legal Studies* 25: 233–59.

Lanjouw, Jean, and Mark Schankerman. 2001. Characteristics of Patent Litigation: A Window on Competition. *Rand Journal of Economics* 32: 129–51.

Lemley, Mark A. Rational Ignorance at the Patent Office. 2001. *Northwestern University Law* Review 95: 1495–1532.

Lemley, Mark A., and Bhaven Sampat. 2012. Examiner Characteristics and Patent Office Outcomes. *Review of Economics and Statistics* 94: 817–27.

Lemley, Mark A., Kent Richardson, and Erik Oliver. 2017. The Patent Enforcement Iceberg. Stanford Public Law Working Paper. Stanford, CA.

Lichtman, Douglas. 2004. Rethinking Prosecution History Estoppel. *University of Chicago Law Review* 71: 151–82.

Mann, Ronald. 2014. The Idiosyncrasy of Patent Examiners: Effects of Experience and Attrition. *Texas Law Review* 92: 2149–76.

Melero, Eduardo, Neus Palomeras, and David Wehrheim. 2017. The Effect of Patent Protection on Inventor Mobility. Working Paper.

Priest, George L. and Benjamin Klein. 1984. The Selection of Disputes for Litigation. *Journal of Legal Studies* 13: 1–55.

Righi, Cesare, and Timothy Simcoe. 2017. Patent Examiner Specialization. Working Paper.

Sampat, Bhaven, and Heidi Williams. 2015. How do patents affect follow-on innovation? Evidence from the human genome. NBER Working Paper 21666.

Studdert, David, Michelle Mello, Atul Gawande, Tejal Gandhi, Allen Kachalia, Catherine Yoon, Ann Louise Puopolo, and Troyen Brennan. 2006. Claims,

Errors, and Compensation Payments in Medical Malpractice Litigation. *The New England Journal of Medicine* 354: 2024–33.

Tu, Shine. 2014. Patent Examination and Litigation Outcomes. *Stanford Technology Law Review* 17: 507–48.

Vishnubhakat, Saurabh, Arti K. Rai, and Jay P. Kesan. 2016. Strategic Decision Making in Dual PTAB and District Court Proceedings. *Berkeley Technology Law Review* 31: 45–124.

Platform Procedure

Using Technology to Facilitate (Efficient) Civil Settlement

J.J. PRESCOTT AND ALEXANDER SANCHEZ

2.1 Introduction

This chapter examines the empirical relationship between party litigation costs and the substantive outcomes of legal disputes.[1] We hypothesize that reducing litigation costs will change case outcomes for at least some types of disputes by altering the dispute resolution process and by inhibiting party default. When litigation costs are high relative to the stakes of a case, the case's final outcome is more likely to be driven by the parties' costs than by the factual and legal merits of their disagreement, leading perhaps too often to default judgments or even failures to file meritorious claims. If such outcomes are less likely to be accurate—assuming that substantive law is efficient, and that parties bargain in the shadow of this law—then reducing the litigation costs that parties bear should improve the accuracy of litigation.

We test this proposition empirically in a context that is highly policy-relevant: the introduction of court-based "online dispute resolution" (ODR) tools, a step being taken by a growing number of courts. We cannot test whether the outcomes of cases become more accurate following the

[1] Professor, University of Michigan Law School, and Manager, Small Claims Division and Dispute Resolution Department, Franklin County Municipal Court, Columbus, Ohio, respectively. We are grateful to the Third Century Global Initiatives Grant Program at the University of Michigan for funding the UM Online Court Project, of which this research is a part; the staff at Court Innovations Inc. and at the Franklin County Municipal Court for sharing their data, expertise, and time; and Patrick Balke, Simmon Kim, and German Marquez Alcala for excellent research assistance. We are also grateful to Yun-chien Chang, Florencia Marotta-Wurgler, Rory Pulvino, and Kyle Rozema for very helpful comments and suggestions on earlier drafts. Disclosure: Prescott is a cofounder and equity holder of Court Innovations Inc., a University of Michigan startup that develops and implements online case resolution systems, including the online platform technology evaluated in this chapter.

implementation of such online "platform" technology because we have no reliable measure of outcome accuracy. We can, however, use our data to study whether the introduction of platform technology affects the substantive outcomes of cases. A change in outcomes and in particular a reduction in the likelihood of a default judgment would suggest that ODR tools enhance system accuracy by dampening the propensity of parties to forgo dispute resolution altogether in favor of an inefficient status quo outcome. We find that reducing litigation costs by implementing ODR software in the small claims context reduces the likelihood of default and, presumably, other inefficient non-negotiated or status quo outcomes.

The chapter aims to better understand whether litigation costs affect how real-world courts arrive at efficient or accurate outcomes in resolving disputes. "Efficient" law is typically taken to refer to optimal substantive legal rules—essentially, rules that maximize social welfare by realigning incentives and allocating risk so that behavior and other outcomes comport with society's preferences (Posner 1972; Rubin 1977). In abstract analyses, procedural costs or complications are usually assumed away or presumed to be fixed or orthogonal to how the substantive law arrived at by courts will operate in the world. Courts have an obvious role in designing substantive rules, interpreting legislation, and applying law so as to achieve this sort of efficiency, and whether they carry out this task well is the subject of a large and mature literature (e.g., Hadfield 1992; Posner 1972; Priest 1977; Rubin 1977). Nevertheless, despite the tendency of commentators to focus on substantive law, scholars have long understood the important role that litigation costs play in whether justice systems operate efficiently.

One classic example of how these costs can affect the *real-world* efficiency of substantive legal rules can be seen in the implications of the Coase Theorem, which reminds us that the initial allocations of rights matter to whether final allocations are efficient because the difficulty of transferring rights makes them "sticky" (Coase 1960; Cole and Grossman 2002; Rubin 1977). Another means by which litigation costs can alter the development of efficient substantive legal rules involves the selection of disputes for litigation (Chang and Hubbard 2018; Lee and Klerman 2016; Priest and Klein 1984). The work of Priest, Klein, and others has thrown into sharp relief the fact that the costs of litigation alone (including risk) can dramatically affect the set of cases courts will have the opportunity to decide, and hence, the set of possible rules that might emerge (Rubin 1977). Courts necessarily have a distorted picture of the world as a result of the selected cases they see (but see Helland, Klerman, and Lee 2018), so the prospect of efficient rules emerging naturally seems somewhat remote unless court procedures and, ultimately, their decision-making is somehow robust to this selection or adjusts in response to it.

A final way in which administrative or transactional litigation costs matter to the efficiency of how courts rule is related to the consequences of case selection, but it seems to us conceptually distinct—and it receives much less attention. When the costs of using courts to decide disputes—relative to the stakes of a case—are sufficiently high, the substantive legal rule a court *would* apply actually becomes irrelevant if one or more of the parties refuses to litigate. In these cases, the result is a de facto legal rule that enforces the status quo or initial allocation of rights (Rhee 2006). This is true even when the de jure substantive rule is extremely favorable to the party seeking relief. If, for example, the litigation costs of using a court to resolve a dispute are $100 and the stakes of the case in question are $200, a risk-neutral plaintiff must anticipate a greater than 50 percent chance of winning in order to make bringing the lawsuit financially worthwhile. If the efficient substantive rule would produce a 35 percent chance of the plaintiff winning, and a reasonable, but inefficient, alternative substantive rule would produce a 25 percent chance of the plaintiff winning, then a court "rules" inefficiently regardless of the choice it would have made because the plaintiff's decision not to proceed on account of the costs of litigation equates to a 0 percent chance of winning.

Of course, if one assumes that the "costs" of using a court are fixed and necessary, then this status quo-enforcing result is welfare-maximizing (Rhee 2006). Using courts to resolve disputes expends resources, and therefore avoiding these costs by an extreme rule may be optimal from society's perspective. Some research even suggests that decreasing barriers to accessing the legal system may have surprisingly regressive effects, for example, by potentially crowding out those litigants who would benefit most from such access (Niblett and Yoon 2017). But the use and design of courts and their processes are choices and involve trade-offs, and there is no good reason to assume that restructuring them to reduce litigation costs must necessarily produce offsetting negative consequences elsewhere in the system. For this reason, pursuing reforms that reduce the administrative costs of litigation—and, more fundamentally, reconceiving how cases are managed and how information flows between parties and the court—is integral to the efficient application of the law and to accurate substantive outcomes.

According to this argument, courts that are managed poorly and that are unnecessarily costly and time-consuming for litigants to use rule "inefficiently" in cases with sufficiently small stakes. High relative litigation costs cause more disputes to default to the status quo. Policies that minimize litigation costs not only free saved resources to be used elsewhere but also result in more cases being decided by courts according to substantive legal rules (or being negotiated to settlement under them). The selection inefficiency that arises from litigation costs is especially acute for what are often referred to as "minor disputes," such as cases involving civil infractions, minor misdemeanors, small claims, and so on. For these cases, the costs of using courts for dispute resolution can have the effect of robbing an efficient substantive rule of any actual significance. This notion echoes the phenomenon of the "vanishing trial," in which the replacement of public adjudication with private, often confidential, settlements may hinder the development of substantive law and the provision of justice (Fiss 1984; Kotkin 2007; Lothes 2005; Luban 1995; Resnik 2006). Generally speaking, for both issues, the concern is that coercive, extralegal conditions, like high litigation costs, are restricting the use of the legal system and producing inefficient or inaccurate outcomes. The takeaway is simply that one important way to pursue the efficient application of the law by courts is through the adoption of structures and procedures that reduce or eliminate *unnecessary* litigation costs that the parties would otherwise bear.

In the empirical work below, we consider the ability of courts to reduce litigation costs by introducing online platform technology, focusing on the effects that reducing these costs and increasing access to justice have on the outcomes of cases. Specifically, we evaluate the effects of a large state court's implementation of court-assisted ODR for its small claims docket to reduce the costs of litigation and facilitate quickly negotiated settlements (in the shadow of what might be efficient substantive law). ODR tools, in theory, enhance court efficiency and the parties' experiences by giving parties on-demand access to a private and secure online platform to negotiate an agreement that resolves their case.[2] Court-assisted ODR eliminates procedural inefficiencies and barriers to court access and saves litigants time and effort. We find that the likelihood of a

---

[2] We also present some tentative evidence that installing ODR tools may increase the average duration of cases as cases become more likely to resolve via negotiation than to end in default, although the size and sign of this effect may vary depending on where in the duration distribution the case would otherwise appear.

small claims case ending in default declines significantly in the wake of ODR implementation, presumably because defendants are empowered by the technology to negotiate their way to better outcomes—ones that are more likely to be based on the relevant merits of a case rather than on its expected litigation costs alone.[3]

The chapter proceeds as follows: In Section 2.2, we provide background information on small claims cases in the Franklin County Municipal Court in Columbus, Ohio, the court from which our data derive, and the operation and implementation of the online platform in the fall of 2016. In Section 2.3, we describe our data and empirical approach. In Section 2.4, we present our empirical findings. In Section 2.5, we discuss these findings in light of related data and analysis. We conclude that because parties will demand greater efficiency in the years ahead and because a majority of cases in the United States are minor ones like the small claims cases we study, the arrival of platform technology presents a critical opportunity. Implementing ODR tools on a broader scale will reduce the administrative, psychological, and other costs of litigation, ensuring parties benefit more fully from their substantive legal rights.

2.2   Background

The Franklin County Municipal Court (FCMC) Small Claims Division (located in Columbus, Ohio) oversees the resolution of an average of 6,000 small claims cases annually (FCMC Annual Report 2016 p. 64). The parties in these cases are identified using the standard terms "plaintiff" and "defendant," but behind these labels—whether they are entities

---

[3] Although we assume in the work below that ODR tools have the potential to improve accuracy primarily by reducing the costs of accessing courts for litigants, ODR may affect accuracy directly by changing how parties exchange information, prepare for litigation, and arrive at settlement. Our empirical work below captures both of these effects, although for minor cases that otherwise would have defaulted absent ODR, we suspect that the cost-reduction theory is more important. For these cases, it is most likely the costs of litigation that led to default, not concern over an inaccurate outcome conditional on choosing to litigate. In addition, we implicitly assume that litigation costs reduce accuracy by deterring negotiation and litigation in the shadow of the law, resulting in inaccurate default outcomes. But ODR tools, by reducing litigation costs, could also encourage nuisance suits—and, particularly in this context, nuisance defenses asserted for their settlement value—which would contribute to *inaccurate* outcomes. While we cannot discount this possibility, we have seen nothing in our data, including in negotiation communications, to support this idea. It is also at odds with the court's experiences.

or not—are people trying to achieve a resolution to an ongoing dispute. The types of cases filed in the Small Claims Division include, for example, a city attorney's attempt to collect unpaid income tax from a city taxpayer, a former friend's claim for repayment of a personal loan, and a businessperson's action to recover on a past due account.

FCMC's small claims docket and operations are functions of various state statutes, court rules and policies, and interpretive case law, all of which dictate which claims the court can address and how to resolve them. As in many jurisdictions, Ohio's small claims courts have limited jurisdiction, the precise scope of which is defined by statute (O.R.C. § 1925). Small claims courts are built around the idea that requiring a full panoply of costly procedures is unnecessary to achieve accurate outcomes in small-dollar civil disputes; rather, these cases can be appropriately handled more quickly and less formally than cases with larger stakes (Ohio Bar Foundation 2006 p. 2). In Ohio, small claims cases are restricted to actions for money damages up to $6,000 and not requiring responsive pleadings. They entail limited discovery and involve trials that are held, in theory, between 15 and 40 days from the date a plaintiff files (O.R.C. § 1925.04). Small claims courts are consciously designed to reduce litigation costs for both plaintiffs and defendants. By increasing the likelihood that plaintiffs file meritorious cases and defendants appear in court to defend themselves, this approach allows the law—or the parties negotiating under the law—rather than litigation costs to determine the outcomes of disputes.

Nevertheless, on average, more than 40 percent of the 6,000 or so cases on the FCMC's small claims docket in a year—roughly 2,400 cases annually—are closed with a default judgment for one party's failure to appear at trial (FCMC CourtView Case Statistics).[4] A default judgment looks like an efficient procedural device that closes a case with minimal time and effort by a decision-maker (Chang and Hubbard 2019),[5] but this inference of "efficiency" is misleading if the substantive outcomes of these default judgments are highly inaccurate. In low-stakes small claims

---

[4] We assembled these calculations using FCMC's CourtView case management software.

[5] Even a default judgment comes with its own procedural requirements and administrative costs: decision-makers must still review service, determine damages, and enter judgment. Clerical staff must docket the outcome, generate notices, and mail entries. Additionally, even though the case may be closed, the judgment may be vulnerable and subject to attack through the use of other procedural devices, which would require additional decision-maker and administrative resources (Ohio Courts Statistical Report 2016).

cases, this possibility seems especially likely because a party's litigation costs (including the opportunity costs of traveling to and appearing in court) may swamp the upside to the party of accurately resolving a dispute involving only a few hundred dollars. In fact, 40 percent is a higher default rate than occurs in other Ohio civil courts.[6] In Franklin County specifically, a large fraction of small claims outcomes are determined by parties apparently avoiding the costs of litigation, broadly construed, rather than by the merits of the dispute. Even if default judgments are sometimes just low-cost concessions (i.e., full admissions of liability) by defendants, as some surely are, it is just as likely that many of those defaulting have viable defenses or counterclaims. These litigants simply (and rationally) decline to raise them because the costs of appearing in court to answer a complaint are too high.

When the stakes of a lawsuit are especially small, even streamlined small claims litigation may prove prohibitively costly for one or both litigants. A judge or magistrate personally hears small claims cases that proceed to trial in a courtroom.[7] Some trials span hours, others days. After trial, the decision-maker either rules from the bench or issues a written decision.[8] The use of a court to resolve a dispute—even a small claims court—amounts to a private and public investment. In exchange for a careful weighing of facts and law and a relatively accurate outcome, the parties and publicly provided court personnel must use resources that could have served other valuable aims (Supreme Court Task Force on Funding 2015 p. 14).[9] To appear in court in person, litigants must overcome a wide range of barriers, including economic costs—forgone wages, transportation

[6] For example, the default rate for civil cases in the Franklin County Common Pleas Court General Civil Division is 26.8 percent (3,851 defaults/14,384 civil cases). Admittedly, these cases may differ systematically on important grounds other than simply the stakes of the dispute.

[7] Jury trials are not permitted in Ohio small claims cases (O.R.C. § 1925.04(a)).

[8] A decision-maker's efficiency is also limited by the decision-maker's statutory authority to grant appropriate relief. For example, in Ohio, a small claims judge is limited to awards of money damages, even if the plaintiff and defendant desire some other form of relief, such as specific performance (O.R.C. § 1925.02(A)(1)). Moreover, even if the court successfully resolves a case, the nature of the outcome may not only allow but actually lead to further litigation, consuming additional administrative time and effort.

[9] In addition to resolving cases, courts also provide processes for enforcing and collecting on a judgment if the judgment debtor does not voluntarily comply with the court's order. These processes typically require more time and third-party involvement from employers, banks, and perhaps courts in other jurisdictions.

outlays, and childcare expenses to attend their hearing during business hours—as well as psychological challenges—enduring confusion over legal technicalities and the fear of public speaking. (Bulinski and Prescott 2016; Prescott 2017). Not surprisingly, a party's litigation costs also hinge on the court's operations and the behavior of court personnel. If litigants find it especially time-consuming or difficult to communicate with clerks or the judge to resolve a case, the costs of using the court to resolve a dispute are even higher.[10]

Of course, defaulting outright or fully litigating to judgment are not the only options for resolving a dispute. Largely to reduce litigation costs (including litigation risk) even further (i.e., beyond what the streamlining of the small claims court process has achieved), parties often negotiate and settle their disputes before trial. Settlement can happen organically, but courts often also make dispute resolution tools and processes available as an alternative to traditional adjudication (Ohio Sup. Ct. Rule 16, n.d.). FCMC is one of these courts. Based on its experience with the mediation services it provides, the court believes that it is most effective at resolving disputes when parties define their own processes and resolve their own disputes without decision-maker intervention.[11] Dispute resolution tools lower litigation costs while still allowing the merits of the dispute to control the outcome.[12] Court-facilitated party negotiation or in-person mediation

---

[10] Likewise, litigants can make choices that delay the resolution of a case and that require more court resources, sometimes because these costs fall on third parties (like court personnel and taxpayers, which litigants in many cases will simply ignore) and sometimes in pursuit of the strategic goal of raising their opponent's litigation costs.

[11] The Dispute Resolution Department provides alternative dispute resolution services before a plaintiff files a lawsuit, at any stage of a lawsuit (including post-judgment), and across all civil case types in the municipal court (http://smallclaims.fcmcclerk.com/home/medi ation). The Department receives more than 2,000 mediation requests and referrals annually (Franklin County Municipal Court 2016 p. 64). In 2016, 58 percent of the total 869 judge-referred mediations were resolved via a negotiated settlement either before trial (256) or through mediation (246), and 91 percent of mediated agreements resulted in the court's disposal of the case without judicial intervention (Memo to Municipal Court Judges 2017).

[12] Dispute resolution tools may also reduce litigation costs even when a case does not settle outright in the immediate aftermath. Negotiation, document exchange, and other communication facilitate an understanding of the evidence, position, and priorities of the other side. This exchange can reduce the time and effort that goes into later litigation, too, especially if there is some sort of partial settlement in place during the adjudication in which the parties agree to ignore certain issues or agree to certain factual predicates.

by court personnel or affiliated mediators are two avenues to lower litigation costs and resolve cases earlier, though they are far from the only ones.

Over the last few years, advances in platform technology have made it possible for courts to offer new dispute resolution services to litigants. For example, online dispute resolution (ODR) tools enhance access to justice by reducing litigation costs. Specifically, they eliminate the need for litigants to go to court in person and allow negotiation and mediation to occur remotely and outside of regular business hours. All of these benefits translate to less missed work, lower transportation and childcare costs, and a reduction in the fear and confusion that can accompany visiting courthouses and speaking publicly in a formal setting. By giving cost-sensitive litigants in low-stakes cases realistic resolution options beyond engaging in a full-blown civil trial or just defaulting to the status quo—whether streamlined small claims trials, in-person mediation services, or an ODR platform over which parties can exchange information, offer proposals, and agree on terms—parties are better able to achieve their goals in light of the facts and the law. Our aim in this chapter is to explore this idea empirically by studying whether the introduction of platform technology in a small claims court affects the litigation process and disposition outcomes by making it easier for parties to negotiate and settle cases using facts and arguments and, in so doing, avoid often-inaccurate default outcomes.

The Small Claims Division of FCMC succeeded in launching the first court-connected ODR platform in the United States for small claims cases in October 2016. The court sought to provide the public a user-friendly process to resolve civil disputes through direct negotiation and without any need for parties to go to court. The platform's dual goals were thus to save court and litigant resources and facilitate accurate outcomes by reducing the number of default judgments. The court also sought to enhance litigant control through the platform by making it easier to resolve cases without decision-maker intervention.

The court piloted the platform by making it available initially only to litigants in Columbus Income Tax Division (CITD) cases. The court focused on these cases for three reasons. First, CITD is the single highest volume plaintiff in the Small Claims Division with an average of 2,000 to 3,000 cases filed annually (roughly 33 percent of small claims suits).[13]

---

[13] The Columbus Income Tax Division became the first e-file plaintiff in FCMC's Small Claims Division in 2017. CITD filed a total of 38 percent (2,206) of all small claims cases (5,760) that year.

Second, in 2016, 47.5 percent of the city's tax cases resulted in a default judgment for CITD on account of the defendant's failure to appear—as compared to an average default rate of less than 40 percent for other small claims cases.[14] Finally, CITD informed court officials that some city tax defendants did not dispute the alleged amount owed in their small claims cases but instead expressed a desire to arrange payment plans with the city. Prior to the implementation of the ODR platform, these small claims defendants had only two options to seek resolution without litigation: attempt to contact and negotiate with the city directly (by phone or in person) or wait to appear in court and attempt to negotiate in the courtroom halls. While both avenues do yield agreements that resolve cases, the process is nonetheless costly: parties still have to coordinate schedules or travel to court in order to discuss settlement terms.

The Small Claims Division's online platform stresses usability and flexibility. It imposes no procedural rules on the parties, and no third-party decision-making or other outside interventions occur without party consent. The platform, which is web-based and mobile device-friendly, mimics common text messaging apps used on smartphones—complete with text bubbles and a document upload/attachment feature. The text-message style of communication is familiar to most users. For individuals who have questions or need additional information about online negotiation, alternatives to negotiation, or the small claims process generally, the platform also supplies answers to frequently asked questions and provides informative videos that explain the small claims and dispute resolution processes. The ODR platform is entirely party-driven. Individuals can negotiate anywhere, anytime, and for any length of time they choose. Individuals are not required to negotiate; all parties must decide independently to use the platform and coming to an agreement using the ODR platform is entirely optional. Negotiations may be terminated at any time as well, which allows the parties to continue with traditional legal options and processes.

The court notifies defendants in eligible cases about the availability of the online platform through an informational postcard included with each notice and summons processed by the Small Claims Division. A link to the platform is also available on the Clerk of Court's website at

---

[14] After a defendant defaults, the city may charge a post-judgment collection fee of no more than 30 percent of the judgment in addition to post-judgment statutory interest if the judgment is referred to a private collection agency (Columbus City Council Ordinance No. 0130-2009).

www.fcmcclerk.com. The ODR workflow is simple.[15] The platform has three user roles: a defendant, a plaintiff, and a court administrator. The defendant initiates negotiation with the plaintiff by entering personal and case information. The defendant then selects between different types of messages, including: (1) proposing a discounted lump sum payment, (2) proposing a discounted short-term payment plan, (3) proposing a long-term payment plan, and (4) indicating an interest in resolution but disputing the claims or amount owed. The defendant may also make settlement proposals in these preliminary communications (such as suggesting a total dollar amount to be paid or a monthly payment plan schedule) as well as offer explanations or informal defenses.

Once the defendant submits this information, the platform automatically e-mails or texts the defendant a unique link to that defendant's private negotiation space on the platform. The plaintiff in the pilot—the city attorney's office—has access to an online dashboard to identify new negotiations, ongoing negotiations, and completed negotiations (i.e., agreements). The plaintiff receives notice of a new communication on the dashboard containing the defendant's name and case number. The plaintiff may respond to defendant communications directly through the negotiation space. The defendant receives an e-mail and/or text message notification each time the plaintiff enters a message in the negotiation space. Parties may continue to exchange information, documents, offers, and counteroffers until either a mutually acceptable agreement is reached or a party terminates the negotiation.[16]

2.3   Data and Empirical Strategy

To examine the consequences of the Small Claims Division's adoption of its ODR platform, we collect case-level data from FCMC and from Court

---

[15] The platform operates independently from FCMC's case management system and without internal court-IT resources. Administrative supervision by court personnel is limited to correcting user-entered case numbers, contacting individuals whose cases are ineligible (such as criminal or traffic cases), and identifying any need for language assistance for the parties (foreign language or American Sign Language). The parties enter all critical data in the negotiation space, and all user-entered data are stored securely.

[16] Agreements and other documents requiring party signatures may be signed electronically using a touchscreen, a touchpad, or a mouse. The platform electronically fastens agreement terms and signatures to a single document that may be filed either on paper or online with the court. The negotiation space is no longer accessible once an agreement is reached or a party terminates the negotiation.

Innovations, the company that operates and maintains the court's ODR platform.[17] We are able to match these data to demographic information using census and other data resources. We begin with basic information about *all* small claims cases filed in FCMC's Small Claims Division in 2016 (first claim filed January 4, 2016) and most of the cases filed in 2017 (last claim filed November 9, 2017).[18] The data include a total of 10,804 cases. Most of these cases have standard dispositions, including "agreed judgment entry" (settlement), "dismissal" (defendant prevails, although this category includes some cases that settled out-of-court and about which the court has no information), and "judgment for the plaintiff" (plaintiff prevails, including default judgments). However, 1,598 of the cases filed during our sample period had not yet been fully resolved as of November 9, 2017,[19] and a few hundred other cases were assigned

---

[17] The name of the platform is Matterhorn. More information about the platform can be found at: https://getmatterhorn.com (accessed July 9, 2019).

[18] We obtained these data from FCMC in two batches. We received the first batch in May 2017 and the second in November 2017. The November 2017 batch includes only cases filed after FCMC extracted the May batch of cases. After the receipt of the second batch, we used the case numbers to scrape FCMC's public online searchable case database to determine whether any of the May batch of cases had been resolved in the period between the first and second batches. Any case that was filed and resolved (disposed) between January 4, 2016, and November 9, 2017, is categorized as a disposed case in our data. Cases filed after January 4, 2016, but having no disposition recorded by November 9, 2017, are categorized as undisposed cases in our data.

[19] Addressing the 1,598 undisposed observations is one of the chief empirical challenges in this chapter. One option for undisposed cases is simply to drop them from the analysis. Unfortunately, this approach may introduce selection bias because cases that are undisposed at the end of the sample period are more likely to be of longer duration or to have been filed later in the sample period and are thus different in other unobserved ways from disposed cases. With respect to our default judgment analysis, the natural way to include unresolved cases is to treat the lack of a disposition as its own outcome or as some outcome other than default. If cases that are likely to default take systematically longer to resolve, however, one concern is that too many cases that will *eventually* default may be miscategorized at the end of the sample period, creating a spurious decline over time in the likelihood of a default disposition. This possibility does have the potential to confound our analysis, but various robustness checks confirm the substance of our findings. Moreover, simple calculations of how long it takes for cases to default indicate that these "likely to default" cases are perhaps a bit shorter in duration than other cases on average, especially when compared to dismissals. Roughly equal numbers of cases result in dismissals and defaults in our data (these two categories make up more than 90 percent of disposed cases), yet in the pre-launch period, duration in the average dismissal case is over 105 days, whereas cases that default average between 80 and 85 days. There is generally greater variance in the duration of cases with "dismissal" outcomes as well. We also explore case duration below, and of course, we can only measure the duration of cases that close. We are nevertheless able to test the robustness of our duration findings in

nonstandard dispositions (e.g., bankruptcy, transfer, and a few other unknown dispositions) or dispositions that are apparently relevant only to platform-ineligible cases.[20] In our baseline analyses below, we study the set of cases that closed with the most common dispositions, a total of 8,955 small claims lawsuits. Table 2.1 shows the breakdown of our analysis sample by filing date, disposition, and ODR use.

Our empirical design includes only data from a single court, but we can leverage the court's implementation strategy to make plausible causal inferences. We use a simple difference-in-differences approach in our analysis. In effect, we separately calculate the outcomes for cases that are plausibly exogenously *eligible* for the ODR platform (as city tax cases) and for *ineligible* small claims cases in both the pre-adoption period and the post-adoption period. We then compare whether any difference in the relevant outcome between eligible and ineligible cases before the adoption of the platform diverges from any difference we measure between the two categories of cases after the adoption. The Small Claims Division launched its ODR platform on October 21, 2016.[21] In our descriptive tables and in our regression analyses below, we consider a case to be

a few different ways, including by survival analysis that is robust to certain time-to-disposition censoring concerns.

[20] The raw data have 33 unique case disposition values. We recode all cases as falling into six disposition types: agreed judgment entry, dismissal, bankruptcy, judgment for plaintiff, judgment for defendant, and transfers/other terminations. It is typically easy to classify these cases into these aggregated disposition types. However, 26 cases have raw disposition values that were uninformative or confusing. We manually checked the final dispositions for these cases. No litigants used the platform in resolving these rarer, nonstandard cases. We assume that these cases are sufficiently atypical that they are unlikely to have been affected in any way by the introduction of the ODR platform. Platform use is associated only with our three primary disposition types: agreed judgment entry, dismissal, and judgment for the plaintiff. This last category—judgment for the plaintiff—is primarily made up of cases in which the defendant defaults. We also have 110 cases with "judgment for the defendant" dispositions, which are disputes in which the plaintiff loses following a trial or the defendant prevails on a counterclaim. None of these cases were ODR-eligible. We exclude them from our sample in the analysis that we present, but including them as dismissals does not materially affect our results. We also exclude the 76 bankruptcy cases, 63 transfer cases, and 13 cases that were reclassified as non-small claims cases. We wind up with a total of 10,542 disposed and undisposed cases in our analysis, as reported in Table 2.1.

[21] Technically, the platform was available as of October 1, 2016, but potential users were not notified on paper of the platform's availability for at least another two weeks, and the first use of the system by an eligible defendant did not occur until October 21, 2016, so we take this as our official launch date. Our results are robust to using October 1, 2016, as the beginning of the post-period. Results relying on this alternative timing (and all other robustness checks discussed below) are available from the authors upon request.

Table 2.1 *Disposition count*

	Eligible Pre-ODR	Eligible Post-ODR	Ineligible Pre-ODR	Ineligible Post-ODR	All Groups
Total Number of Cases					
All	1,815	2,205	2,856	3,666	10,542
Disposed	1,815	1,616	2,853	2,671	8,955
Case Count by Disposition Type					
Agreed Judgment Entry	218	165	124	165	672
Dismissal	711	718	1,353	1,232	4,014
Judgment for Plaintiff					
By Default	886	733	1,331	1,247	4,197
By Trial	0	0	45	27	72
Undisposed	0	589	3	995	1,587
ODR Use by Disposition Type					
Agreed Judgment Entry	0 (0)	19 (17)	0 (0)	0 (0)	19 (17)
Dismissal	3 (2)	51 (28)	0 (0)	11 (4)	65 (34)
Judgment for Plaintiff					
By Default	1 (0)	20 (6)	4 (0)	6 (1)	31 (7)
By Trial	0 (0)	0 (0)	0 (0)	0 (0)	0 (0)
Undisposed	0 (0)	44 (4)	0 (0)	4 (1)	48 (5)

Notes: Pre-ODR and post-ODR classifications are determined by a case's filing date in relation to the online dispute resolution (ODR) platform implementation date (i.e., October 21, 2016). Eligibility is determined by the plaintiff's identity (eligible if the City of Columbus Income Tax Division is the plaintiff). "ODR Use" indicates a case in which the defendant accessed the Small Claims Division's ODR platform. In parentheses, we report the number of cases that reached agreement while using the ODR platform. Dispositions and ODR agreements are distinct: reaching an agreement through the ODR platform does not necessarily indicate that a case is disposed, nor does it preclude the litigants from seeking an agreed judgment entry (or any other disposition) in person.

pre-ODR (or pre-launch, pre-adoption, or pre-implementation) if the lawsuit was filed before this date (i.e., cases filed from January 4, 2016, to October 20, 2016);[22] post-launch cases were filed on or after this date (October 21, 2016, to November 9, 2017). Thus, the post-ODR period is over 90 days longer (and has more cases) than the pre-ODR period.

Our empirical strategy implicitly uses ineligible small claims cases as a control group for treated eligible small claims cases and assumes that any changes in law, procedure, or court management that affect only city tax cases do not correlate with the timing of the adoption of the platform.[23] This identifying assumption is nontrivial. City tax small claims cases, our treatment group, are filed by a single agency (and presumably by a limited number of CITD repeat-player personnel). Any changes in how CITD litigates its small claims cases (or levies taxes in Columbus, Ohio, more generally) that happen to be correlated with FCMC's adoption of the ODR platform may produce a spurious relationship between the implementation of court-assisted ODR and various case outcomes. Yet there is no evidence that CITD's rules, personnel, litigation strategy, or resources changed in any notable way at the time of the court's adoption of the ODR tools *beyond* the behavioral adjustments rooted in the newly available technology itself. Any change in tax laws, rules, or regulations at the city level that might plausibly result from the availability of the ODR platform—and which might be considered to be additional "enforcement tools"—would not affect the small claims docket during our sample period.[24]

To ensure that any differences over our sample period in case outcomes (i.e., default) between eligible and ineligible cases are the result of FCMC's ODR platform, we also collect and control for certain litigant characteristics, including the income level of the defendant's

---

[22] Tables 2.1 and 2.2 (somewhat confusingly) show that 8 cases (4 eligible; 4 ineligible) are classified as "using ODR" despite the fact that these cases were filed "pre-ODR." These are straddle cases. They were filed weeks or months before FCMC implemented the ODR platform, but the defendants were able to find the platform on the court's website at a later date and initiate court-assisted online negotiation. Our findings are robust to different ways of treating these eight cases, including dropping all straddle cases, treating only the eligible CITD pre-ODR cases as post-ODR cases, and treating all of these straddle cases as post-ODR cases.

[23] To ensure that other secular trends do not account for our findings, some of our regressions include eligibility status-specific (eligible vs. ineligible) linear trends and squared linear trends as regressors. Our results are also robust to including only linear trends as controls.

[24] Admittedly, CITD could have changed how it treated eligible cases after ODR implementation *in anticipation* of changes in defendant litigation behavior, including the likelihood that some number of defendants were likely to invoke the option of negotiating with the CITD using FCMC's online negotiation tools.

neighborhood,[25] the defendant's gender,[26] and whether the defendant is an organization (e.g., business) or an individual.[27] These data also make it possible to identify heterogeneous effects, if any, by defendant gender, type, or neighborhood income. For the sake of brevity, we do not report results from these analyses because we find little evidence to suggest that the effects of reduced litigation costs resulting from the implementation of ODR tools varied significantly by defendant demographics.

We are also able to match case-level data from the court to more information than simply whether a defendant had access to FCMC's ODR platform (by case type and date) and how court records show the case resolved. From the developer of the platform, Court Innovations, we obtained information on whether the defendant "used" the ODR platform, the sort of interactions that occurred (e.g., how often the parties interacted, how many messages passed between the parties during online negotiation, at which times), and whether the parties arrived at an ODR-based "agreement." All ODR activity necessarily occurs after implementation and only for eligible cases,[28] and we do not have comparable data for non-ODR interactions. Therefore, at best, we can use this information to explore

[25] We link defendant individual and organization addresses to U.S. Census tracts, which generally contain 1,200 to 8,000 people, ideally a population of about 4,000. We then use Federal Financial Institutions Examination Council (FFIEC) data on median household income percentage (calculated by dividing the tract-level median family income by the MSA/MD-level median family income) to code neighborhood income level as follows: median family income percentage (MFIP) > 0 and < 50 percent as "low," MFIP $\geq$ 50 percent and < 80 percent as "moderate," MFIP $\geq$ 80 percent and < 120 percent as "middle," and MFIP $\geq$ 120 percent as "upper." See www.ffiec.gov/censusapp.htm (accessed July 9, 2019). This approach to coding defendant neighborhood income level is likely to be less accurate in the context of businesses and other entities because owners may live elsewhere. Name or address information is initially missing for almost 1,400 cases. For most cases with defendant name information missing, the defendant is an organization (e.g., business). To associate each defendant with a single name, we scrape party information from FCMC's public online case management portal, following the court's rules for selecting a single name (entity or individual) when cases have multiple defendants.

[26] We code defendant gender using Gender-API.com's gender-matching algorithm, which uses government data, social-network information, and machine learning to predict an individual's gender using first name and country of residence.

[27] Our data on defendant type (individual vs. entity) are relatively complete. Whenever name information is missing, we discovered that an entity (e.g., business) is almost invariably the true defendant in interest, but there are many cases with multiple defendants.

[28] There are, however, approximately 21 disposed cases in which litigants attempted to "use" the ODR platform but did so despite having an ineligible case (4 pre-launch; 17 post-launch). We explore the robustness of our results to our treatment of these observations. In the results below, we treat these cases as not involving ODR, but our conclusions are robust to treating them as observations involving ODR and also to dropping these observations altogether.

possible mechanisms underlying any effect we detect, conscious of the fact that selection or compositional changes, rather than ODR availability, may explain differences in outcomes across eligible-case subgroups (i.e., among eligible cases, litigants who opt to use ODR might differ from those who decide against using it on many unobservable dimensions).[29] Table 2.2 presents, by eligibility and timing, the number of ODR cases during our sample period and demographic summary statistics.[30]

The primary focus of our empirical analysis is whether the availability of an ODR platform has an effect on case outcomes—in particular, the likelihood that the defendant defaults. Default is a status quo-preserving outcome and therefore likely to be inaccurate and inefficient as a legal "ruling." If litigation costs are driving this inefficiency, then a reduction in the costs of litigation (in this case, access to an online negotiation platform) should make default relatively less attractive for defendants, encouraging them at the margin to negotiate in the shadow of substantive law.[31] We present evidence that reducing the costs of litigation lowers the likelihood of a default outcome. These results lead to our exploring a

[29] For example, if we were to find that ODR availability reduces the likelihood of a case ending in default, that reduction might occur across all eligible cases or only for those who choose to use the platform. Unfortunately, among the eligible cases, litigants who decide to use ODR to negotiate next steps in their lawsuit might be especially prone to resolving their cases actively or might be especially tech-savvy or excellent negotiators. Therefore, to draw an inference about the role ODR tools play in determining case outcomes, we must compare all eligible users to all ineligible users—because, by assumption, this categorization is exogenous.

[30] A total of 163 cases have defendants that use the ODR platform in some way during the sample period. Of this number, 48 cases were undisposed at the end of the sample period, leaving 115 fully resolved. Among disposed cases, 8 ODR cases had been filed *before* the platform was launched (4 were eligible and 4 were ineligible), and another 17 cases involved defendants who attempted to use the ODR system to resolve their case despite their case being ineligible (i.e., CITD was not the plaintiff).

[31] One difficulty with this theory is that whether ODR reduces litigation costs may depend in part on whether the plaintiff agrees to participate, and it is initially unclear why a plaintiff *would* participate if refusing to engage is likely to lead to a default judgment or, more generally, to systematically produce plaintiff-friendly outcomes. One potential answer is that fashioning an online agreement may be quick and easy and, ex ante, the plaintiff may not be able to predict which cases will default and which will proceed to a costly trial. In such an environment, efficient negotiation may be the best strategy for all cases. It may also be that a default judgment, although a legal "win" for the plaintiff, is still a costly outcome for plaintiffs generally because of the expense and delay that accompany enforcing a default judgment. In other words, a default may on average be both inaccurate and costly to both parties relative to other potential outcomes.

follow-up question about the case-duration effects of making ODR tools available to litigants. When a defendant defaults, the case tends to close relatively quickly; default can occur in as few as 40 days. As a consequence, reducing default may have the unintended effect of increasing average case duration, which might strike some observers as a drawback but which is also consistent with system efficiency.[32]

2.4 Empirical Results

We hypothesize that a reduction in litigation costs will lower the likelihood of a case ending in a default judgment. To test this proposition, we estimate a series of regressions in which the dichotomous outcome, default, is primarily a function of whether the platform is operational at the time of the case's filing (*post-ODR*), whether the case is (or would have been) eligible for negotiation on the ODR platform (*ODR-eligible case type*), and an interaction of these two indicator variables (*post-ODR × ODR-eligible case type*). We construct our measure of default using online documents available through FCMC's public case management portal that note whether a case was "submitted" to a factfinder before a judgment in favor of the plaintiff.[33] To ensure that our results are not due to a poor measure of default, we also study whether ODR availability affects whether the plaintiff—i.e., CITD—prevails outright in general, also a decent proxy for default in this particular setting.[34] Our case-level controls include indicators for the defendant's gender, type

---

[32] Innovations that cause cases to conclude more slowly may seem socially (and privately) undesirable, but this is not necessarily true if the longer process achieves a more accurate outcome. When litigation costs are so high that defendants choose to default quickly, cases with longer durations (so long as there is evidence that the parties are actively pursuing resolution and ending up somewhere other than the status quo) may be superior. Put another way, when the "price" of litigation drops, defendants may "buy more" by accessing the court system and the tools it offers, and this choice may improve overall social welfare even if resolution takes more time on average.

[33] Specifically, these documents indicate, at least some of the time, whether a case with a disposition of "judgment for the plaintiff" was actually submitted to a factfinder (i.e., did not default) after some sort of hearing involving both the defendant and the plaintiff.

[34] We consider the "judgment for the plaintiff" disposition to be a reasonable proxy for default given the high percentage of default judgments in this category of cases (over 80 percent). Although we do not report the effects of ODR availability on the likelihood of any "judgment for the plaintiff," the results are very similar to our results reported in our tables below that look only at the subset of cases with objective evidence of default. This is reassuring as we are not entirely confident in our principal way of identifying whether a case ended in a default judgment.

Table 2.2 *Sample descriptive statistics*

	Eligible Pre-ODR	Eligible Post-ODR	Ineligible Pre-ODR	Ineligible Post-ODR	All Groups
Number of Cases					
All cases	1,815	2,205	2,856	3,666	10,542
Used ODR	4	134	4	21	163
Number of Disposed Cases					
All cases	1,815	1,616	2,853	2,671	8,955
	(100.0%)	(73.3%)	(99.9%)	(72.9%)	(84.9%)
Used ODR	4	90	4	17	115
	(100.0%)	(67.2%)	(100.0%)	(81.0%)	(70.6%)
Mean Time (Days) to Disposition					
All cases	99.73	90.87	91.29	75.45	88.20
	(62.52)	(58.94)	(75.07)	(54.32)	(64.60)
Used ODR	138.00	109.79	94.00	72.00	104.63
	(74.98)	(66.18)	(91.06)	(41.32)	(65.18)
Defendant Income Level					
Low	281	323	434	493	1,531
Moderate	578	664	725	937	2,904
Middle	512	632	705	933	2,782
Upper	340	447	678	874	2,339
Missing	104	139	314	429	986

Defendant Gender

Male	1,148	1,395	1,415	1,843	5,801
Female	536	629	1,045	1,300	3,510
Missing	131	181	396	523	1,231

Defendant Type

Business	195	255	357	482	1,289
Individual	1,620	1,950	2,499	3,184	9,253

Notes: Pre-ODR and post-ODR classifications are determined by a case's filing date in relation to the online dispute resolution (ODR) platform implementation date (i.e., October 21, 2016). Eligibility is determined by the plaintiff's identity (eligible if the City of Columbus Income Tax Division is the plaintiff). "Used ODR" indicates a case in which the defendant accessed the Small Claims Division's ODR platform. There are some defendants who "used" ODR even though their cases had filing dates in the pre-ODR period (8 cases: 4 eligible, 4 ineligible) or were classified as ineligible in the post-ODR period (21 cases, of which 17 were disposed). The first group involves cases that were *filed* before ODR implementation but were nonetheless active post-ODR and in which defendants were able to use the platform before the case closed. Defendants in the second group apparently located the platform and initiated ODR inadvertently. We explain the data and coding rubric for defendant neighborhood income level, defendant gender, and defendant type in the text. The percentages of all cases and "used ODR" cases that are disposed and standard deviations are reported in parentheses in the second and third panels, respectively, from the top.

(individual or organization), and neighborhood income as well as various time controls, including eligibility status-specific time trends.

We estimate logit regressions because of the dichotomous nature of the outcome variable. We report the results of analyzing the sample of disposed cases as odds ratios in Table 2.3.[35] The baseline odds presented in the table describe the default judgment odds for an ineligible (i.e., non-CITD) case filed before ODR implementation.[36] The odds ratio estimates in the first two rows capture the factor by which the baseline default odds change for each case type (i.e., post-ODR cases and ODR-eligible cases); an odds ratio estimate below one indicates that the odds of a particular category of cases ending in a default judgment (relative to all other alternative dispositions) are relatively lower than for the baseline case type. The baseline odds across specifications confirm that defaults are very common in FCMC's Small Claims Division. A default outcome is about as likely to occur as all other dispositions combined for an ineligible case filed prior to the implementation of ODR technology.[37] Across the columns, the analysis also hints that post-ODR cases (including those that are ineligible for ODR, according to later columns) and city tax (CITD) cases may be less likely to end in default all else equal, although the estimates are not statistically significant.

[35] Odds tell us the probability that a case will end in a default judgment relative to the probability a case will end in any other disposition, taking into account observables—i.e., $\Omega(x) = p(default|x)/(1 - p(default|x))$. An odds *ratio* can be interpreted as the factor by which the baseline odds are expected to change with a one-unit increase in a particular variable, all other variables held constant—i.e., $\Omega(x, x_k + 1)/\Omega(x, x_k)$. Odds ratios are the exponentiated coefficients estimated by the logit regression (Long and Freese 2014). Since we use binary indicator variables in our analysis, an odds ratio less than one indicates that the particular case type described by the binary variable is less likely to be resolved by default than the baseline default odds. Consequently, the magnitudes of our odds ratio estimates are quite different from the predicted probabilities of default we present in Table 2.4.

[36] For example, the baseline odds in column (1) are 0.929, which tells us that for every ineligible case filed before ODR implementation that does not default, 0.929 cases of the same type end with a default judgment. Columns (2) and (3) have very similar baseline odds. Therefore, default is nearly as likely an outcome for ineligible cases prior to ODR as any other disposition, which is consistent with the court's basic summary statistics.

[37] When we run logits on different permutations of controls—including no controls—the baseline odds ratio alternates between being below one and above one but is seemingly always above 0.80 regardless of the reference category of cases, consistent with the fact that default is very common.

Table 2.3 *Default judgment: logit results*

	(1)	(2)	(3)	(4)	(5)	(6)
Post-ODR (0 = No, 1 = Yes)	0.780	0.884	0.909	0.729	0.785	0.816
	(0.168)	(0.193)	(0.201)	(0.180)	(0.196)	(0.206)
ODR-Eligible Case Type (0 = No, 1 = Yes)	0.960	0.813	0.813	0.876	0.793	0.793
	(0.129)	(0.116)	(0.116)	(0.131)	(0.126)	(0.126)
Post-ODR × Eligible Case Type		0.530**	0.573**		0.687+	0.746
		(0.094)	(0.102)		(0.135)	(0.147)
Used ODR (0 = No, 1 = Yes)			0.324**			0.328**
			(0.084)			(0.095)
Baseline Odds	0.929	0.987	0.988	1.219	1.261	1.261
	(0.119)	(0.127)	(0.128)	(0.193)	(0.201)	(0.201)
Controls						
Filed Year and Month Dummies	✓	✓	✓	✓	✓	✓
Eligibility-Status Linear and Squared Time Trends	✓	✓	✓	✓	✓	✓
Gender				✓	✓	✓
Neighborhood Income Level				✓	✓	✓
Defendant Type (Business/Individual)				✓	✓	✓
No. of Observations	8,941	8,941	8,941	7,233	7,233	7,233

Notes: The table reports results from logit regressions in which the dichotomous outcome variable is equal to one if the disposition of the case was "judgment for the plaintiff" by default (according to the court's public online case management system) and zero otherwise (all other dispositions). Estimates are shown as odds ratios (i.e., exponentiated coefficients of the logistic regression) for all but the interaction term, for which the table presents a ratio of odds ratios. Heteroskedasticity-robust standard errors are reported in parentheses. This analysis only includes closed cases (with dispositions). +, *, **, represent significance at the 10%, 5%, and 1% level, respectively.

51

The results of our difference-in-differences specifications are displayed in columns (2) and (5) of Table 2.3. The estimates of interest are the odds ratio transformations of the coefficients on the *post-ODR* × *ODR-eligible case type* interactions.[38] In column (2), the estimate on *post* × *eligible*— 0.530—indicates that the default odds are nearly halved for eligible cases after the implementation of ODR and after we take into account potentially unrelated trends over time by accounting for post-ODR changes in ineligible case outcomes.[39] This estimate is highly statistically significant and tells us that our difference-in-differences framework is helpful in understanding the effect of introducing ODR in small claims courts. In column (5), we include our additional defendant demographic controls. These admittedly reduce the statistical significance of the transformed interaction coefficient, but this shift may be the result of lost observations from missing values (approximately 20 percent of the sample is omitted by including all three categories of controls). In fact, when we repeat the specification in column (2) on the smaller sample used in column (5), the estimate on the interaction increases from 0.530 in column (2) to 0.653 (versus 0.687 in column (5)) and is less precisely estimated. Importantly, linear probability model (OLS) versions of these regressions produce substantively similar results.

In columns (3) and (6) of Table 2.3, we present the results from adding an indicator for whether a defendant in the case actually accessed the online negotiation platform.[40] Individuals with ODR-eligible cases must *choose* whether to use the court's ODR tools—and so use is very unlikely

---

[38] Technically, the transformed coefficient on the interaction term is a ratio of odds ratios. Ai and Norton (2003) and others have highlighted the difficulties of properly interpreting interaction coefficients in nonlinear models such as logistic regression. Marginal effects (i.e., changes in probabilities) are nonlinear functions of both estimated coefficients and independent variable values. However, presenting estimates as multiplicative effects (e.g., odds ratios) avoids the problem of interpreting the sign and statistical significance of the interaction coefficient (Buis 2010), and in any event interpreting the coefficient on an interaction of two indicator variables in a differences-in-differences setting such as this one may be relatively straightforward (Puhani 2012).

[39] As Table 2.3 indicates, the analysis in column (2) controls for month and year effects and eligibility status-specific time trends and trends squared. (These results are robust to omitting the trends-squared controls.) If we estimate the same equation without including any time controls, the estimate that results is still well below one (0.869) but only statistically significant at the 10 percent level.

[40] ODR use in this setting, by and large (i.e., ignoring the handful of pre-implementation and ineligible cases in which parties attempted to access the negotiation platform), can only occur after a court implements an online platform and only with respect to eligible (CITD) cases. Consequently, the use indicator is implicitly a triple interaction, which

to be random. Therefore, any correlation between ODR use and default judgment ought to be interpreted descriptively. From the analysis we learn that cases negotiated via the platform have even lower default odds than eligible cases post-implementation. This association is not surprising. It may be explained by selection: defendants who are unlikely to default under any circumstances may also be more likely to use the negotiation platform when resolving their dispute. Still, it is also consistent with defendants' use of the platform to engage with plaintiffs rather than defaulting by choosing to ignore the complaint.

It is worth noting that the inclusion of the ODR-use indicator reduces the magnitude and statistical significance of the primary difference-in-differences interaction estimate somewhat, but it does not appear to account entirely for the association ODR access has on its own with lower default rates. This pattern is consistent with a few different stories: 1) ODR use may indirectly reduce litigation costs for nonusers by reducing court crowding and mitigating (in this context) the plaintiff's overall litigation burden, and 2) ODR eligibility—including the receipt by mail of the notice announcing the negotiation platform's availability—may independently reduce the likelihood of default, perhaps by making courts appear more open and inviting or by encouraging other forms of negotiation. Regardless, the possibility that the mere availability of ODR tools may reduce the likelihood of default even for those who do not use the platform is a puzzling one and may counsel caution with a causal interpretation of our *post × eligible* estimates if one assumes that eligibility can only reduce default via ODR use.

In Table 2.4, we report the predicted probabilities of default by treatment group for each column in Table 2.3.[41] Conducting a comparison of predicted probabilities averaged across individuals by group allows us to calculate the average marginal effects of implementing FCMC's ODR tools on the likelihood of default—notwithstanding the difficulties associated with interpreting interaction coefficients in nonlinear models (Ai and Norton 2003). We accomplish this by computing a difference-in-differences estimate from group-level averages of individual-level

leaves our *post × eligible* estimate to capture the effect of ODR implementation for eligible cases in which the defendant did not access the negotiation platform.

[41] Rather than inferring changes in the probability of default directly from the coefficients of the logistic regression, we calculate the predicted probability of default for each observation in our sample using the logistic results, report the average for each case type (i.e., ineligible pre-ODR, ineligible post-ODR, eligible pre-ODR, and eligible post-ODR), and then test for differences between these averages.

Table 2.4 *Predicted probability of default judgment*

	Predicted Probability		Pre-ODR vs. Post-ODR			
	Pre-ODR	Post-ODR	Difference over Time	95% Confidence Interval		Diff-in-Diffs
Column (1)						
Ineligible	0.503	0.441	−0.061	−0.165	0.042	-
Eligible	0.493	0.431	−0.061	−0.164	0.042	-
Column (2)						
Ineligible	0.530	0.501	−0.030	−0.133	0.074	−0.144**
Eligible	0.480	0.307	−0.173	−0.280	−0.067	(0.036)
Column (3)						
Ineligible	0.524	0.500	−0.023	−0.128	0.082	−0.127**
Eligible	0.473	0.323	−0.150	−0.262	−0.039	(0.038)
Column (4)						
Ineligible	0.539	0.462	−0.078	−0.195	0.040	-
Eligible	0.507	0.429	−0.077	−0.194	0.039	-
Column (5)						
Ineligible	0.557	0.498	−0.059	−0.177	0.059	−0.088*
Eligible	0.501	0.354	−0.146	−0.276	−0.017	(0.044)
Column (6)						
Ineligible	0.549	0.499	−0.050	−0.170	0.071	−0.069
Eligible	0.492	0.374	−0.119	−0.254	0.017	(0.045)

Notes: The table shows average predicted probabilities of default, conditioned on eligibility status, calculated using logistic regression results. Each row corresponds to the specification denoted by the respective column in Table 2.3. The first two columns depict the average adjusted predicted probabilities of default for cases filed pre-ODR and post-ODR, respectively. The next three columns depict the difference in the predicted probabilities across the two periods as well as the 95% confidence interval (lower bound and upper bound) for this difference, respectively. The final column shows the difference in the predicted probabilities of default between eligible and ineligible cases across the two periods. We use pairwise comparisons to test if the difference between the two differences is significant; we present delta-method standard errors in parentheses below the relevant difference-in-differences estimates. +, *, ** represent significance at the 10%, 5%, and 1% level, respectively.

predicted probabilities.[42] Not surprisingly, given the content of Table 2.3, the marginal effects on the likelihood of default from reducing litigation costs by allowing online negotiation are large and statistically significant. With respect to column (2), ODR availability reduces the likelihood of default by an estimated 14.4 percentage points. When we control for defendant demographics in column (5), the magnitude of the marginal effect drops, but it is still economically important: an 8.8 percentage-point reduction in the likelihood of default.

Tables 2.3 and 2.4 analyze only disposed cases. This is an important limitation. Reducing litigation costs by implementing ODR might have the effect of simply drawing out cases that would eventually default, perhaps past the end of the sample period, or speeding up cases that would have eventually settled or been resolved in court, perhaps pulling them into the sample of disposed cases. In either case, the reduction in the likelihood of default could be at least a partial artifact of a change in the composition of the post-ODR comparison groups. At first blush, this seems unlikely. The percentages of undisposed cases for post-ODR-eligible cases and ineligible cases are almost identical: approximately 26.7 percent and 27.1 percent, respectively. Comparing disposition rates in pre- and post-ODR periods of equal length for both eligible and ineligible cases, eligible cases became relatively more likely to resolve within the sample period, but not by much.[43] There could be more complicated compositional shifts at play, but the most likely story that might confound our results is that ODR availability pulled forward only cases that were

---

[42] Ai and Norton (2003) contend that an interaction effect in nonlinear models is best captured by the cross-difference of the expected value of the outcome variable (or the difference-in-differences in terms of predicted probabilities). Table 2.4 reports the average adjusted predicted probabilities of default by eligibility and pre/post-ODR status as well as the difference between the pre- and post-ODR probabilities for eligible and ineligible cases. The difference between these two differences can be interpreted as the average marginal effect of the interaction across all observations.

[43] In the 290-day time period between January 4, 2016, and October 20, 2016 (i.e., the entire period before ODR implementation in our sample), there were 4,617 cases filed. Of these, 29.7 percent (847 of 2,856) of ineligible cases and 37.7 percent (685 of 1,815) of eligible cases were undisposed as of October 20, 2016. In the 290-day time period between October 21, 2016, and August 7, 2017 (i.e., a substantial portion of the period after ODR implementation in our sample), there were 4,386 cases filed. Of these, 33.8 percent (912 of 2,700) of ineligible cases and 39.6 percent (668 of 1,686) of eligible cases were undisposed as of August 7, 2017. In other words, for the same amount of time, the number of undisposed cases is larger after ODR (for a 290-day period), but the proportion of undisposed eligible cases deviates by less than two percentage points between the two time periods.

unlikely to default (perhaps by facilitating quick and easy negotiation), reducing the fraction of post-ODR cases that end in default among disposed cases.

To examine this particular concern and other selection possibilities, in unreported work, we include undisposed cases in two separate analyses. In both, we rerun the analysis in Table 2.3 with key differences: in the first, we redefine all undisposed cases as having a non-default disposition; in the second, we assume the opposite, redefining all undisposed cases as ending in a default judgment. Our findings are surprisingly robust to both of these strong assumptions. Treating all undisposed cases as defaults actually strengthens our findings, reducing the interaction estimate in column (2) to 0.452 from 0.530 and in column (5) to 0.579 from 0.687, both still highly statistically significant. Treating all undisposed cases as ending in something other than default pushes the estimates in the other direction, increasing them to 0.633 and 0.814, respectively, with the former statistically significant, but the latter no longer statistically significant at conventional levels.[44] On the whole, we find the consistency in these patterns encouraging.

The primary message of Tables 2.3 and 2.4 is that FCMC's Small Claims Division's implementation of ODR seems to have produced a sizeable reduction in the likelihood that a small claims case ends in default. This evidence aligns with the proposition that platform technology reduces the costs of using the courts, leading to more accurate case outcomes. We find that when defendants actually use ODR, cases are even less likely to default, relative to other eligible cases, although this correlation could be the result of selection—i.e., those who choose to use ODR tools may be more likely to be tech-savvy, better educated on

---

[44] We also experimented with a third test: including all undisposed eligible cases as defaults and all undisposed ineligible cases as not ending in a default judgment. We consider this to be a very strong test since it assumes the worst possible arrangement of undisposed cases. With the sets of controls we include in Table 2.3, we continue to find results consistent with Table 2.3. In fact, only by removing the time trends do we find a reversal of our key result (i.e., the exponentiated estimate on *post* × *eligible* becomes greater than one). This makes intuitive sense. Of the total 1,597 undisposed cases in our sample, only three were filed pre-ODR. The undisposed cases filed post-ODR rise in number steadily over time (e.g., 9 undisposed cases were filed in January 2017, 39 in March 2017, 121 in May 2017, 291 in September 2017, 430 in October 2017). Because the undisposed cases are not distributed more equally across time (e.g., pre-ODR and post-ODR), the default odds for eligible cases post-ODR absorb the effect that ought to be attributed to time. This effect is amplified when all eligible undisposed cases are assumed to default and all ineligible undisposed cases are assumed to end in something other than default.

average, and more likely to answer a small claims complaint. On the whole, our results are quite robust to how we treat undisposed cases, the timing of ODR implementation, the inclusion or exclusion of various controls, and even our modeling choices—for instance, if we replace our logit with a linear probability model, we find very similar numbers.[45] In particular, we estimate coefficients on the interaction indicator that are very similar to the marginal effects we calculate in Table 2.4.

One potentially interesting extension of this analysis involves investigating case duration as a distinct outcome. If reducing litigation costs has the effect of altering the distribution of case dispositions—i.e., it reduces the likelihood of default judgments—one unexpected consequence of implementing ODR might be *longer* case durations because defaults can occur quickly relative to longer negotiation and litigation paths. But there is no clear prediction for how a reduction in litigation costs will affect case duration. Lower litigation costs (e.g., from eliminating the need to schedule appointments with a city attorney and from adding communication opportunities outside of business hours) may result in shorter case durations for cases that would never have ended in a default judgment. At the same time, lower access costs may also cause defendants to find responding actively to a complaint more attractive post-ODR implementation, increasing average duration *by* reducing default. In effect, longer duration would capture a shift in which the defendant faces a lower per-unit cost and so "buys more." It is thus an empirical question whether the reduction in litigation costs through procedural tools like an online negotiation platform affects duration, but it is an important one from the perspective of courts, litigants, and policymakers.

---

[45] To further investigate the possibility that implementing court-assisted ODR changes case outcomes, we also examine whether the availability of online negotiation affects the likelihood of "dismissal" and "agreed judgment entry" dispositions. We hypothesize that, because the ODR platform allows defendants to present evidence directly to the plaintiff and attempt to convince the party to dismiss the case, dismissal rates might increase. Without the platform, parties instead often negotiate in the courthouse prior to trial at a point when the plaintiff is more invested—given the time already expended and travel already incurred—and when the defendant may not have the time or evidence at hand to persuade the plaintiff to dismiss. Under these circumstances, an agreed judgment entry seems more likely. Our data are consistent with this story. We find that ODR availability increases the likelihood of a case ending in dismissal and reduces the likelihood of an agreed judgment entry. Importantly, however, the substantive outcomes themselves may not differ all that much. Dismissals often follow settlements, too (dismissals do not only occur when the defendant prevails outright) and agreed judgment entry may be used solely to allow for enforcement after the parties leave the courthouse (if the defendant complies before the trial date, a judgment is unnecessary).

To begin to investigate this issue in a way that lends itself to intuitive interpretation, we regress case duration in days on the indicator variables we use to study default—i.e., *post-ODR*, *ODR-eligible case type*, and *post-ODR × ODR-eligible case type*—using ordinary least squares. As before, our regressions include controls for a defendant's gender, type, and neighborhood income as well as time controls, including eligibility status-specific time trends. Our estimated interaction coefficient represents the change in time-to-disposition in days for eligible cases following the exogenous reduction in litigation costs that accompanies ODR implementation. As before, to explore the role ODR might play in altering the small claims litigation landscape, we also add (endogenous) regressors in some of our regressions, cutting the data by whether the defendant in the case actually accessed the ODR tools and also by whether the parties were able to come to an agreement using the negotiation platform.

We report the results of this OLS analysis in Table 2.5. Column (4) presents the results of our preferred specification, which omits endogenous regressors but does control for time effects and eligibility status-specific time trends.[46] Statistically insignificant point estimates indicate that duration (for disposed cases) is slightly shorter after ODR implementation and that CITD cases generally take an extra week or two to resolve. Our difference-in-differences coefficient estimate of the interaction between *post* and *eligible* shows that cases with defendants who have access to FCMC's ODR platform took on average around 14 days longer to resolve. This estimate is statistically significant at the 5 percent level. If our assumptions (identifying and otherwise) are correct, this longer case duration can be interpreted as the causal result of making small claims cases less costly to litigate.

The welfare implications of such a finding are ambiguous. While cases of longer duration are more expensive and more burdensome on litigants (and perhaps also on courts) all else equal, they are also consistent with higher litigant welfare because case duration is an equilibrium outcome. In particular, if litigation becomes less expensive for defendants to pursue, one might expect fewer defendants to opt for default and instead to seek court-facilitated negotiation. Longer durations may represent better access and, ultimately, the achievement of more accurate outcomes. Thus, there is nothing socially problematic with litigation costs

---

[46] Columns (1) through (3) present the results of analysis that does not control for time effects and trends. We do not discuss these results here but include them for later comparison with results in Table 2.6.

Table 2.5 *Case duration: OLS results*

	(1)	(2)	(3)	(4)	(5)	(6)
Post-ODR (0 = No, 1 = Yes)	-15.210**	-15.207**	-15.205**	-4.243	-5.155	-5.713
	(1.969)	(1.969)	(1.969)	(7.887)	(7.847)	(7.779)
ODR-Eligible Case Type (0 = No, 1 = Yes)	10.224**	10.212**	10.191**	9.150+	9.143+	9.118+
	(2.253)	(2.253)	(2.253)	(5.386)	(5.385)	(5.384)
Post-ODR × Eligible Case Type	4.983+	3.581	3.582	14.040*	12.229+	12.775*
	(2.979)	(2.991)	(2.991)	(6.371)	(6.385)	(6.368)
Used ODR (0 = No, 1 = Yes)		25.437**	48.059**		21.013**	49.932**
		(8.007)	(11.745)		(7.649)	(10.553)
Agreement through ODR (0 = No, 1 = Yes)			-38.186*			-48.806**
			(15.289)			(14.012)
Constant	100.692**	100.754**	100.757**	104.377**	104.375**	104.365**
	(2.650)	(2.649)	(2.651)	(5.777)	(5.777)	(5.778)
Controls						
Gender	✓	✓	✓	✓	✓	✓
Neighborhood Income Level	✓	✓	✓	✓	✓	✓
Defendant Type (Business/Individual)	✓	✓	✓	✓	✓	✓
Filed Year and Month Dummies				✓	✓	✓
Eligibility-Status Linear and Squared Time Trends				✓	✓	✓
No. of Observations	7,243	7,243	7,243	7,243	7,243	7,243

Notes: The table reports results from OLS regressions in which the outcome variable is the time (in days) between the case's filing and disposition dates. Heteroskedasticity-robust standard errors are reported in parentheses. This analysis only includes closed cases (with dispositions). +, *, ** represent significance at the 10%, 5%, and 1% level, respectively.

and average case duration being negatively correlated. A reduction in costs can induce a defendant to initiate negotiation or mediation or to appear to defend a case—which is usually socially valuable. In fact, when default is common, reform that improves access to justice seems likely to increase duration, at least in the kinds of disputes in which engagement cannot resolve a case any faster than a case can end in default. By contrast, Prescott (2017) finds that platform-based online case resolution technology reduces the duration of cases involving civil infractions alleged by the government, which, critically, are disputes that can be actively resolved before default would otherwise occur.

In columns (5) and (6) of Table 2.5, we probe the data to develop hypotheses to account for the increase in duration for eligible cases post-ODR implementation. ODR use and arriving at an agreement are intermediate outcomes in themselves and therefore endogenous, so these correlations ought to be interpreted descriptively. When we include an indicator for whether a case actually involved ODR as a regressor, we learn that cases negotiated through the platform took even longer to resolve—about 21 days longer.[47] While this difference could be explained by selection, it may also indicate that defendants use the platform to engage with plaintiffs rather than default by choosing to ignore a complaint. If this hypothesis is true, one would expect longer durations for eligible cases after ODR implementation. If we further cut the data by whether the case is resolved by an online agreement (i.e., using the negotiation space), we find that ODR use leading to an agreement is associated with much *shorter* durations relative to ODR cases that are resolved without an online agreement, perhaps because litigation continues in some cases to formal adjudication. In other words, defendants who *actively* access the platform but do not settle seem more likely to litigate rather than default on their cases relative to litigants who do not use ODR tools.[48]

---

[47] In column (5) of Table 2.5, the point estimate and statistical significance of the *post × eligible* estimate drop somewhat relative to column (4), indicating that ODR users account for a larger-than-average share of the increase in case duration for the post-ODR-eligible cases.

[48] In unreported work, we also examine the patterns in the distribution of duration changes across different disposition categories (e.g., agreed judgment entry, dismissal, and judgment for the plaintiff). The results point to further complexity. The availability of ODR may reduce marginal litigation costs via online negotiation, and court-assisted ODR may extend the length of small claims cases on average. But there may be a good deal of variance around this average. Duration may drop if an agreement occurs quickly or may increase by a good deal if negotiation occurs before (and ultimately simply delays) adjudication. In our regressions that include (endogenous) regressors for disposition type, if we look solely at eligible cases involving defendants who choose not to use ODR to negotiate their dispute (this group may not be representative, and so this correlation is just suggestive), we detect

We present OLS analysis in Table 2.5 because the estimates are easy to interpret and because it is straightforward to control for time effects and eligibility status-specific time trends in such a framework. However, there are two significant concerns with this approach that require further investigation. First, the sample we analyze above includes only disposed cases, which may generate an important selection bias if the composition of disposed versus undisposed cases changes following ODR implementation.[49] Second, the use of OLS itself is less than ideal when analyzing duration as an outcome because, among other issues, time-to-disposition measures are unlikely to satisfy OLS's normality assumption and OLS is not well-suited to deal with the censoring of disposition dates.

We address these concerns in two ways. First, we test the robustness of our general conclusion that lower litigation costs increase duration (presumably by reducing default and increasing engagement) by rerunning modified OLS models designed to account for undisposed cases—or at least detect if they might explain our findings.[50] In general, our OLS findings in Table 2.5 on the average increase in duration do not appear to be particularly robust when we try to account for undisposed cases in our analysis. But one of our robustness checks suggests that this shift may be because the reduction in litigation costs produces heterogeneous offsetting duration effects on different types of cases.

We start by treating undisposed cases as if they had closed on the last day of the sample, including an additional indicator control for whether the case was actually undisposed. In unreported results, we find a point estimate that is almost as large (9.2-day increase versus 14.4-day increase), but no longer statistically significant.[51] To investigate this further, we redefine our outcome

---

no reliable evidence that the availability of ODR tools alone affects case duration. Changes in case duration appear to be channeled through cases that actually use the platform (i.e., when litigants take advantage of the technology to reduce litigation costs), generally resulting in a longer time to disposition. These results are difficult to interpret, and alone do not point in any reliable way to easier or more efficient litigation.

[49] For example, if using ODR tools reduces only the duration of relatively protracted cases, our estimate of the coefficient on the interaction between *post* and *eligible* might be positive. The reduction in duration would manifest only as long-lived *undisposed* cases that transform into somewhat less-long-lived *disposed* cases, increasing the average duration of disposed cases, even though the overall duration of eligible cases drops as a result of ODR implementation.

[50] For space reasons, we do not report these and many other robustness results. We also do not explicitly discuss some of our many sensitivity checks—for example, ensuring that our OLS duration estimates are robust to the exclusion of weekend days.

[51] Specifically, we assume all undisposed cases in our sample are disposed on the data collection date (i.e., November 9, 2017) and include them in our OLS analysis. If we also include an indicator variable that accounts for ODR use (to match column (5) in

measure for all cases (i.e., both disposed and undisposed) as indicators for whether a case closes within 3 months, between 3 months and 6 months, between 6 months and 9 months, and between 9 months and 12 months of when it is filed. Linear probability models produce (unreported) evidence consistent with offsetting changes in the duration distribution. Specifically, we detect increasing duration at the left end of the distribution (i.e., relatively short cases get longer) but evidence of the opposite change at the other end of the distribution.[52] This exploratory analysis hints that duration may increase (in our OLS estimates) primarily through the lengthening of relatively short-lived cases and that ODR tools might actually reduce the duration of long-lived cases but not by enough to compensate for the larger share of now more protracted but initially very short-lived cases. These findings point to there being a complicated relationship between litigation costs and case duration.

Our second strategy to address the potential selection bias of excluding undisposed cases in our duration work is to employ survival analysis, specifically, a Cox proportional hazards model, which requires a proportional hazards assumption but is robust to non-informative right-hand censoring (i.e., undisposed cases). The disposition hazard function represents the disposition rate for a particular case as a function of time in days and a matrix of time-dependent and time-independent controls. As before, we use a difference-in-differences approach, and we include defendant gender as a covariate and stratify the model on defendant type and average neighborhood income level.[53]

Table 2.6 presents the results from our Cox analysis, displayed as exponentiated coefficients, or hazard ratios,[54] with values greater than one

---

Table 2.5), we find that accessing the negotiation platform is associated with a statistically significant (at the 5 percent level) increase in duration of more than 11 days. If we further add a variable that accounts for reaching an agreement through the platform, we find that an online agreement is associated with a statistically significant (at the 10 percent level) decrease of nearly 18 days.

[52] This evidence is consistent with a higher likelihood of post-ODR-eligible cases resolving within between 6 and 9 months of their filing but a lower or unchanged likelihood of cases resolving during other months (e.g., between 0 and 3 months after filing).

[53] We use stratification for the defendant type and income information rather than include them as covariates because, as controls, they violate the proportional hazards assumption for Cox models. We tested the proportionality assumption for all variables in this analysis using both Schoenfeld residuals and Kaplan-Meier curves.

[54] As before, the exponentiated coefficient of the *post* × *eligible* interaction is actually a ratio of hazard ratios.

Table 2.6 *Case duration: Cox proportional hazards results*

	(1)	(2)	(3)	(4)	(5)	(6)
Post-ODR (0 = No, 1 = Yes)	0.937$^+$	0.937$^+$	0.937$^+$	0.906**	0.906**	0.906**
	(0.032)	(0.032)	(0.032)	(0.028)	(0.028)	(0.028)
ODR-Eligible Case Type (0 = No, 1 = Yes)	0.929*	0.929*	0.929*	0.452**	0.457**	0.457**
	(0.029)	(0.029)	(0.029)	(0.025)	(0.025)	(0.025)
Post-ODR × Eligible Case Type	0.906*	0.931	0.931	0.968	0.996	0.996
	(0.041)	(0.043)	(0.043)	(0.046)	(0.048)	(0.048)
Used ODR (0 = No, 1 = Yes)		0.662**	0.432**		0.386**	0.113**
		(0.062)	(0.056)		(0.105)	(0.051)
Agreement through ODR (0 = No, 1 = Yes)			2.457**			9.563**
			(0.450)			(5.301)
Eligible Case Type × Analysis Time				1.008**	1.008**	1.008**
				(0.001)	(0.001)	(0.001)
Used ODR × Analysis Time					1.005**	1.012**
					(0.002)	(0.003)
Agreement through ODR × Analysis Time						0.988**
						(0.004)
Controls						
Gender	✓	✓	✓	✓	✓	✓
Neighborhood Income Level	✓	✓	✓	✓	✓	✓
Defendant Type (Business/Individual)	✓	✓	✓	✓	✓	✓
No. of Observations	8,497	8,497	8,497	8,497	8,497	8,497

Notes: The table reports results from the (extended) Cox proportional hazards model with "failure" occurring when a case is disposed. Estimates are shown as hazard ratios (i.e., exponentiated coefficients of the Cox regression) for all but the interaction terms, for which the table presents ratios of hazard ratios. Heteroskedasticity-robust standard errors are reported in parentheses. This analysis includes all cases (disposed and undisposed). $^+$, *, ** represent significance at the 10%, 5%, and 1% level, respectively.

indicating a higher rate of case disposition. In column (1), the estimate on our interaction term is 0.91 (which is statistically significant at the 5 percent level). This estimate tells us that once we account for changes in disposition rates experienced by both ineligible and eligible cases (i.e., changes not directly attributable to ODR implementation), the availability of the negotiation platform reduces the disposition rate on any particular day by approximately 9 percent on average, which equates to a longer duration period between filing and disposition.[55] Column (2) adds a variable for a defendant's use of the negotiation platform. Use is associated with a statistically significant hazard ratio of 0.66, indicating that eligible cases filed after ODR implementation experience a further reduction in their disposition rate when defendants use the platform. By contrast, column (3) shows that when negotiation over the platform ends in an agreement, cases resolve relatively quickly.

Columns (1) through (3) of Table 2.6 follow the specification choices of our previous analyses; however, some of our key independent variables may violate the proportional hazards assumption.[56] To account for this, we add three additional specifications with new regressors: linear interactions with analysis time for each variable that violates this assumption. We present these results in columns (4) through (6). Column (4) reports estimates from our base difference-in-differences specification with time

[55] We do not control for time effects or time trends in Table 2.6 for the practical reason that there are computational limits to the number of stratification dimensions one can use. To help in assessing the likely consequences of this exclusion, columns (1) through (3) in Table 2.5 report OLS results from specifications that also omit these controls. In the OLS context, the inclusion of time controls and trends strengthens our results, so their absence in the survival setting may be considered conservative. To explore the robustness of our approach in Table 2.6 for controlling for potential confounders, we run a series of Cox models in which we stratify on varying subsets of our controls (other than gender, which satisfies the proportional hazards assumption and so is included in all models as a control variable). The resulting point estimates on our *post* × *eligible* interaction are usually lower than 0.91 in magnitude (i.e., the longer duration effect is even stronger) but are less precise—in most cases, the interaction estimate is not statistically significantly different from one at conventional levels.

[56] Failing to satisfy the proportional hazards assumption indicates that the relative hazard may not be constant over time. Although some of the variables we use in our analysis that we report in columns (1) through (3) of Table 2.6 appear to violate the proportional hazards assumption for Cox models, Allison (2010) argues that the relative hazards can nevertheless be interpreted as an "average effect" over the relevant time period and are therefore not necessarily incorrect. Interacting these problematic variables with a measure of time—as we do in the specifications corresponding to columns (4) through (6) in Table 2.6—is sufficient to correct for the problem, but the estimates this approach produces are more complicated to interpret (as the relative hazard ratios are now functions of time).

interactions for the *eligible* variable. In general, the variables without time interactions describe a similar effect to the first iteration of this model: introducing ODR tools decreases the disposition rate for eligible cases filed after ODR implementation (i.e., ODR increases case duration). However, the hazard ratio for *eligible* is now dependent on time (in this case, days). The time-dependent relative hazard ratio for eligible cases is 1.008t, meaning that each additional day a case is undisposed results in a disposition rate that is 0.8 percent higher. Thus, although ODR-eligible cases are initially associated with lower disposition rates (and, therefore, longer case durations), this effect diminishes over time.[57]

2.5   Possible Mechanisms

Our analysis so far has stressed the effects of ODR access and use on case dispositions and duration. We have contended that access to an online negotiation platform has made it easier for people to resolve their disputes, lowering litigation costs and reducing barriers to using courts, and thereby increasing parties' willingness to pursue litigation. When pursuing a meritorious small claim is rational, parties are more likely to negotiate in the shadow of substantive law, and the outcomes of disputes will be more efficient. But does court-assisted ODR actually reduce litigation costs? How has it worked on the ground? In this part, we present additional data suggesting that access to ODR tools has resulted, in the main, in more effective communication between parties and has made courts more responsive and accessible by eliminating the need to go to court physically during regular business hours. These additional pieces of evidence dovetail well with the major thesis of this chapter that difficult, frustrating, and inaccessible court procedures (i.e., high litigation costs) are more likely to end with default in low-stakes cases, reducing the accuracy of courts and law generally.

In Table 2.7, we present supplementary information on the content of actual negotiations occurring over FCMC's Small Claims Division's ODR

---

[57] Similar conclusions follow from the estimates we present in columns (5) and (6) in Table 2.6. The indicators for eligibility status, ODR platform use, and whether an agreement was reached on the ODR platform are associated with higher hazard rates as analysis time increases. While eligible cases and cases in which parties made use of the court's ODR tools have much lower disposition rates initially than ineligible cases or cases that are not negotiated over the platform, the disposition rates of the former increase linearly with time, suggesting that after a certain period, they become more likely to be disposed on any given day than their counterpart cases that remain undisposed.

Table 2.7 *ODR content statistics*

	Eligible Pre-ODR	Eligible Post-ODR	Ineligible Pre-ODR	Ineligible Post-ODR	All Groups
All ODR Cases					
Total No. of Cases	4	132	4	21	161
Mean No. of Negotiations	1.25	1.10	1.50	1.00	1.10
Mean No. of Exchanges					
Both Parties Total	10.75	11.30	2.25	1.95	9.84
Sent by Defendant	6.25	5.96	1.50	1.24	5.24
Sent by Plaintiff	4.00	4.92	0.00	0.14	4.15
Disposed ODR Cases					
Number of Cases	4	89	4	17	114
Mean No. of Negotiations	1.25	1.10	1.50	1.00	1.11
Mean No. of Exchanges					
Both Parties Total	10.75	11.70	2.25	1.76	9.85
Sent by Defendant	6.25	5.92	1.50	1.12	5.06
Sent by Plaintiff	4.00	5.16	0.00	0.18	4.19
Disposed ODR Cases w/ Agreement					
Total No. of Cases	2	51	0	5	58
Mean No. of Negotiations	1.00	1.16	–	1.00	1.14
Mean No. of Exchanges					
Both Parties Total	16.50	13.27	–	2.00	12.41
Sent by Defendant	9.50	6.27	–	1.00	5.93
Sent by Plaintiff	6.00	6.02	–	0.00	5.50

Notes: Pre-ODR and post-ODR classifications are determined by a case's filing date in relation to the online dispute resolution (ODR) platform implementation date (i.e., October 21, 2016). Eligibility is determined by the plaintiff's identity (eligible if the City of Columbus Income Tax Division is the plaintiff). An "ODR case" indicates a case in which the defendant accessed the Small Claims Division's ODR platform. The total number of cases reported is 161 (as opposed to 163, as reported in Table 2.2) because two cases represent two distinct matters, and it is impossible in our data to distinguish which negotiations and exchanges are associated with each case in these two pairs.

platform. In particular, we calculate the average number of communications between the parties in all ODR cases, in disposed ODR cases, and in ODR cases ending in agreements. Negotiations producing online agreements involved relatively few exchanges (on average between 13 and 14 for post-ODR-eligible cases), meaning that negotiations were not protracted and were not strategically used as a dilatory tactic to extend the life of cases. Whether negotiations resulted in short- or long-term arrangements, each party received the benefit of avoiding costs associated with scheduling calls or meetings or appearing in court. Importantly, decision-maker intervention was avoided when the parties came to agreement using the ODR platform, allowing court staff to focus resources elsewhere—a spill-over benefit that may have led to more effective case processing for parties not opting for ODR. Even when exchanges by the parties over the platform do not result in an agreement, these communications may still amount to quick, efficient discovery—reducing confusion and clarifying issues—and therefore may reduce the psychological and financial costs of resolving the underlying dispute, especially because communication between the parties can occur asynchronously.

ODR-platform technology also responds to the public's demand for choice and on-demand service (reducing litigation costs of a particular sort). For instance, FCMC's court-assisted ODR enhances access to justice by allowing parties to participate in negotiations at a time of day of their choice (and they do not need to agree with each other on a particular time).[58] Under the traditional litigation model, a trial is scheduled for a particular date and time. In FCMC's Small Claims Division, small claims cases were held Mondays through Thursdays at 1:30 p.m. or 2:00 p.m. during the period of this study. Rescheduling is costly and results in delays. By contrast, the ODR platform is accessible 24/7, and rescheduling is never necessary. The communication behavior of our sample of ODR-using defendants reveals that the traditional time for small claims trials is not ideal for a large majority of litigants. In Figure 2.1, we show when defendants initiated negotiation for the first time and when each defendant message was sent by the hour of the day.

---

[58] FCMC's platform is designed to place parties in control of not only *when* they address their case but how they approach that task as well. A traditional trial is costly in part because it requires parties to surrender self-determination in exchange for a decision that is guided by rules of procedure and substantive case law. Court-connected negotiation, in contrast, allows parties to retain self-determination at an early stage with the knowledge that they may proceed to court if their negotiations are unsuccessful.

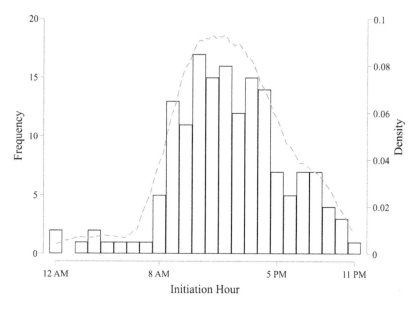

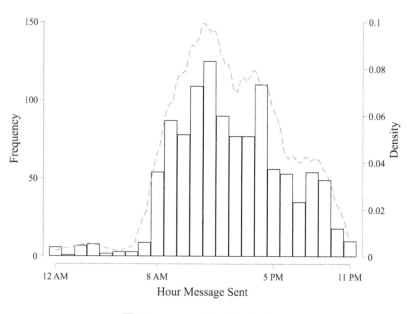

Figure 2.1   ODR exchange timing.

We can draw a couple of conclusions from these data. First, there is great heterogeneity in when defendants *choose* to engage with the court's tools and with the plaintiff. Second, many defendants prefer to "litigate" their case outside of traditional business hours. Leaving aside the financial costs of travel and missing work and the confusion that accompanies going to a courthouse, the traditional one-"time"-fits-all approach is clearly costly in and of itself for defendants.

Our data also allow us to study individual negotiations that took place on FCMC's platform. The exchanges are enlightening, as they regularly reveal the source of the dispute (often confusion or miscommunication), how parties try to resolve their dispute using the platform, and how the availability of the platform allows defendants to engage in a way likely to reduce default and improve the accuracy of the final disposition. In one case, although the defendant had two jobs and would have been unable to come to court either to negotiate with the CITD or for any in-court adjudication, the parties resolved the dispute online in about three hours. In another case, the complaint had its source in a misunderstanding between the defendant and plaintiff and was resolved quickly online. In a third dispute, the defendant was out of the country when he received notice of the small claims suit against him, yet he was easily able to communicate with the plaintiff online and resolve the case. A fourth example involves a quick online agreement for a defendant who, because of family obligations to three special-needs children, would have been unable to appear in court without great difficulty. In the negotiations themselves, defendants sometimes express gratitude for the availability of FCMC's platform. These data points are anecdotes, but they do provide meat to the claim that adopting court-assisted ODR tools can reduce the financial and psychological costs of litigation.[59]

2.6   Conclusion

This chapter has sought to examine how litigation costs can distort case outcomes, particularly in low-stakes cases. In these cases, even modest litigation costs can induce parties to choose "optimally" to default. When litigation costs are fixed, default may be privately and socially optimal,

---

[59] From the court's perspective, the availability of the online negotiation platform has allowed parties to leverage civil procedure to generate positive substantive outcomes that would not have been possible otherwise.

even if substantively inaccurate. However, when courts are in a position to use technology or other innovations to reduce parties' litigation costs, the outcomes of disputes may improve, tracking on-the-books law more closely. In our empirical work, we study the consequences of a large court's experiment with court-assisted ODR, which takes the cost-reducing aspirations of small claims courts one step further by making an online negotiation space available to litigants, facilitating access to the court and easing communication between the parties. Our conclusions regarding case outcomes are straightforward. The availability of ODR-platform technology reduces the likelihood that a typical defendant's case ends in a default judgment, particularly when the defendant in question actually employs the technology to negotiate and resolve the case. We estimate complicated and at best tentative effects on case duration. Even so, they at least hint that although total litigation costs may not have gone down, the payoff of investing in a case may have increased, making parties more willing to use the courts. In light of this evidence, reform focused on reducing litigation costs in small-stakes cases may not only improve litigant satisfaction with using the court system but may also lead to more accurate case outcomes.

References

Allison, Paul D. 2010. Survival Analysis in *The Reviewer's Guide to Quantitative Methods in the Social Sciences*, edited by Gregory R. Hancock and Ralph O. Mueller. New York: Routledge, pp. 413–24.

Ai, Chunrong, and Edward C. Norton. 2003. Interaction Terms in Logit and Probit Models. *Economic Letters*, 80: 123–29.

Buis, Maarten L. 2010. Stata Tip 87: Interpretation of Interactions in Nonlinear Models. *Stata Journal*, 10(2): 305–08.

Bulinski, Maximilian A., and J.J. Prescott. 2016. Online Case Resolution Systems: Enhancing Access, Fairness, Accuracy, and Efficiency. *Michigan Journal of Race and Law*, 21: 205–49.

Chang, Yun-chien, and William H. J. Hubbard. 2018. Does the Priest and Klein Model Travel? Testing Litigation Selection Hypotheses with Foreign Court Data. https://papers.ssrn.com/sol3/papers.cfm?abstract_id=3127728 (accessed July 7, 2019).

  2019. Speedy Adjudication in Hard Cases and Low Settlement Rates in Easy Cases: An Empirical Analysis of Taiwan Courts with Comparison to U.S. Federal Courts in *Selection and Decision in Judicial Process around the World: Empirical Inquiries*, edited by Yun-chien Chang. New York: Cambridge University Press, ch.3.

Coase, Ronald H. 1960. The Problem of Social Cost. *Journal of Law and Economics*, 3: 1–4.

Cole, Daniel H., and Peter Z. Grossman. 2002. The Meaning of Property Rights: Law versus Economics? *Land Economics*, 78: 317–30.

Columbus City Council Ordinance No. 0130-2009. 2009. https://columbus.legistar .com/LegislationDetail.aspx?ID=1036010&GUID=7C333922-3097-4674-BF0E-D3DF82E485EA (accessed July 19, 2019).

Fiss, Owen M. 1984. Against Settlement. *Yale Law Journal*, 93: 1073–90.

Franklin County Municipal Court. 2016. Annual Report. www.fcmcclerk.com/docu ments/annual-reports/FCMC_AR_2016.pdf [pg. 17] (accessed July 7, 2019).

Hadfield, Gillian. 1992. Bias in the Evolution of Legal Rules. *Georgetown Law Journal*, 80: 583–616.

Helland, Eric, Daniel Klerman, and Yoon-Ho Alex Lee. 2018. Maybe there Is No Bias in the Selection of Disputes for Litigation. *Journal of Institutional and Theoretical Economics*, 174(1): 143–70.

Lee, Yoon-Ho Alex, and Daniel Klerman. 2016. The Priest-Klein Hypotheses: Proofs and Generality. *International Review of Law and Economics*, 48: 59–76.

Long, Scott J., and Jeremy Frees. 2014. *Regression Models for Categorical Dependent Variables Using Stata*, 3rd ed. College Station, TX: Stata Press.

Lothes, Alison. 2005. Quality, Not Quantity: An Analysis of Confidential Settle-ments and Litigants' Economic Incentives. *University of Pennsylvania Law Review*, 154: 433–75.

Luban, David. 1995. Settlements and the Erosion of the Public Realm. *Georgetown Law Journal*, 83: 2619–62.

Kotkin, Minna J. 2007. Outing Outcomes: An Empirical Study of Confidential Employment Discrimination Settlements. *Washington and Lee Law Review*, 64: 111–63.

Memo to Municipal Court Judges. 2017. 2016 Mediation Results. Franklin County Municipal Court Dispute Resolution Department. June 13, 2017.

Niblett, Anthony, and Albert H. Yoon. 2017. Unintended Consequences: The Regressive Effects of Increased Access to the Courts. *Journal of Legal Studies*, 14: 5–30.

Ohio Bar Foundation. 2006. *Small Claims Court, A Citizens Guide*. 8th ed. www.supremecourt.ohio.gov/jcs/interpretersvcs/forms/english/5.pdf [pg. 2] (accessed July 7, 2019).

Ohio Courts Statistical Report. (2016). www.supremecourt.ohio.gov/Publications/ annrep/16OCSR/2016OCSR.pdf (accessed July 19, 2019).

Ohio Revised Code, § 1925 (2016).

Ohio Sup. Ct. Rule 16, www.supremecourt.ohio.gov/JCS/disputeResolution/ resources/medDirectory.xlsx; https://www.supremecourt.ohio.gov/LegalRe sources/Rules/superintendence/Superintendence.pdf (accessed July 7, 2019).

Posner, Richard A. 1972. *Economic Analysis of Law*. New York: Little, Brown.

Prescott, J.J. 2017. Improving Access to Justice in State Courts with Platform Technology. *Vanderbilt Law Review*, 40: 1993–2050.

Puhani, Patrick A. 2012. The Treatment Effect, the Cross Difference, and the Interaction Term in Nonlinear "Difference-in-Differences" Models. *Economic Letters*, 115: 85–7.

Priest, George L. 1977. The Common Law Process and the Selection of Efficient Rules. *Journal of Legal Studies*, 6: 65–82.

Priest, George L., and Benjamin Klein. 1984. The Selection of Disputes for Litigation. *Journal of Legal Studies* 13: 1–55.

Resnik, Judith. 2006. Uncovering, Disclosing, and Discovering: How the Public Dimensions of Court-Based Processes Are at Risk. *Chicago-Kent Law Review*, 81: 521–70.

Rhee, Robert J. 2006. A Price Theory of Legal Bargaining: An Inquiry into the Selection of Settlement and Litigation Under Uncertainty. *Emory Law Journal*, 56: 619–92.

Rubin, Paul H. 1977. Why Is the Common Law Efficient? *Journal of Legal Studies*, 6(1): 51–63.

Supreme Court of Ohio. 2016. Ohio Courts Statistical Report. www.supremecourt.ohio.gov/Publications/annrep/16OCSR/2016OCSR.pdf (accessed July 7, 2019).

Supreme Court Task Force on Funding of Ohio Courts. 2015. Report & Recommendations. www.supremecourt.ohio.gov/Boards/courtFunding/Report.pdf [pg. 14] (accessed July 7, 2019).

Speedy Adjudication in Hard Cases and Low Settlement Rates in Easy Cases

An Empirical Analysis of Taiwanese Courts with Comparison to US Federal Courts

YUN-CHIEN CHANG AND WILLIAM H. J. HUBBARD

3.1 Introduction

This chapter empirically compares civil litigation in the United States and Taiwan.[1] Our goals are twofold. First, as part of the focus of this book on the efficiency of courts, we present Taiwan and the United States as examples of two basic paradigms for controlling costs and delay in civil litigation. Debates about cost and delay among US lawyers almost inevitably involve calls for promoting settlement and alternative dispute resolution (such as mediation and arbitration), on the one hand, or (less frequently) calls for limitations on time-consuming or expensive procedures (such as discovery or trial), on the other hand. Loosely speaking, we can think of these approaches to reducing costs and delay as *avoiding* the cost of litigation, on the one hand, and *reducing* the cost of litigation, on the other hand. Taiwan and the United States provide a dramatic contrast given the almost singular approach in the United States on the

[1] Chang: Research Professor & Director of Center for Empirical Legal Studies, Institutum Iurisprudentiae, Academia Sinica, Taiwan. Email: kleiber@sinica.edu.tw. Hubbard: Professor of Law and Ronald H. Coase Teaching Scholar, the University of Chicago Law School. Email: whubbard@uchicago.edu. A draft of this paper was presented at the 2018 Conference on Empirical Legal Studies in Europe held at Leuven on May 31, 2018 and 2018 Conference on Empirical Legal Studies held at University of Michigan, Ann Arbor on November 11, 2018. Two anonymous referees, Tilmann Altwicker, Anu Bradford, Stephen Calkins, Julian Nyarko, Shay Lavie, Stewart Schwab, Keren Weinshall, and Wei Zhang provided valuable suggestions. We thank several Taiwanese judges for granting interviews with us. Hubbard thanks the Jerome F. Kutak Faculty Fund for research support. Rafeh Qureshi provided excellent research assistance. The views expressed in this article are solely of the authors, not of the Judicial Yuan of Taiwan, Academia Sinica, or any other government agencies.

former (avoiding litigation costs) and in Taiwan on the latter (reducing litigation costs).

Second, we take advantage of this comparative exercise to evaluate a theory about litigation delay and settlement failure – a theory that is harder to test in the absence of a comparative perspective. A large share of Taiwanese court cases (over 40 percent) are debt collection actions, and these cases tend to settle even less often than other categories of cases. This might appear surprising, given that debt collection cases tend not to involve major questions of private or asymmetric information, which usually tend to explain why cases do not settle.[2] On the other hand, a standard prediction of the literature on fee-shifting rules is that fee shifting in favor of prevailing parties (known as the English Rule) encourages litigation when the plaintiff has a very high probability of winning. Given that Taiwan follows the English rule and most debt collection plaintiffs prevail at trial, one might be tempted to conclude that fee shifting rules explain this pattern. Yet the comparison to the United States is instructive here: despite having patterns of settlement that are generally sharply different from Taiwan, the US data on debt collection cases looks almost identical to the Taiwanese data, despite the United States employing the opposite fee shifting rule. In our analysis below, we attempt to explain this striking similarity between litigation patterns in the United States and Taiwan.[3]

This chapter's comparative examination of Taiwanese and US courts is powered by two large data sets of rich, case-level data. One contains all civil cases rendered by courts of first and second instance in Taiwan in 2010–2015 ($N = 798,801$).[4] Our second data set is administrative data on federal civil cases filed in the United States in 2010–2013.[5]

While the comparative exercise in this chapter is limited to two court systems, we have the benefit of large administrative data sets of detailed information on these court systems. This allows us to be highly selective in choosing the most similar subsets of cases from each system for

---

[2] See Section 3.5 for further discussion.

[3] To be sure, there are other aspects of court behavior for which parallels exist between Taiwan and the United States. One of us, for instance, in Chang et al. (2017), demonstrates that Taiwanese judges, American judges, and American juries exhibit the same pattern in assessing pain and suffering damages, despite coming from different legal and personal backgrounds.

[4] Our Taiwan data are described in detail in Chang and Hubbard (2019). In short, our data set comprises all civil cases decided by the courts of Taiwan other than the Supreme Court.

[5] Our US data are described in detail in Hubbard (2017).

comparison with the other. For example, the institutional environment in the United States makes low-stake cases either ineligible to be or unworthy of being filed in federal courts, but it is not the case in Taiwan. Using detailed information on case stakes (available in the Taiwanese data) and on jurisdictional basis (available in the US data), we are able to identify a subset of cases in each system with amounts in controversy in excess of 75,000 USD. The subset of cases with comparable stakes in the two countries provides a more even playing field to compare the working of courts on filed cases.

With its preliminary, yet detailed, examination of Taiwanese data, this chapter paints a picture of a court system that embodies an approach to judicial "efficiency" very different from that in the United States: low settlement rates and lots of trials, but relatively low costs of adjudication in terms of both money and time. The Taiwanese courts are a surprising institution to many lawyers from the United States, who find the high trial rates and fast disposition times a far cry from the familiar patterns in data on the US federal courts. Of course, a cross-country comparison of courts is never an apples-to-apples comparison. We emphasize that we provide the juxtaposition to illustrate how different – and sometimes, how similar – the systems are, not to presume that any prescriptive conclusions can or should flow from the comparison. We also try to account for differences in the underlying cases or terminology used in the two systems, so as to minimize the mismatch between the two data sets.

The rest of the chapter is structured as follows: Section 3.2 provides an overview of the Taiwanese court system. Section 3.3 contrasts the patterns of case disposition in diversity cases in US federal courts and high-stake cases in Taiwanese courts. Section 3.4 shows that despite their lower rates of settlement and higher rates of trial and appeal, when dealing with cases with comparable stakes, courts in Taiwan reach final judgments significantly faster than the US federal courts. In Section 3.5, we note that despite these obvious differences, there are subtle similarities between how courts in Taiwan and the United States address the challenge of efficiently resolving high volumes of cases, with a particular focus on debt-collection cases. Along the way, we acknowledge the numerous challenges researchers face when comparing court administrative data from different jurisdictions, and explain the ways in which we address these challenges.

Section 3.6 concludes, noting that Taiwan and the United States offer prototypical examples of two contrasting approaches to judicial efficiency: *reducing* the cost of adjudication, or *avoiding* the cost of the adjudication, respectively. While the contrasts are illuminating, so are the points of similarity, which suggest to us that some categories of litigation, such as debt-collection actions, are so common, yet so distinctly unlike other types of disputes, that empirical researchers would be well advised to analyze that category separately. We also note a possible convergent evolution in procedure: although further investigation is warranted, our study suggests that the seemingly non-substantive procedural device of default judgment in Taiwan may end up filling the niche occupied by summary judgment for the plaintiff in the United States.

3.2   Overview of the Courts of Taiwan

Taiwan is a civil-law country. Most of its private law resembles that in Germany, with influences from Japanese law (Chang 2016, pp. 227–28; Chang, Chen, and Wu 2017; Chang, Garoupa, and Wells 2018; Huang 2009, p. 251; Wang 2002). American law has only occasionally been referenced in legal reforms. Taiwan has a unitary legal system, unlike the United States' federal system. In addition to a constitutional court in charge of abstract, centralized, ex post constitutional review, there are administrative courts that deal with disputes between citizens and governments regarding public-law matters; ordinary courts that handle civil and criminal cases; and IP courts.

Our focus is on the courts that handle civil law disputes. Taiwan has 22 district courts (courts of first instance) and 6 high courts (courts of second instance). The Taiwan Supreme Court reviews questions of law in appeals from the high courts.

As is typical for a civil-law system, there is no sharp distinction between pretrial and trial phases litigation; the entire lawsuit could be considered the "trial." Judges and attorneys meet once every few weeks for a few times, rather than meeting on consecutive days (Langbein 1985).

There is no American-style discovery in Taiwan, although there are rules for disclosure of information early in the process. Most attorneys charge flat fees collected beforehand. Contingent fees are legal but are used in less than 5 percent of cases (Chang and Tu 2019 forthcoming). Bigger law firms charge by the hour about half of the time (Chang and Tu 2019 forthcoming). Most attorneys charge 1,500 USD–2,500 USD per case, per court instance (i.e., appeal is a separate fee), even in high-stake cases.

There are three types of court procedures: small-claim procedure, summary procedure, and ordinary procedure. Small-claim procedures apply when the amount at stake is below 100,000 NTD (approximately 3,333 USD). Small-claim cases are handled by a single judge in one of the 22 district courts. This kind of case can be appealed to a three-judge district court panel on questions of law.

Summary procedures apply when the amount at stake is below 500,000 NTD (approximately 17,000 USD) or in certain types of cases specified in Article 427 of the Taiwan Code of Civil Procedure. This type of case is also handled by a single judge. Cases can be appealed to a three-judge district court panel for trial de novo, and the court may permit appeal to the Supreme Court.

A case applying ordinary procedures is handled by a single judge in a district court. Ordinary procedures apply when the amount at stake is equal to or above 500,000 NTD.[6] Appeals are handled by a three-judge panel in one of the six high courts. The review of facts and laws is de novo. Cases with more than 1,000,000 NTD (approximately 33,000 USD) at stake may be appealed to the Supreme Court for questions of law. Appellants have to be represented by attorneys in the Supreme Court. The Taiwan Supreme Court has discretionary jurisdiction (Eisenberg and Huang 2012).

The filing fee is pro rata (about 1 percent of the amount claimed in the first instance and 1.5 percent of the amount claimed in the second instance), meaning the higher the stakes, the more expensive (in absolute terms) it is to use litigation to resolve the dispute. Filing fees are two-thirds refunded if parties settle (including through mediation) in court before adjudication. If the plaintiff wins partially, filing fees are allocated on pro rata basis between the parties. If plaintiffs win entirely, filing fees are the sole responsibility of defendants.

3.3   Patterns of Settlement, Judgment, and Appeal

To many American lawyers and judges, efficiency means more settlements and case dispositions (such as summary judgment) that avoid the tremendous expense of trial. Viewed in this light, the courts of Taiwan might seem terribly inefficient. As we show below, settlement rates are

---

[6] Summary procedures, however, will always apply to certain types of cases even when the amount at stake is above 500,000 NTD (see Article 427 of the Taiwan Code of Civil Procedure).

low in Taiwan, and summary judgment is very rare. Rather, most cases end with a judgment by the court after a complete trial. In this section, we document the strikingly low rates of settlement and summary judgment in civil cases in Taiwanese courts and correspondingly high rates of trial and appeals.

The settlement, trial, and appeal rates reported in this section refer to what we call "high-stake cases," which we define as cases with stakes exceeding 75,000 USD.[7] One important distinction is that the data from Taiwan are data from a unitary court system, including everything from the proverbial dog-bite case to real estate development contracts and sovereign immunity actions. Our US federal court data, due to the limits of federal subject matter jurisdiction, include a narrower, and usually higher-stakes, swath of litigation. To account for this, when juxtaposing data from Taiwan and the United States in this part, we limit ourselves to high-stakes cases in each court system. For Taiwan, we obtain stakes directly from the "stakes" variable in the Taiwanese data.[8] We limit our analysis of US data to cases within the diversity jurisdiction, as such cases have a requirement that the "amount in controversy" (i.e., plaintiff's claimed stakes) exceed 75,000 USD.[9] Because administrative data from the US federal courts does not otherwise contain a consistently coded measure of stakes, we use diversity jurisdiction as a proxy for high stakes to make our US data comparable in terms of stakes to our Taiwanese data. We omit lower-stakes cases because unlike Taiwan, which has a unitary court system, the United States has separate state court systems that handle the vast majority of lower-stakes cases. High-stakes cases allow us to isolate those cases from Taiwan whose stakes makes them most comparable to the type of litigation most generally associated with US federal courts.[10] (See Appendix 3A for overall settlement, trial, and appeal rates in lower courts in Taiwan.)

[7] Throughout this chapter, we use an exchange rate of 30:1 for New Taiwan dollars to United States dollars, which approximates the exchange rate during the time frame of the data. Thus, the high-stake cases in Taiwan have stakes above 225,000 NTD. We do not take into account purchasing power parity in this chapter.
[8] Plaintiffs in Taiwan are required to plead the stakes of the case, and filing fees are assessed as a percentage of stakes. Thus, plaintiffs have incentives not to excessively overclaim stakes.
[9] See 28 USC §1332(a).
[10] To this end, we also exclude categories that, under US doctrine, are excluded from the US courts, such as family law and probate matters. Ideally, of course, we would compare the remaining Taiwanese cases to data from state courts. Unfortunately, there is no comparably comprehensive dataset of US state court data as there is with US federal court data.

3.3.1   Settlement

Settlement can occur in many ways. Parties can settle out of court after filing a lawsuit. If they prefer to keep the settlement terms strictly confidential, plaintiffs can withdraw their cases. Hence, "withdrawal" as a case outcome can represent settlement. Of course, plaintiffs may withdraw when finding out that they (at the time) do not have a winning case.[11] Parties can also settle before the judge is assigned to handle their case. Judges, in fact, are encouraged by the Taiwan Code of Civil Procedure to actively promote settlement.

There is also a separate mediation procedure. Voluntary agreements reached in the mediation procedure also count as settlements. Mediations are handled by summary court judges if the disputes are originally filed as mediation applications. If, during trial, both parties agree to have their disputes transferred to the mediation procedure, either the judge assigned the case or a judge in the summary court handles the mediation. In principle, a mediating judge chooses one to three mediators to start mediating (parties may object to the choice; mediators are chosen from a list of mediators prepared by each district court); the judge will personally participate in the mediation once it is likely that both parties can reach an agreement. The judge may also mediate the dispute throughout by herself.

We treat settlements, withdrawals, and successful mediations as "settlements" for our purposes. All of them contrast with a judicial judgment in which the court renders a verdict that declares a winner and awards (or declines to award) damages or issues an injunction.

Even when one defines "settlement" in this broad way, settlement rates in Taiwan are low. In Figure 3.1, we visually demonstrate the rate of the three components of our broad definition of settlement for high-stake cases in the courts of first instance in 2010–2015. Judge-approved settlement in court is what we call settlement "narrowly defined," and it is not even the largest component of settlement "broadly defined." It should be clear from the graphs that the rates of plaintiff withdrawal are the major factor in determining the rates of broadly defined settlement rates. Both narrowly defined settlement rates and successful mediation rates are below 12 percent in all case types. The settlement rate broadly defined

---

[11] Helland et al. (2017) find that 13 percent of disputes were "abandoned" without settlement after a lawyer was hired and that 6 percent of disputes for which suit was filed were abandoned without settlement.

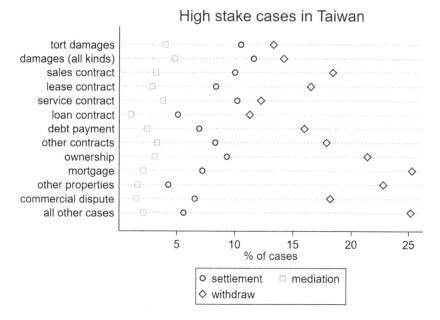

Figure 3.1   Settlement (narrowly defined), mediation, and withdrawal rates by dispute type for high-stake cases in the Courts of First Instance in Taiwan, 2010–2015.
Source: Civil Cases Administrative Data (Judicial Yuan, Taiwan)

in Taiwan (17 percent–35 percent) is much lower than that in the United States, where, in diversity cases, settlement rates exceed 70 percent[12] (see Table 3.1). Settlement rates broadly defined in Taiwan are also lower than those in Japan (50 percent–70 percent between 1952 and 2015), whose civil procedure rules are very similar to those in Taiwan (Chang 2017).[13]

3.3.2   Trial and Other Adjudications (Summary and Default Judgments)

Trial rates in Taiwan are not directly comparable to "trial" rates in the United States. Because Taiwan has a civil-law tradition, the entire

---

[12] In our data from the Administrative Office of the US Courts, among diversity cases that we code as "settled," the cases are coded as "Dismissed: Voluntary" (15.4%); "Dismissed: Settled" (71.4%); "Dismissed: Other" (11.3%); and "Judgment on Other" (1.9%).

[13] Given the similarities in procedure between Japan and Taiwan, we do not attribute the low settlement rates in Taiwan solely to its procedural differences from the United States.

Table 3.1 *Outcomes in first-instance courts*

	Merits Js as % of Terminations	% of Merits Js Plaintiff Win	% of Merits Js Plaintiff Partial Win	Settled as % of Terminations	Other as % of Terminations	Total Terminations
Taiwan Ordinary Courts (Civil Division), 2010–2015						
Total	64.9	53.9	13.9	23.6	11.5	718,079
High Stakes	56.4	34.2	33.2	25.5	18.1	92,820
Debt-Collection	75.4	93.2	4.4	14.4	10.2	319,428
Non-Debt-Collection	56.5	41.9	31.8	31.0	12.5	398,651
US Federal Courts, 2010–2013						
Total	12.2	56.9	3.1	70.3	17.5	588,111
Diversity	7.3	43.7	3.1	74.1	18.6	358,285
Debt-Collection	64.1	95.1	0.1	30.1	5.8	13,659
Non-Debt-Collection	10.9	51.5	3.3	71.3	17.8	574,451

Notes. All cells except for in the last column are in percentages. "Settlement" refers to settlement broadly defined by this chapter. "Other" refers to non-merits judgments in non-settled cases. Plaintiff win rate is the number of judgments favoring the plaintiff divided by all merits judgments. A case that is both high-stake and (non) debt-collection will be included in both rows. High-stake cases include cases where ordinary procedures apply and more than 75,000 USD is at stake. In Taiwan, one of the three procedures (ordinary, summary, and small-claim) may apply to debt-collection and non-debt-collection cases. The non-debt-collection cases in the United States comprise all the cases not used that are not under the "debt-collection" row. The "total terminations" column in the "non-debt-collection" row and the "debt-collection" row add up to the "Total" row.

Sources: Civil Cases Administrative Data (Judicial Yuan, Taiwan). Federal Court Cases: Integrated Data Base (US Federal Judicial Center).

litigation is the "trial," and thus any case not settled is resolved by the "trial." This stands in contrast to the United States' common law tradition, in which trial is a distinct (and distinctively labor-intensive) phase of litigation. Thus, when discussing "trial" rates, and especially given that we are comparing statistics from Taiwan and the United States, we define our terms somewhat more precisely.

We use the term "merits judgment" to reflect a decision by the court in which the court determines which party prevails on the plaintiff's claims.[14] This is in contrast to settlements, in which the parties resolve the plaintiff's claims on their own, and what we label "other" outcomes, in which the case is terminated without a resolution on the merits, such as a dismissal due to a jurisdictional defect.[15] Thus, while "summary judgment" would be considered a "trial" outcome in Taiwan, summary judgment would be considered an alternative to "trial" in the United States. Nevertheless, a summary judgment qualifies as a "merits judgment" in either setting. The relative prevalence of merits judgments, as we define them, and settlements is basically flipped in Taiwan and the United States. In high-stakes cases in Taiwan, merits judgments are 56.4 percent of cases and settlements are 25.5 percent; in diversity jurisdiction cases in the United States, merit judgments are 7.3 percent of cases and settlements are 74.1 percent (see Table 3.1).

This leaves the question of how the rates of full-blown trials – "trials" in the American sense of the term – compare. Our US data separately code trial verdicts as a distinct outcome, but, because there is no distinct category of "full-blown trial" in Taiwan, our Taiwanese data do not. Thus, we must construct trial rates by eliminating merits dispositions that do not involve a complete trial. It turns out to be an easy task in Taiwan, as summary judgments can be treated as essentially nonexistent.

The primary means of merits adjudication in the United States is summary judgment. Of what we have designated "merits judgments," most are summary judgments (see Table 3.2). Summary judgment also

---

[14] In the United States, this includes all merits judgments entered by the court, even if based on a jury verdict.

[15] More specifically, the "other" outcome in Taiwan includes cases dismissed procedurally, cases transferred to other courts, and other procedural dispositions. In the United States, these cases mostly comprise cases transferred to another district, dismissed for want of prosecution, dismissed for lack of jurisdiction, multidistrict litigation transfers, or cases labelled statistical closing. A small number of cases (about 5 percent altogether) include cases remanded to a US agency, judged on award of arbitrator, appealed to district court (reversed or affirmed) or stayed pending bankruptcy.

exists as a procedural device for accelerated adjudication in Taiwan, although its scope of application is narrower than in the US, Article 249 Section 2 of the Taiwan Code of Civil Procedure stipulates that "where the plaintiff's claim, given the facts that he/she alleges, is manifestly without legal grounds, the court may, without oral argument, issue a judgment dismissing the action with prejudice." That is, unlike in the United States, summary judgment cannot be used to grant judgment in favor of the plaintiff.

Summary judgment is very rare in Taiwan. Our administrative data do not distinguish summary judgments from other court verdicts, but, at our request, Lawsnote.com, a legal service provider in Taiwan, used Article 249 Section 2 as the keywords to search from the universe of cases in 2000–2017 and provided us with a complete list of cases that ended with summary judgments.[16] Based on this search, we find that summary judgments have been used only 483 times in district courts in 2000 January–2017 June. That is, less than 30 times per year throughout Taiwan, out of a total of approximately 75,000 merit judgments per year that are resolved through summary judgments.[17] In other words, the rate at which summary judgment is granted in the courts of Taiwan is essentially zero.[18]

Another means for abbreviating the process of adjudication is default judgment. In the ordinary procedure, per Article 385 Section 1 of the Taiwan Code of Civil Procedure, "where one of the parties fails to appear at the oral-argument session, the court may, on the appearing party's motion, enter a default judgment based on the appearing party's arguments; where the party who fails to appear is summoned and fails to appear again, the court may also on its own initiative enter a default judgment based on the appearing party's arguments." In the summary and small-claim procedures, in principle there will be only one oral-argument session. If one party fails to show up in that session, the court

---

[16] Lawsnote.com collects cases from the official website of the Judicial Yuan, which publishes essentially all civil cases (there are no unpublished or unreported civil cases in Taiwan; only a tiny fraction of specific types of civil cases are not published for privacy reasons).

[17] In 2010–2015, the average merit judgment each year was 77,675. Note that the number of summary judgments Lawsnote.com tallied includes quite a few instances of divorce litigation, while our 2010–2015 administrative data do not contain family- and inheritance-related litigation.

[18] Appendix 3B summarizes our interviews of several Taiwanese judges regarding why summary judgments were so rarely utilized.

Table 3.2 *Trial rates in first-instances courts*

	Total Terminations	All Merits Js (% of Term.)	SJs (% of Merits Js)	DJs (% of Merits Js)	Full-Blown Trials (% of Merits Js)
Taiwan, Ordinary Courts (Civil Division), Ordinary Procedure Only, 2010–2015					
All Cases	215,022	124,346 (57.8%)	0* (0%)	35,234 (28.3%)	89,112 (71.7%)
High-Stakes Cases	85,916	48,453 (56.4%)	0* (0%)	NA	NA
Debt-Collection Cases	46,125	26,725 (57.9%)	0* (0%)	18,686 (69.9%)	8,039 (30.1%)
Non-Debt-Collection Cases	168,897	97,621 (57.8%)	0* (0%)	16,548 (17.0%)	81,073 (83.0%)
US Federal Courts, 2010–2013					
All Cases	588,110	71,737 (12.2%)	23,132 (32.2%)	24,109 (33.6%)	4,820 (6.7%)
Diversity Cases	358,285	26,211 (7.3%)	11,270 (43.0%)	5,773 (22.0%)	2,776 (10.6%)

Debt-Collection	13,659	8,756	(64.1%)	380	(4.3%)	6,600	(75.4%)	37	(0.0%)
Non-Debt-Collection	574,451	62,981	(11.0%)	22,752	(36.1%)	17,509	(27.8%)	4,783	(7.6%)

Notes: DJ = default judgment. Strictly speaking, the domain of debt-collection cases in this table is not exactly the same as that in other tables and figures where the source is Judicial Yuan Administrative Data. Debt-collection cases in the latter are defined by the authors based on the information provided in the raw administrative data. Debt-collection cases in this table are defined by the statistical department of the Judicial Yuan based on the same raw administrative data. Nonetheless, they should be largely overlapping. For unknown reasons, the total number of cases provided to us in descriptive statistics tables by Judicial Yuan is 215,022, while the total number of cases contained in the administrative data is 220,009.

As explained in the text, the number of summary judgments in Taiwan is very low each year. A case that is both high-stake and (non) debt-collection will be included in both rows. High-stake cases include cases where ordinary procedures apply and more than 75000 USD is at stake. In this table, (non) debt-collection cases are included only when the ordinary procedure applies. The non-debt-collection cases in the United States comprise all the cases not used that are not under the "debt-collection" row. The "total terminations" column in the "non-debt-collection" row and the "debt-collection" row add up to the "All cases" row.

Sources: Taiwan Judicial Yuan internal descriptive statistics provided to one of us (Chang). Federal Court Cases: Integrated Data Base (US Federal Judicial Center).

85

may also on its own initiative enter a default judgment based on the appearing party's arguments. Default judgments are somewhat common in civil cases in Taiwan. As we see in Table 3.2, a default judgment is the outcome of about 28 percent of all merits judgments handled in the ordinary procedure. The number for the cases in our US data is about 34 percent of all merits judgments.

After adjusting for summary judgments and default judgments, we treat the remaining merits judgments as outcomes from full-blown trials. In diversity cases in the US federal courts, the full-blown trial rate is 11 percent, while in high-stake cases in Taiwan, the full-blown trial rate is probably higher than 80 percent (see Table 3.2).[19] We see that the discrepancy in complete trials between Taiwan and US federal court is still very large.

3.3.3   Appeal

We estimate appeal rates in the US federal courts by comparing the number of case terminations at the first-instance level to the number of terminations at the second-instance level. Our administrative data on Taiwanese courts track whether each first-instance case was appealed. As we see in Table 3.3, appeal rates are very high among high-stakes cases in Taiwan (about 28 percent of all terminations and 48 percent of all merits judgments). By contrast, appeals occur in a smaller share of cases in the US federal courts than in Taiwan. Although for some categories of cases appeal rates are high, for most types of disputes in our dataset of US cases, the rate of appeal is below 5 percent of all terminations, and 23 percent of all merits judgments (see Table 3.3). Note that because settlements are much more common in the United States, appeals are a much larger share of merits judgments than terminations are.

* * *

In short, civil litigation in Taiwan is characterized by low settlement rates, infrequent summary judgments (with default judgments appearing

---

[19] We do not have separate data on high-stakes cases for default judgments. Assuming that the higher the stake, the lower the default judgment rate, the default judgment rate among high stake cases is likely to be lower than the average default judgment rate (17 percent) for all non-debt-collection cases. This will make the full-blown trial rate for all non-debt-collection cases higher than 80 percent.

Table 3.3 Comparison of appeal rates from first-instance courts to second-instance courts in high-stakes civil cases in Taiwan and diversity jurisdiction cases in the United States, by nature of dispute

Nature of Dispute	Taiwanese Courts 2010–2015		US Courts 2010–2013		
	% of Terminations	% of Merits Js	% of Terminations	% of Merits Js	Nature of Suit
Tort damages	31.2	49.5	5.8	34.1	Torts - Property
Damages	24.9	43.1	1.0	27.6	Torts - Personal Injury
Loan contract	9.1	16.5			Student Loans
Debt payment	19.2	41.6	7.0	18.1	and Recovery of
Sales contract	28.0	54.1			Overpayments
Lease contract	33.3	55.8	8.1	26.8	Contract
Service contract	43.3	67.8			
Other contracts	28.4	52.1			
Ownership	28.9	47.2			
Mortgage	22.8	39.0	4.8	7.8	Real Property
Other properties	32.0	49.4			
Commercial dispute	35.9	61.7			
Other types	31.0	57.3			
Total	27.7	47.8	3.0	23.4	
Debt-Collection	12.4	24.0	7.0	18.1	
Non-Debt-Collection	30.6	51.9	3.1	23.9	

Notes: High-stakes cases are defined as cases with stakes greater than 75,000 USD (based on an exchange rate of 30 NTD : 1 USD) for Taiwanese and cases within the diversity jurisdiction for US federal court cases. That is, non-debt-collection cases in this table contain only diversity jurisdiction cases in the United States.
Sources: Civil Cases Administrative Data (Judicial Yuan, Taiwan). Federal Court Cases: Integrated Data Base (US Federal Judicial Center).

to be more common than summary judgments), and relatively high rates of trial and appeal.

3.4   Speed in Resolving Cases

To lawyers accustomed to the American context, a pattern of low settlement rates and high trial rates would seem to be a recipe for procedural inefficiency and expense. In this part, we see that courts in Taiwan bring cases to final judgment with impressive alacrity. Furthermore, the swift disposition of cases in the courts of first instance does not appear to lead to lengthy appeals, followed by do-overs after reversals for sloppy mistakes the first time through. Thus, it appears that the Taiwanese court system manages to be effective, notwithstanding low settlement rates.

Courts in Taiwan are fast. The mean duration of a case in Taiwanese courts of first instance is 100 days. The median handling period for all first-instance cases is 56 days. Even among high-stakes cases, which are more comparable to the disputes likely to appear in US federal court, the mean duration is 223 days, and the median is 143 days. For comparison, the mean duration in our US data is 487 days and the median is 242 days – nearly twice as long (see Figure 3.2 for comparison).

Appeals in Taiwan, too, are slightly faster than appeals in the United States. The mean duration of high-stakes cases in Taiwanese courts of second instance is 303 days, and the median is 222 days. In our US data, the corresponding durations are a mean of 303 days and a median of 257 days (see Figure 3.3 for comparison).

Of course, haste may make waste, and speed to resolution in any given instance of the court must be balanced against the likelihood of appeal and possibility of further expense and delay if errors in the lower court are exposed, thereby requiring further litigation. Bringing cases to judgment quickly may be counterproductive if sloppy rulings invite appeals and require correction by courts of appeal.

Because appeal rates are higher in Taiwan than in the United States, this concern merits attention. When comparing time to resolution, what ultimately matters to the parties in terms of resolving disputes efficiently is the total duration of the case, including any appeals. Because appeals happen more often in Taiwan, the differences between Taiwan and the United States in total case duration are not as great as the numbers above suggest. As noted above, 28 percent of high-stakes cases (terminations)

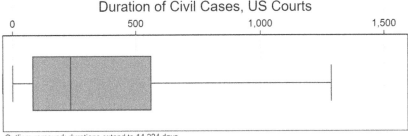

Outliers removed; durations extend to 14,224 days

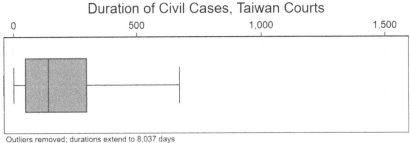

Outliers removed; durations extend to 8,037 days

Figure 3.2   Duration of first-instance high-stake cases.
Notes: Only high-stake cases in the ordinary procedure of the first instance in Taiwan
are included. Both debt-collection cases and other cases are included in both
jurisdictions. Taiwan, 2010–2015; United States, 2010–2013.
Sources: Civil Cases Administrative Data (Judicial Yuan, Taiwan). Federal Court Cases: Integrated
Data Base (US Federal Judicial Center)

are appealed from the first instance to the second instance in Taiwan.
Thus, adding the length of appeal to 28 percent of cases raises the average
duration of cases to 308 days. For the United States, its appeal rate is so
low (3.1 percent) that the average duration barely budges (it rises to 496
days, from 487).

Then there is the issue of the Supreme Court. In the United States,
Supreme Court merits review of civil judgments of the federal courts is
negligible (fewer than 50 cases per year, out of over 200,000 civil actions
filed in federal district courts per year). But in Taiwan, 46 percent of
high-stakes cases in the courts of second instance are appealed to the

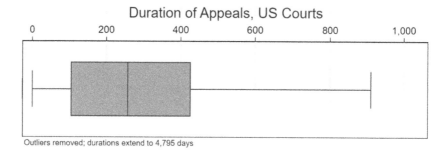

Figure 3.3   Duration of second-instance high-stake cases.
Notes: Only high-stake cases in the ordinary procedure of the second instance in
Taiwan are included. Both debt-collection cases and other cases are included in both
jurisdictions. Taiwan, 2010–2015; United States, 2010–2013.
Sources: Civil Cases Administrative Data (Judicial Yuan, Taiwan). Federal Court Cases: Integrated
Data Base (US Federal Judicial Center)

Supreme Court. Given the average duration of cases in the Supreme
Court of 24–45 days (up from 24 days in 2010–45 days in 2015),[20] this
raises the expected duration of a filed case to 329 days (based on the
high-end estimate of 45 days in the Supreme Court). Nonetheless, the
courts of Taiwan retain a considerable advantage in speed – 329 days is
less than two-thirds of the United States average of 496 days.

[20] Data source: Judicial Yuan Statistical Yearbook 2016, available at www.judicial.gov.tw/
juds/year105/03/02.pdf (last visited January 15, 2018). There were barely any oral arguments at the Taiwan Supreme Court during our research period. This explains the speed
of the Supreme Court.

Additionally, there is the possibility of reversal and remand. If haste indeed makes waste, we would expect higher reversal rates on appeal in Taiwan. (Other factors, however, confound our analysis here, because Taiwan, like most civil law jurisdictions, has de novo review of both facts and law on appeal; in the United States, factual findings in the court of first instance are subject to deference.) On average, the appellant prevails in whole or in part in 32 percent of appeals of high-stakes cases (terminations) in Taiwan. The corresponding figure for the United States is 9.1 percent. This means that only about 28%*32% = 9% of the high-stake-case decisions by the courts of first instance in Taiwan, and 0.3 percent of the decisions of US district courts, were changed in total or in part by appeals. Even if we assume (contrary to reality) that every time an appellant prevails on appeal, there is a second, full-length litigation in the court of first instance, incorporating this factor into the expected durations yields 349 days for Taiwan and 511 days for the United States – still a large advantage for Taiwan.[21]

Finally, we note that while reversal in the Supreme Court of Taiwan is also a possibility, it constitutes an unlikely event, as one might expect. As we noted above, appeals to the Supreme Court are uncommon, and as Figure 3.4 shows, successful appeals are even less common. In 2010–2015, about 70 percent of the appeals to the highest court in Taiwan were flat-out dismissed with standard-template written opinions.[22] Most of the non-dismissed cases were remanded to the second-instance courts, which did not necessarily change the final outcome of the cases. So far, no study has chronicled the true reversal rates of first-instance or second-instance court decisions. But no more than 46%* (1–70%) = 14% of the second-instance decisions (and 28%*46% = 12.9% of first instances decisions) involving high stakes could have been changed during the research period. Thus, given that the upper bound for remands from the Supreme Court is 14 percent of second-instance decisions, and even if every one of those remands required a full retrial in

---

[21] The calculation is 329 days + (9.1%) (223 days) = 349 days for Taiwan, and 496 days + (0.3%) (487 days) = 511 days for the United States.

[22] In Supreme Court practice in Taiwan, "dismissal" could be on the merits of the appeal, or because the appeal does not conform to the formal requirements of an appeal to the Supreme Court, which are provided under Articles 467–469 of the Taiwan Civil Procedure Code. The liberal construction of the formal appeal requirements gave the Supreme Court de facto discretionary jurisdiction before the Civil Procedural Code was amended to give some discretion in taking cases. See Eisenberg and Huang (2012) for an empirical study of discretionary jurisdiction of the Taiwan Supreme Court.

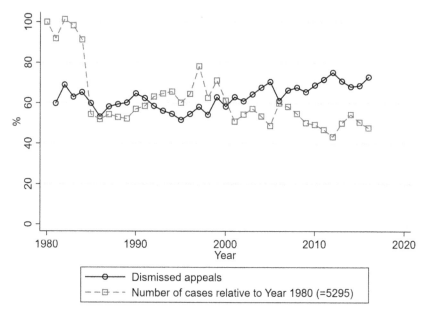

Figure 3.4   Rates of dismissals in Taiwan Supreme Court, 1980–2016.
Notes: All kinds of Supreme Court cases are included. We cannot limit the types of cases to high-stake ones, because we do not have the raw data and have to rely on available published descriptive statistics. Note that only cases with more than 1,000,000 NTD (roughly 33,000 USD) at stake can be appealed to the Supreme Court of Taiwan. Appealed cases filed at the Supreme Court are very likely to have high stakes or close to high stakes, as we have defined the term. Furthermore, note that according to the Annual Reports of Judicial Statistics, very few debt-collection cases were filed at the Supreme Court.
Source: Annual Reports of Judicial Statistics, published by Judicial Yuan, Taiwan

the court of second instance, this would increase the expected duration of a case in Taiwan to 387 days – still much less than the expected duration in the United States.[23] These very conservative estimates of the difference in expected duration between cases in Taiwan and the United States suggest that although appeals occur more often in Taiwan than in the United States, Taiwan retains its advantage in terms of speed.

---

[23] The calculation is 349 days + (28%) (46%) (303 days) = 387 days for Taiwan. We assume that remand from the US Supreme Court is so rare that it has no effect on expected duration for US cases.

In sum, Taiwanese courts do have higher rates of appeal and reversal. While we cannot know whether this is *caused* by the greater speed of case handling in the courts of first instance, it is consistent with the view that there is a trade-off between speed and accuracy (however defined). Nonetheless, even after accounting for the extent to which the possibility of appeal and remand increases the expected length of litigation, it remains true that cases reach their ultimate conclusions faster in the Taiwanese courts than in the US courts.

* * *

As we have observed, the courts of Taiwan are fast, despite trial rates and appeal rates being much higher than in the United States. It goes without saying that the courts of Taiwan manage this feat by (among other things) employing procedures that are dramatically simplified relative to their American counterparts. Discovery is radically limited. There are no civil juries in Taiwan, and trial procedure and pretrial and posttrial motion practice are simpler or nonexistent in Taiwan. With fewer and simpler moving parts, the product is cheaper and faster to produce.

Although resolving disputes swiftly is good, it is not the only value. After all, dismissing every complaint the moment it is filed would minimize cost and maximize speed of disposition, but would be a disastrous approach to procedure! Many aspects of American procedure reflect an embrace of values that often stand in tension with resolving cases quickly and cheaply.[24] For example, civil juries may increase the time and expense of litigation,[25] but reflect a commitment to a whole host of values associated with lay participation in the civil justice

---

[24] The pursuit of 99 percent justice in the American legal system has led Ramseyer (2015) to praise the Japanese legal system, which does well by making do.

[25] Jury trial requires an expensive and burdensome jury selection process, including the formation of the venire, voir dire of prospective jurors, strikes for cause, and peremptory strikes. The parties must draft and negotiate or litigate the jury instructions, which the court then must deliver to the jury at the outset and end of the trial. Pretrial motions in limine governing the exclusion or admission of evidence take on heightened importance in a jury trial, since (unlike in a bench trial) the judge (who sees the evidence regardless) is not the finder of fact. Nor does the fact that a jury need not give reasons for its verdict necessarily save time, as parties can and do routinely move for judgment as a matter of law (during trial) and judgment notwithstanding the verdict and for new trial (posttrial), all of which may require briefing, deliberation by the judge, and an oral or written elaboration of reasons for granting or denying the motion. See Federal Rules of Civil Procedure 50 and 59.

system.[26] Thus, we make no claims about whether the speedy case processing by the Taiwanese courts is better or worse than the job the US courts do with their cases. Rather, we make a narrower set of observations: First, there is no necessary connection between higher settlement rates and faster resolutions, at least when comparing distinct systems. Second, the speed with which the courts of Taiwan dispatch cases does not appear to be counterproductive, insofar as higher appeal and reversal rates in Taiwan do not lead to higher overall case durations.

3.5 Wasted Energy? Making Sense of High Trial Rates for "Easy" Cases

So far, this chapter has examined a subset of cases in Taiwan and the United States that are roughly comparable in terms of stakes (what we've called "high stakes cases"). We now turn to a different set of cases, which are comparable based on the nature of the dispute (and possibly with respect to stakes as well, but we lack reliable details on stakes from US cases). These are what we call "debt-collection cases." The category of debt-collection cases is intended to capture actions where there is a debt of (usually) undisputed amount in which the debtor has failed to pay. While we cannot perfectly capture this set of cases in our data, there are categories in each of our data sets that serve as strong proxies: in the Taiwan data, the "loan contract" and "debt payment" dispute categories,[27] and in the US data, the "student loan default and recovery of overpayments" nature-of-suit category.[28] This category (which largely does *not* overlap with the high stakes category) captures a surprisingly large set of cases (43 percent of all civil cases in Taiwan[29]; and in the US

---

[26] Just as our analysis here does not make a normative judgment of Taiwan's rejection of broad discovery and civil juries, it does not make a normative judgment on the United States's embrace of these institutions, either.

[27] Loan contract cases clearly arise from monetary loan contracts. Debt payment cases involve a broader array of cases, including payment obligations arising from all kinds of contracts (including loan contracts) and unjust enrichment.

[28] In the US data, this category comprises cases on overpayments, enforcement of judgments, and recovery of defaulted student loans. There are a few additional cases pertaining to overpayments under the Medicare Act and Veteran benefits.

[29] The debt-collection cases in the United States all involve the US government as the creditor. If the debt-collection cases in Taiwan are limited to those in which the central or a local government is the plaintiff, only 801 and 1,608 cases will be left, respectively. As we think the nature of this type of cases, rather than the nature of the plaintiff, is driving

federal courts, while it made up less than 5 percent of all cases in the 2010s, in the 1980s it made up 10–23 percent of all cases).

Unlike the results in Sections 3.3 and 3.4, which reveals striking differences between outcomes in civil litigation in Taiwan and the United States, this part identifies striking similarities between the court outcomes in these countries. In the context of debt collection, the United States looks more like Taiwan: in both countries, settlement rates are low, and most cases end in a court judgment.

A priori, this might seem to be the last area in which the United States would look more like Taiwan. Debt-collection cases do not provide a context where the usual explanations for settlement failure in US litigation would apply. These are not cases with asymmetric information (and in many such cases, maybe no uncertainty at all).[30] Further, these are not "close" cases, which are the type of cases that the canonical Priest and Klein (1984) model predicts will go to trial.

Despite this, we rarely see these cases settle. In Taiwan, only 14 percent of debt-collection cases end in settlement, with 75 percent proceeding to a judgment on the merits (see Table 3.1). The failure of what should be routine cases to settle might suggest inefficiency in the courts' handling of these cases. Furthermore, the large numbers of these cases – debt-collection cases make up 41 percent of the total caseload of the Taiwanese courts in our data – indicate that inefficiencies here could have a major impact on the court system as a whole. Yet, we see a similar pattern in our US data, which (as shown above) is otherwise quite dissimilar from the Taiwan data. In the United States, only 30 percent of debt-collection cases end in settlement, with 64 percent proceeding to a judgment on the merits (including default judgments; see Table 3.1).

Nor can the explanation be fee-shifting rules, notwithstanding the established theoretical prediction that the English rule encourages litigation when the plaintiff has a very high probability of winning (see generally Spier 2007). Given that Taiwan follows the English rule, the Taiwanese data is consistent with this prediction – but the United States exhibits the same patterns despite the United States employing the opposite fee-shifting rule.[31]

---

the result, we decide not to limit the debt-collection cases in Taiwan to government versus natural persons.

[30] See Bebchuk (1984) and Reinganum and Wilde (1986) for a discussion of how asymmetric or private information leads to bargaining failure.

[31] For most cases, the United States follows the "American rule" that each party, win or lose, pays its own attorney fees.

This suggests that the patterns we see in the data may have more to do with the nature of debt-collection cases than with any special feature of the US or Taiwanese courts. As one of us has argued elsewhere (Hubbard 2018), debt-collection cases may present an example of litigation that arises due to bargaining failure in the absence of asymmetric information or beliefs. Imagine a routine debt-collection action in which the liability for the debt and the amount of the debt is undisputed, but the defendant can't (or at least won't) pay. A defendant in this case, as in other types of cases, knows that he benefits from delay. Nonetheless, unlike in other types of cases with asymmetric information and/or divergent expectation, in debt-collection cases, the outcome is certain to be unfavorable to the defendants. Anything that delays the inevitable allows the defendant to retain use of whatever assets of his are in jeopardy of being used to satisfy the debt. If the plaintiff attempts to negotiate, this only benefits the defendant – negotiation allows for delay, which is exactly what benefits the defendant and harms the plaintiff. The only way to avoid a negotiation process in which the defendant can always delay is for the plaintiff to push forward with litigation, which the plaintiff knows she is going to win for sure. In litigation and unlike in out-of-court negotiation, delay requires defending the case, and defending the case is costly (Prescott and Sanchez 2018). Because delay is more costly in litigation, the plaintiff forgoes negotiation in favor of litigation, expecting that because litigation is costly, the defendant may forgo defending the case. Thus, litigation occurs, even though there are no divergent beliefs or uncertainty preventing settlement.

If this view of debt-collection cases is correct, we would expect that courts would not be able to rely on settlement to bring a swift resolution, but would be able to use default judgments to quickly resolve what are (by assumption) simple cases. This is what we see in the data. In debt-collection cases, litigation proceeds to court judgments, but it is still handled quickly. The average time to judgment in debt-collection cases is 59 days in Taiwan (the median is 46 days) and 193 days in the United States (the median is 118 days).

Importantly, this speed is achieved in part because default judgments are very common in debt-collection cases. In this aspect of civil litigation, the United States and Taiwan are similar to each other. As we see in Table 3.2, a default judgment is the outcome in about 70 percent of merits judgments in debt-collection cases in Taiwan and 75 percent in the United States. During litigation, as long as the defendant neither appears in court nor responds to the plaintiff's complaint, courts can use default judgments to proceed quickly in ruling in favor of plaintiffs. This device becomes central in debt-collection cases, because in these cases, defendants have neither incentive to settle nor incentives to respond to plaintiffs' complaint or show up in court, as these efforts are pure costs with extremely low expected benefits, while being sued and losing in itself incurs little costs. (Court fees, which are roughly 1 percent of plaintiffs' claims, are shifted, but attorney fees are not.) Bankrupt and thus judgment-proof defendants would not care about paying court fees, either. As a result, settlement rates are low but default judgments are common.

We note here that we suspect that default judgments, while technically not summary judgments, are in some cases serving the same purpose as summary judgment for the plaintiff. As noted above, summary judgments in Taiwan can be used by judges only to rule in favor of the defendants. But there are surely cases where the facts are undisputed and the plaintiff is entitled to judgment without extensive hearings. Indeed, the original rationale for summary judgment in the United States was to provide an expedited means for granting judgment to plaintiffs seeking to enforce undisputed debts.[32] It is somewhat ironic that this use of summary judgment is expressly excluded from the scope of summary judgment in Taiwan. Yet the high rates of default judgment and the rapid disposition of debt-collection cases in Taiwan suggest that the Taiwanese courts have adapted their procedures to effectively control cost and delay in this context.

Turning to appeals, we see that although the default judgment procedure is fast, and default judgments indicate that defendants are not having their proverbial day in court, defendants in debt-collection cases do not appeal. After a verdict that grants everything in the plaintiff's claim, only 1 percent of the defendants appeal.[33] Full-win-for-the-plaintiff cases

---

[32] See Wright, Miller, and Kane (2018, p. 10A–§ 2711) ("A device with some of the characteristics of the contemporary summary judgment first was introduced in England in the Bills of Exchange Act of 1855 for cases involving liquidated claims on certain commercial instruments to expedite the legal enforcement of debts. Its use gradually expanded in England so that by the time of the adoption of the Federal Rules of Civil Procedure in 1938 in the United States it had become available in virtually all actions at law except for certain torts and breach of promise to marry proceedings."). Of course, today the pattern is much different in US federal court. In our data on diversity cases, 65 percent of all cases terminated by summary judgment were terminated in favor of the defendant.

[33] Taiwanese law does not allow non-adverse appeals. For such appeals in US state courts, see Heise (2018).

account for 93 percent of all merit judgments. Overall, 3 percent of the losing parties in debt-collection cases in the court of first instance appeal (unreported in tables); in contrast, 24 percent of debt-collection cases handled in the ordinary procedure in the court of first instance involve appeals (Table 3.3). By contrast, appeal rates in all other categories are much higher – the overall appeal rate in non-debt-collection cases (merit judgments) is 52 percent; see Table 3.3. Likewise, in our US data, the appeal rate for our debt-collection category is 18 percent, as compared to a higher appeal rate (24 percent) for other categories we examine.

* * *

Summing up the aforementioned findings, we see that the low settlement rates in debt-collection cases appear to be the product of the distinct litigation strategies in that setting, rather than the product of any ineffi- ciency in the Taiwanese system – or the American system, for that matter. Indeed, it is the similarity of how these cases are resolved across two otherwise very different systems that suggests that it is something distinct about those cases that is driving outcomes. We see that courts use strat- egies for reducing the cost of trial in this ultra-low-settlement setting. In the United States, these techniques include default judgments and sum- mary judgment in favor of plaintiffs. In Taiwan, because there is no summary judgment in favor of plaintiffs, these kinds of disputes go to "trial" – but trial in this context often consists of default judgments that are rendered within a very short time. Moreover, defendants rarely appeal.

Furthermore, this part offers a cautionary tale of comparative civil litigation studies: Empiricists always endeavor to compare apples to apples, but in some countries, oranges are functionally equivalent to apples. In this case, default judgments may fill a niche reserved for summary judgments in the US context – granting an early judgment to a plaintiff with a straightforward claim.[34]

3.6   Conclusion

In this study, we have taken advantage of fine-grained court data to look at comparable subsets of court data from two court systems, Taiwanese

---

[34] Of course, default judgments cannot be rendered if both parties attend the oral arguments and make a case for their positions. We do not claim that judges grant default judgments in circumstances in which doing so would be improper.

courts and the US federal courts. This "matching" approach allows us to better distinguish between differences due to the composition of observed cases, rather than differences due to different handling of otherwise similar cases in different court systems. Other jurisdictions may not have been chronicled with such fine-grained data we have; this study benefited from the high-quality data we were able to collect.

Our examination of Taiwanese courts reveals several obvious ways in which their case flow differs from that in the US courts. First, while parties in Taiwanese courts have two ways – settlement and mediation – to voluntarily solve their disputes with the help of judges and/or mediators, neither one works particularly well, from a comparative law point of view. Among high-stakes cases, which are most comparable to the cases in the US courts, settlement and mediation each account for less than 15 percent of almost all major case types. Even taking into account plaintiff withdrawal as a form of settlement, the settlement rate broadly defined is below 30 percent of all terminations. Second, summary judgments for defendants are an available legal device but are almost never used. Default judgments, however, are often used, particularly in debt-collection cases, and in some settings may be the functional equivalent of summary judgments in Taiwan. Third, appeal rates in the first instance are substantial (almost 30 percent for high-stake cases), and reversal is not infrequent.

Second, debt-collection cases may be a "white elephant" and may need to be treated separately. This type of case takes up 40 percent of the total caseload in Taiwan, although it is a small portion of the US federal court caseload. Parties in this type of lawsuit on both sides of the Pacific Ocean, however, behave in strikingly similar fashion. They rarely settle, even though there is barely asymmetric information or divergent expectations. Even the summary judgment rate of this type is much lower than that of other types in US federal courts. In addition, plaintiff win rates in this type of case are very high. These results suggest two conclusions. One, our comparative analysis reveals that court procedures cannot explain the distinctive features of debt collection litigation, which has similar patterns in Taiwan and the United States despite their differences in procedure. We tentatively conclude that parties in the debt collection context have incentives to avoid settlement that lead to high litigation rates. Two, debt-collection cases are outliers, and their sheer numbers may shift many key summary statistics. Analyzing this type of case separately would give researchers a better sense of the real picture of civil litigation.

Taiwan presents a vivid example of a court system in which trials and appeals are frequent, settlement is rare, and yet case resolution comes swiftly. Low settlement and summary judgment rates are not a sign of the parties' or the court's inability to resolve cases quickly, but rather a product of the fact that even if a case goes to trial, it is resolved fairly quickly and at low expense. This stands in contrast to the view in some common-law contexts that increasing the speed and reducing the cost of litigation involves reducing trials and appeals. This suggests more than one path to improving case handling by courts: either reducing trials and appeals to avoid their cost, or reducing their cost.

As a normative matter, of course, our analysis points toward no firm conclusions. A full normative analysis would require consideration of social costs and benefits, and we do not assess here the benefits of slower and more expensive procedures or more frequent merits judgments or appeals. Nonetheless, comparative analysis of the potential cost efficiencies generated by different design choices can inform our thinking about potential reforms. This chapter conducts this analysis for two highly distinct court systems, and also notes potential methodological considerations for future studies on the speed and effectiveness of courts.

References

Bebchuk, Lucian Arye. 1984. Litigation and Settlement Under Imperfect Information. *The RAND Journal of Economics* 15(3): 404–15.

Chang, Yun-chien. 2016. The Evolution of Property Law in Taiwan: An Unconventional Interest Group Story. In *Private Law in China and Taiwan: Economic and Legal Analyses* 212–244, edited by Yun-chien Chang, Wei Shen, and Wen Yeu Wang. Cambridge: Cambridge University Press.

  2017. Empirical Description of Civil Litigation in Japan in 1952–2015. In *Festschrift for Former Supreme Court President Chi-Bin Wu*. Taipei: New Sharing [in Chinese].

Chang, Yun-chien, Weitseng Chen, and Ying Chieh Wu. 2017. *Property and Trust Law in Taiwan*. Alphen aan den Rijn: Wolters Kluwer.

Chang, Yun-chien, Theodore Eisenberg, Tsung Hsien Li, and Martin T. Wells. 2017. Pain and Suffering Damages in Personal Injury Cases: An Empirical Study. *Journal of Empirical Legal Studies* 14: 199–237.

Chang, Yun-chien, Nuno Garoupa, and Martin Wells. 2018. Drawing the Legal Family Tree: An Empirical Comparative Study of 108 Property Doctrines in 154 Jurisdictions. Working Paper.

Chang, Yun-chien, and William Hubbard. 2019. New Empirical Tests for Classic Litigation Selection Models. Working Paper.

Chang, Yun-chien, and Su-hao Tu. 2019, forthcoming. Two-way Selections Between Flat-fee Attorneys and Litigants: Theoretical and Empirical

Analyses. *European Journal of Law and Economics.* https://doi.org/10.1007/s10657-017-9566-3 (accessed July 7, 2019).

Eisenberg, Theodore, and Kuo-Chang Huang. 2012. The Effect of Rules Shifting Supreme Court Jurisdiction from Mandatory to Discretionary–an Empirical Lesson from Taiwan. *International Review of Law & Economics* 32(1): 3–18.

Heise, Michael. 2018. When Winning Is Not Enough: Prevailing-Party Civil Appeals in State Courts. In *Selection and Decision in Judicial Process around the World: Empirical Inquires*, edited by Yun-chien Chang. Cambridge: Cambridge University Press.

Helland, Eric, Daniel Klerman, Brendan Dowling, and Alexander Kappner. 2017. Contingent Fee Litigation in New York City. *Vanderbilt Law Review* 70(6): 1971–92.

Huang, Kuo-Chang. 2009. Does Discovery Promote Settlement? An Empirical Answer. *Journal of Empirical Legal Studies* 6(2): 241–78.

Hubbard, William H. J. 2017. The Effects of Twombly and Iqbal. *Journal of Empirical Legal Studies* 14: 474–526.

2018. Stalling and Stonewalling in Litigation. *Unpublished working paper.*

Langbein, John H. 1985. The German Advantage in Civil Procedure. *The University of Chicago Law Review* 52(4): 823–66.

Prescott, J. J., and Alexander Sanchez. 2018. Platform Procedure: Using Technology to Facilitate (Efficient) Civil Settlement. In *Selection and Decision in Judicial Process around the World: Empirical Inquiries*, edited by Yun-chien Chang. Cambridge: Cambridge University Press.

Priest, George L., and Benjamin Klein. 1984. The Selection of Disputes for Litigation. *The Journal of Legal Studies* 13(1): 1–56.

Ramseyer, J. Mark. 2015. *Second-Best Justice: The Virtues of Japanese Private Law.* Chicago, IL: The University of Chicago Press.

Reinganum, Jennifer F., and Louis L. Wilde. 1986. Settlement, Litigation, and the Allocation of Litigation Costs. *The RAND Journal of Economics* 17(4): 557–66.

Spier, Kathryn E. 2007. Litigation. In A. M. Polinsky and S. M. Shavell (Eds.), *Handbook of Law and Economics*, Volume 1, pp. 259–342. Elsevier.

Wang, Tay-sheng. 2002. The Legal Development of Taiwan in the 20th Century: Toward a Liberal and Democratic Country. *Pacific Rim Law & Policy Journal* 11: 531–60.

Wright, Charles Alan, Arthur R. Miller, and Mary Kay Kane. 2018. *Federal Practice and Procedure.* 4th ed. Vol. 10A. New York: Thompson West.

Appendix 3A

Overall Picture of Civil Litigation in Lower Courts in Taiwan

In the text, we present summary statistics regarding high-stake cases and debt versus non-debt-collection cases. In this Appendix, we include figures and tables that show the overall trends in the courts of first and second instance in Taiwan.

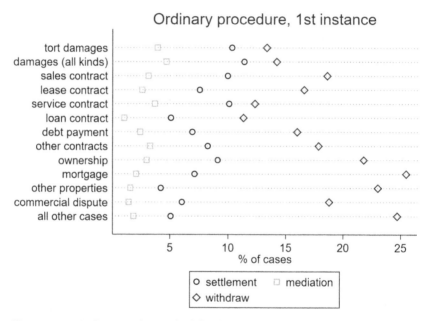

Figure 3A1 Settlement (narrowly defined), mediation, and withdrawal rates by dispute type for ordinary procedure cases in the Courts of First Instance in Taiwan, 2010–2015.

Notes: All cases (not just high-stake and debt-collection cases) are included in this figure. Debt-collection cases are loan contract and debt payment in the Y axis.

Source: Civil Cases Administrative Data (Judicial Yuan, Taiwan)

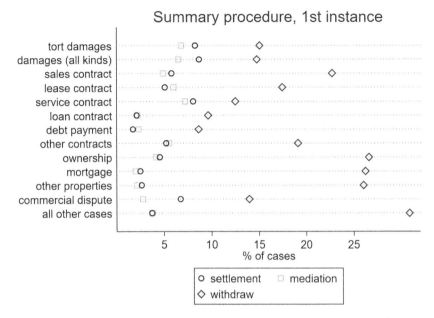

Figure 3A2 Settlement (narrowly defined), mediation, and withdrawal rates by dispute type for summary procedure cases in the courts of first instance in Taiwan, 2010–2015.

Notes: Debt-collection cases (loan contract and debt payment in the Y axis) and non-debt-collection cases are both included in this figure.

Source: Civil Cases Administrative Data (Judicial Yuan, Taiwan)

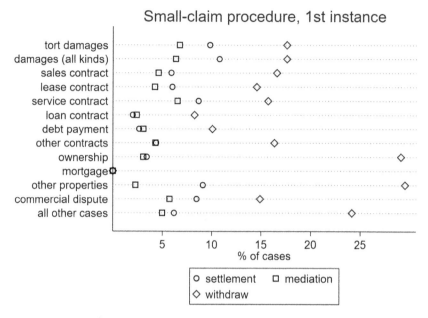

Figure 3A3   Settlement (narrowly defined), mediation, and withdrawal rates by dispute type for small-claim procedure cases in the courts of first instance in Taiwan, 2010–2015.

Notes: Debt-collection cases (loan contract and debt payment in the Y axis) and non-debt-collection cases are both included in this figure.

Source: Civil Cases Administrative Data (Judicial Yuan, Taiwan)

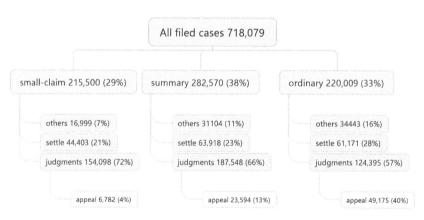

Figure 3A4   Overall appeal rates in courts of first instance in Taiwan, 2010–2015.

Source: Civil Cases Administrative Data (Judicial Yuan, Taiwan)

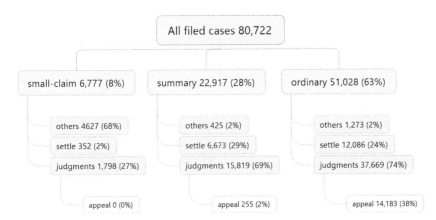

Figure 3A5   Overall appeal rates in courts of second instance in Taiwan, 2010–2015.
Source: Civil Cases Administrative Data (Judicial Yuan, Taiwan)

Table 3A1 *Appeal rates in civil cases in Taiwanese courts, by nature of dispute in 2010–2015*

| | Appeal Rate from First-Instance Courts to Second-Instance Courts | | | | | |
| | % of Terminations | | | % of Merit Js | | |
Nature of Dispute	Small Claims Procedure	Summary Procedure	Ordinary Procedure	Small Claims Procedure	Summary Procedure	Ordinary Procedure
Tort damages	6.2	18.2	27.0	10.2	26.7	43.3
Damages	5.8	16.4	22.4	9.8	23.4	38.2
Sales contract	5.8	13.0	23.3	8.9	27.7	45.7
Lease contract	8.5	16.1	35.7	13.1	42.2	56.5
Service contract	13.2	25.9	35.9	22.6	2.3	57.9
Loan contract	0.8	1.8	5.9	0.9	2.1	9.0
Debt payment	1.3	1.7	15.5	1.6	24.0	33.2
Other contracts	5.3	13.0	31.3	7.9	27.0	54.3
Ownership	8.3	14.8	25.0	13.7	9.8	42.6
Mortgage	0.0	5.7	17.5	0.0	29.7	30.7
Other properties	4.6	17.5	26.8	12.5	39.9	43.4
Commercial dispute	8.3	24.3	28.2	13.3	26.0	47.9
Other types	8.2	13.3	27.2	15.1	12.6	51.8
Total	3.3	8.6	23.3	4.4	26.7	39.5
Debt-Collection	0.9	1.7	8.4	1.1	2.2	14.0
Non-Debt-Collection	6.9	15.4	27.4	11.1	27.3	46.6

Source: Civil Cases Administrative Data (Judicial Yuan, Taiwan).

Table 3A2 Outcomes in second-instance courts

	Verdicts as % of Terminations	% of Verdicts Appellant Win	% of Verdicts Appellant Partial Win	Settled as % of Terminations	Other as % of Terminations	Total Terminations
Taiwan, Ordinary Procedure, 2010–2015						
Total	73.8	13.0	26.2	23.7	2.5	51,028
Non-Debt-Collection	73.6	12.8	26.3	23.9	2.5	47,052
Debt-Collection	76.3	15.4	25.3	21.1	2.5	3,976
United States, 2010–2013						
Total	55.6	9.1	6.2	25.3	19.1	26,202
Non-Debt-Collection	55.6	9.1	6.2	25.3	19.0	25,886
Debt-Collection	52.5	7.0	4.8	23.1	24.4	316
Diversity	56.5	8.9	5.6	27.3	16.2	11,039

Notes. All cells except for in the last column are in percentages. "Settlement" refers to settlement broadly defined by this chapter. "Other" refers to non-merits judgments in non-settled cases. Plaintiff win rate is the ratio of judgments favoring the plaintiff out of all merits judgments.

Source: Civil Cases Administrative Data (Judicial Yuan, Taiwan).

Appendix Table 3A3 *Distribution of dispute natures in Taiwan, 2010–2015*

Nature of Dispute	(%)						
	Small 1st	Small 2nd	Summary 1st	Summary 2nd	Ordinary 1st	Ordinary 2nd	Total
Tort damages	10.9	19.8	6.2	12.8	15.4	18.2	11.1
Damages	7.7	14.9	3.9	7.4	7.7	6.9	6.4
Sales contract	2.0	3.5	2.0	3.1	4.1	4.2	2.8
Lease contract	1.2	3.2	1.9	3.5	1.2	1.9	1.6
Service contract	3.0	12.1	3.3	10.5	8.8	14.1	5.7
Loan contract	43.5	9.6	31.4	6.2	15.7	3.8	27.7
Debt payment	17.4	7.2	18.6	4.2	5.6	4.0	13.3
Other contracts	7.8	12.7	14.8	22.4	9.4	13.4	11.5
Ownership	3.9	9.9	10.7	18.3	17.2	17.6	11.3
Mortgage	0.0	0.0	0.8	0.6	2.1	1.5	1.0
Other properties	0.0	0.0	1.2	2.3	1.7	2.0	1.1
Commercial dispute	0.9	2.4	0.7	1.8	3.2	3.8	1.7
Other types	1.8	4.7	4.6	7.0	8.0	8.7	5.1
Total %	100	100	100	100	100	100	100
Total N	215,500	6,777	282,570	22,917	220,009	51,028	798,801

Notes: All types of cases included in this table. 1st and 2nd refers to court instances.
Source: Civil Cases Administrative Data (Judicial Yuan, Taiwan).

Appendix 3B

Interview of Taiwanese Judges

Why were summary judgments so infrequently used? Based on interviews with several judges,[35] there are a few plausible explanations.

1. Appellant courts will reverse summary judgments, because appellate courts still have a culture of "favoring substantive verdicts." Summary judgments (thus disallowing parties to present evidence later in trial) are frowned upon.
2. Plaintiffs have paid the filing fee. They may file a formal complaint against judges who use summary judgment to rule in defendants' favor, as they have not had their "day in court." Formal complaints, amidst the judicial reform political movements, are a pain in the neck for judges. To put this in context, President Tsai, a former law professor, put judicial reform high on her agenda once she assumed her post in 2016. In 2017, large-scale meetings over half a year were convened to discuss how to reform the judiciary. Both Judicial Yuan and activist attorney groups monitor judges for misbehavior. A formal complaint would lead to a lot of paperwork for judges.
3. There are very few cases in which judges can know for sure before trials that plaintiffs will not win anything, as presentation of evidence before trial is fairly limited due to lack of a full-blown discovery process.
4. Taiwan's civil procedure is not 100 percent adversarial. Its Civil Procedure Code requires judges to "give parties some heads-up" during trials. If trials have already started and both parties have debated in open court, judges would prefer to write a decision favoring defendants, rather than using summary judgments.
5. There will be pressure from fellow judges. Judges tend to think that it is "too easy" to close cases by summary judgments. Judges are evaluated based on a number of factors, including how many cases they close in a year. Personnel evaluation affects the amount of bonus and promotion to higher courts. Summary judgments may be perceived as cheating.

---

[35] In 2017 June, one of us (Chang) interviewed in person, by phone, or by e-mail two judges in Taipei District Court, two judges in Taoyuan District Court, and one former judge who was a practicing attorney.

How Lower Courts Respond to a Change in a Legal Rule

ANTHONY NIBLETT

4.1 Introduction

Actions speak louder than words.[1] For many years, this was the mantra of the Tax Court of Canada when determining whether or not a worker was an employee or an independent contractor for tax purposes. Irrespective of what label the worker or the hiring firm gave to characterize the relationship, the court consistently held that the actual behavior of the worker and hiring firm in question was the important factor, not the words that taxpayer used to describe their relationship. If it looks like an employee and walks like an employee, then it matters not that she calls herself an independent contractor. In assessing these cases, the Tax Court of Canada relied on a multifactor test, weighing four different factors that described and characterized the true nature of the "total relationship" between the worker and the hirer.

The law changed in 2006. The Federal Court of Appeals in Canada changed the rule. The appeals court held that the Tax Court must *always* take into account how the parties intend to characterize their relationship. But did this rule change actually change the way that the lower courts characterized the relationships between workers and hirers? While the strict words of the legal test may have changed, did the actions of the

[1] Associate Professor and Canada Research Chair in Law, Economics, and Innovation, University of Toronto, Faculty of Law. Email: anthony.niblett@utoronto.ca.

The author is grateful to participants at the CELS Asia symposium on "Do Courts Rule Efficiently?" held in Academia Sinica, Taiwan (June 2017), STILE conference in Siracusa, Italy (July 2017), and CELS Europe (June 2018) especially Yun-chien Chang, Alon Harel, William Hubbard, Michael Livermore, Patricia Popelier, Eric Talley, and Michael Trebilcock for thoughtful and helpful comments and discussion. The dataset here comprises part of a dataset collected by employees and contractors of Blue J Legal. The author is a cofounder of Blue J Legal, a startup bringing machine learning to law. The author particularly wishes to thank Adrienne Staudohar for coding much of the data included here. The author acknowledges generous funding from Canada Research Chair program.

lower courts change at all? Or are the actions of lower courts louder than the words of the appellate court? These are questions we seek to answer in this paper.

We explore the effect of the rule change on the behavior of lower courts. From a theoretical standpoint, one factor has gone from not being relevant at all to being one of five relevant factors. The rule change dictates that the lower court *must* place emphasis on a new factor, in addition to the four factors they were previously using. One might therefore expect that *if* this new factor is taken into account by the lower courts in the way the higher court intended, we will be able to identify cases that were decided one way before the change that are decided differently after the change, now that the court is taking into account the parties' intention. Admittedly, the factor is only one of five factors, but if the factor is relevant and lower courts respond accordingly, we might expect to see similar cases decided differently. If, however, the appeals court ruling had no effect on how lower courts decide the cases, then similar cases will be decided the same before and after the change. Here, we empirically test whether cases are different *after* the change, by exploring whether or not we can correctly predict the outcomes of post-change cases using the putative pre-change rules.

We create a dataset of 525 cases from the Tax Court of Canada (the lower court) to illustrate how they responded to a rule change implemented by the Federal Court of Appeals (a higher, intermediate level appellate court). We have data from a decade before the rule change and a decade after the rule change. We examine what factors influence (or, at least, are correlated with) the outcomes of lower court decisions both before and after the change.

We find only limited evidence that the rule change affected the way that lower courts decide cases. We find that the Tax Court was marginally more likely to issue a ruling that reflected how the parties had themselves characterized the relationship after the change in the law. This small observed impact, however, appears to taper off after about five years.

Importantly, taking this new fifth factor into account – as required by the appeals court – does not explain variation in outcomes that cannot be explained by the four previous factors alone. The cases decided after the rule change can be predicted with a high degree of accuracy using just the four factors that lower courts used before the rule change. Our model for predicting the outcomes of cases correctly predicts 93.3 percent of lower court cases that follow the rule change using the four original factors.

Adjusting the predictive model to also take into account the new fifth factor results in a marginal increase in predictability, correctly predicting the outcomes in 93.7 percent of cases. Ultimately, it appears as though the new legal rule changes little.

While this study may appear narrow in scope, the findings have important implications for the question of whether or not courts behave efficiently. First, much of the literature examining the efficiency of the common law focuses on rules handed down by appeals courts (see, e.g., Gennaioli and Shleifer 2007; Niblett, Posner and Shleifer 2010; Ponzetto and Fernandez 2008).[2] But what if lower courts ignore the rules issued by an appeals court or merely pay lip service to them? It would then matter little if the rules issued by appeals courts were efficient or not. Previous work has explored how lower courts respond to dramatic rule changes. Peltason (1961) and Read and McGough (1979), for example, discuss the response of lower courts in southern states of the United States to the change of the law in *Brown v. Board of Education*. Jacobi and Tiller (2007) and Kim (2007) discuss the discretion that lower courts have in deciding cases.

Second, the particular legal question studied here explores the extent to which courts will enforce contracts as written (Atiyah 1985; Gilmore 1974; Goetz and Scott 1981). The Coase Theorem (1960) holds where transaction costs are very low, parties will behave efficiently provided that property rights are well defined and courts enforce private contracts. But, before the rule change being examined here, the courts did not necessarily enforce the contracts as written or as the parties intended. One might therefore suggest that this lack of public enforcement was not efficient. For example, parties may make investments in reliance upon their contractual obligations, only for the tax authorities to ignore the agreement between the hirer and the worker. On this theory, the rule change – increasing the likelihood that lower courts adhere to the private contract – would appear to be the efficient rule. We do not push this line of argument too far though, as there are competing theories about the efficiency of the law in the context of freedom of contract (see, e.g., Schwartz and Scott 2003; Trebilcock 1993).[3]

---

[2] Posner (1973), Priest (1977), and Rubin (1977) do not explicitly focus on appeals courts, but rather on courts that have the ability to change legal rules.

[3] For an empirical study examining the inconsistency with which courts enforce private contracts, see Niblett (2013).

This paper proceeds as follows. In the next section, we spell out in more detail the nature of the rule change. In Section 4.3, we describe our data. In Section 4.4 we present our empirical findings. We examine how the lower courts respond to the rule change. Section 4.5 concludes.

4.2   The Legal Background: The *Wiebe Door* Factors and the *Royal Winnipeg* Rule Change

Whether or not a worker is characterized as an employee or an independent contractor can have large tax consequences in Canada. On one hand, employees are entitled to employment insurance and other benefits. On the other hand, independent contractors are entitled to take more generous deductions and are subject to other rules about what constitutes income. Hiring firms must accurately characterize their workers in order to ensure that they are making the correct source deductions and providing appropriate benefits.

Taxpayers may face incentives to characterize or label a working relationship as one type of relationship, while in reality the nature of the relationship is such that the worker is actually the other. For example, a music school may hire music teachers, entering into an independent contractor agreement with each these workers to avoid paying taxes associated with hiring employees. But the nature of the relationship between the music school and the music teachers may more accurately reflect an employment relationship. The tax authority (the Canada Revenue Agency) may assess the music school's situation and consider the workers to employees, ordering the music school to back pay the taxes from each of the tax years in question.

4.2.1   The Law Before the *Royal Winnipeg* Decision

For many years, tax courts in Canada held that the label the two parties gave to their agreement was afforded little, if any, weight. The intention of the parties was considered to be largely irrelevant. Courts, instead, looked to the "total relationship" between the hirer and the worker. The leading authority on the question of whether a worker is an employee or an independent contractor has been the 1986 decision of *Wiebe Door Services Ltd. v. Minister for National Revenue*[4] ("*Wiebe Door*"). In *Wiebe*

---

[4] *Wiebe Door Services Ltd. v. Minister for National Revenue* (3 F.C. 553 [F.C.A.1986]).

Door, the Federal Court of Appeal held that there are four general factors courts should examine when looking at the "total relationship" between the worker and the hirer:

1. Does the hirer exercise control over the worker? (*Control*)
2. Who owns the most important tools and equipment? (*Ownership*)
3. Does the worker have a chance of profits and risks of loss? (*Profit and risk*)
4. Is the worker integrated into the hirer's place of business? (*Integration*)

Judges of the Tax Court of Canada were charged with the responsibility of weighing these four factors appropriately. Importantly for our study, *Wiebe Door* does not state that the common intention or understanding of the parties about the legal nature of their relationship is or should be a relevant factor that aides in characterizing the relationship.

4.2.2 The Legal Rule Changed with the *Royal Winnipeg* Decision

In 2006, the Federal Court of Appeal decided a case involving ballet dancers working with the Royal Winnipeg Ballet Company. The ballet company had hired these dancers as independent contractors, but had asked the Minister for National Revenue for a ruling on this point in order to better understand the extent of their legal obligations. The Minister characterized the dancers as employees. The ballet company (and some dancers) appealed this decision to the Tax Court of Canada. The Tax Court upheld the Minister's decision, finding that the four *Wiebe Door* factors indicated that the relationship between the ballet company and the dancers was an employment relationship. The Tax Court held that it was not necessary to take into account "the intention of the parties."[5]

On appeal, the Federal Court of Appeal in *The Royal Winnipeg Ballet v. Minister for National Revenue*[6] ("*Royal Winnipeg*") held that the Tax

---

[5] An aside about language used in this paper: The parties to a contract are not the two litigants in the dispute. We use the word "parties" in this paper to reflect the worker and the hirer who have entered into agreement for the worker to work for the hirer; we use the word "litigants" when we discuss the relevant party who is going to court and the Minister for National Revenue on behalf of the Canadian government.

[6] *The Royal Winnipeg Ballet v. Minister for National Revenue* (346 N.R. 87 [F.C.A.2006]).

Court erred by not considering the intention of the parties. The majority of the court ruled that evidence of the parties' understanding of their contract must *always* be examined and given appropriate weight.[7] The court emphasized that it did not mean that the parties' intention was determinative, but rather was another factor that the lower courts should take into account. Thus, the *Royal Winnipeg* decision of the Federal Court of Appeals added a fifth factor to the analysis. In this paper, we measure how the lower court responded to this change.

4.3   Our Data

We collect publicly available cases from the Tax Court of Canada. CanLii has published Tax Court of Canada cases from 1997 until early 2017. We limit our cases to those where the specific legal issue of whether a worker is an employee or an independent contractor is addressed. The litigants in these cases are the government (usually the Minister of National Revenue) and the taxpayer (either the worker or the hirer). The cases usually follow a similar pattern: the taxpayer declares a position (characterizing the worker as either an employee or an independent contractor) and the government disputes this characterization. Unfortunately, we have no data on how frequently these types of disputes arise. We also have no data on settlement rates or the terms or the timing of settlement in the underlying disputes.

We have data from the 525 cases that were decided by the Tax Court of Canada over the period 1997 to early 2017. Figure 4.1 shows the number of cases in each of the years in our sample. The year, here, reflects when the decision of the Tax Court is handed down, not when the suit is filed. There is some variation in the number of cases in each year. Notably, we see a general trend toward more cases before the change in the law in 2006, but we do not observe any great increase in cases after the change in the law. In the last few years of the sample, we observe fewer cases.

For each of these 525 cases in our dataset, we collect a number of variables of interest. The data are hand coded.

---

[7] A concurring opinion in an earlier Federal Court of Appeal had suggested a change in the law. In *Wolf v. Canada* (4 F.C. 396 [F.C.A 2002]), Noel J.A. had reasoned that the characterization given to the agreement by the parties should hold weight where the relevant *Wiebe Door* factors point in both directions. The majority in the *Wolf* decision, however, focused on the *Wiebe Door* factors.

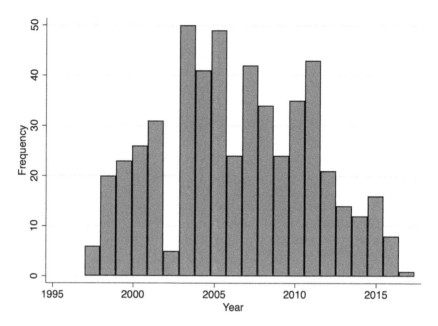

Figure 4.1   Number of Tax Court of Canada cases addressing this specific issue in each year of our sample, 1997–2017.

4.3.1   Dependent Variable: Outcome of Case

The dependent variable of interest here is the outcome of the lower court decision. We code the outcome with the value 1 if the court finds an employment relationship and as 0 if the court finds an independent contractor relationship. The outcomes in our dataset of 525 cases are split roughly evenly, with an employment relationship found in 275 cases (52.4 percent of our universe) and an independent contractor relationship in 250 cases (47.6 percent).

4.3.2   Independent Variables: Facts of Each Case

We have five key independent variables of interest that represent the key factors of each of the cases: the intention of the parties and the four *Wiebe Door* factors.

4.3.2.1   Intention of the Parties

For each case we code the "intention" of the worker and the hirer as measured by the agreement at the time the worker was hired. The variable is dichotomous: coded as 1 if the parties expressly agreed to enter into an employment agreement and 0 if the parties did not. This, of course, may not necessarily reflect the subjective intention of the parties, but it reflects the objective intention as described by the court in the written opinion.[8] In the majority of our cases (466 out of 525, 88.8 percent) the parties do *not* have an employment relationship. The majority of parties in our dataset intended for the relationship to be characterized as an independent contractor relationship at the time the worker started working for the hirer. These cases usually arise in situations where the tax authority claims that the relationship is, in fact, an employment relationship, which has additional tax responsibilities for the taxpaying hirer. The other 11.2 percent of cases are those where the parties enter into an employment relationship, but perhaps the worker claims to be classified as an independent contractor for tax purposes with a view to claiming more generous deductions.

4.3.2.2   *The Four* Wiebe Door *Factors*

For each case we create four variables that describe and reflect the four *Wiebe Door* factors. Each variable is a score that ranges from 0 to 1. We create these scores in the following way:

1. *Control factors* – Courts look to a variety of different aspect of the hirer's ability to control a worker. We track eight different factors that evidence control: (1) whether the worker is supervised or monitored by hirer; (2) whether the worker or the hirer sets the agenda; (3) whether the worker can turn down work from the hirer; (4) whether the worker or the hirer sets the worker's hours or schedule; (5) whether the worker or the hirer determines how the work is to be done; (6) whether the worker is free to work for other companies; (7) whether the worker is prohibited from delegating work to another; and (8) whether the worker is required to adhere to a dress code or wear a uniform. We take the information about these eight factors and create one score that reflects the control factors. We give each factor one point if the factor suggests that the hirer has more control over the worker and zero points if the factor suggests that the worker has

---

[8] Indeed, there is an extensive literature in employment law discussing how firms impose contracting relationship on workers in order to avoid regulatory obligations in a number of jurisdictions (see, for example, Carlson (2001) and Harned, Kryda, and Milito (2010) and references cited within).

more autonomy and independence. For simplicity, here, the overall *control* variable that summarizes these data is simply an average of these eight factors, ranging from 0 (the hirer exerts no control over the worker) to 1 (the hirer exerts substantial control over the worker).

2. *Ownership of tools and equipment* – In each written opinion, the court will outline who owns the important tools and equipment that the worker requires to do her job. This variable takes the value of 1 if the hirer owns the important tools and equipment; 0 if the worker is the owner; and 0.5 if the court indicates that both (or neither) own important tools.

3. *Profit and risk factors* – We measure the profit and risk of the worker by looking at evidence used by the court when analyzing this factor. Courts frequently note whether the worker is paid by commission and whether the worker liable for any losses such as liability insurance or loss of business. We also look to whether the worker is reimbursed for these losses. As with *control* above, we take an average of these scores. The *profit and risk* score ranges from 0 (worker has opportunities for profit, but faces substantial risk) to 1 (hirer assumes all the risk, but yields all profits).

4. *Integration factors* – We measure the integration factors by looking at where the worker performs the tasks (at her home office; at the hirer's workplace; or at mobile locations) and whether the hirer provides the worker with training. Again, we take an average, creating a score that ranges from 0 (worker is not integrated in the hirer's business at all) to 1 (worker is substantially integrated into the hirer's business).

We are fortunate that the written opinions yield so much information about the facts of each case. Judges typically describe each of the four *Wiebe Door* factors in some detail. Further, even before the *Royal Winnipeg* decision, the judges of the Tax Court of Canada would note the intention of the parties. Thus, even though it was not generally seen as an important factor in the cases from 1997 to 2006, we are able to collect data on each of these variables for all cases.

We divide our dataset in two, looking at decisions by the Tax Court before and after the Federal Court of Appeal decision in *Royal Winnipeg*. The data are fairly evenly split between these two time periods. We have 257 cases handed down before the *Royal Winnipeg* decision (1997 to March 2006) and we have 268 decisions after (from March 2006 to February 2017). Table 4.1 provides the means of each of our main variables, both pre- and post-*Royal Winnipeg*.

Table 4.1 *Summary statistics of key variables in aggregate as well as pre- and post-*Royal Winnipeg

	Pre-*Royal Winnipeg* N = 257	Post-*Royal Winnipeg* N = 268	Total N = 525
	Mean	Mean	Mean
Outcome	0.553	0.496	0.524
Binary variable			
0 = independent contractor			
1 = employee			
Intention	0.152	0.074	0.112
Binary variable			
0 = intention to have independent contractor relationship			
1 = intention to have employment relationship			
Wiebe Door factors			
Control factors	0.453	0.446	0.450
Variable ranges from 0 to 1 where:			
0 = hirer has no control over worker			
1 = hirer has full control over worker			
Ownership of tools and equipment	0.350	0.388	0.379
0 = worker owns important tools or equipment			
0.5 = both or neither own tools or equipment			
1 = hirer owns important tools or equipment			
Profit and risk factors	0.541	0.496	0.518
Variable ranges from 0 to 1 where:			
0 = worker has high chance of profit, risk of loss			
1 = worker has little chance of profit, risk of loss			
Integration factors	0.566	0.583	0.575
Variable ranges from 0 to 1 where:			
0 = worker is not integrated in hirer's business			
1 = worker is highly integrated in hirer's business			

There are two notable observations from Table 4.1. First, the four *Wiebe Door* factors do not change markedly from the pre-*Royal Winnipeg* cases to the post-*Royal Winnipeg* cases. This suggests that, on average, the types of cases as measured by the four original factors are similar before and after the change in the law. Second, the percentage of cases where the parties intend the relationship to be characterized as an employment relationship drops after the *Royal Winnipeg* decision (just 7.4 percent of cases after the change, compared to 15.2 percent before the change). This is important because it suggests that the type of cases that the courts are litigating may be different before and after the change in the law. But, much remains unobserved with regard to selection effect. Because we have no data on the background disputes or settlements, it is difficult to say whether this drop is because the government is less willing to dispute characterizations where the parties have an employment contract or, if the government is behaving consistently, and the taxpayer is more willing to settle such cases. Nonetheless, despite this statistically significant change, before the change in the law, the parties did not have an employment contract in 85 percent of cases; while, after the change, the parties did not in about 93 percent of cases.

One selection concern may be that the parties' intention was more likely to digress from the direction suggested by the *Wiebe Door* factors after the change in the law. If there was a greater divergence, this may suggest that the parties are being strategic in choosing what cases to litigate. We do not find evidence that there is greater divergence. To investigate this concern, we can observe the correlation between the parties' intention and the sum of our measure of the four *Wiebe Door* factors before and after the legal change. In both sets of cases, the correlation is negative, but the differences before pre- and post-change are quite small. The correlation cases before *Royal Winnipeg* the correlation is –0.177. After, the correlation is –0.077. Thus, there appears to be less divergence after the change.

Below, in Section 4.5, we discuss further how other potential selection issues may dampen the effect of our results.

4.4 Results

We seek to investigate whether lower courts (the Tax Court) will follow the rule handed down by the higher appeals courts (Federal Court of Appeal). If lower courts are faithful to the appeals court, we should

Table 4.2 *Percentage of cases where the Tax Court of Canada upholds the contractual intention of the hirer and the worker*

	Pre-*Royal Winnipeg*	Post-*Royal Winnipeg*	All Cases
All cases	52.7%	56.3%	**55.0%**
Parties intended employment relationship	79.4%	90.0%	**83.1%**
Parties intended independent contractor relationship	49.1%	53.6%	**51.5%**

observe a higher proportion of cases where the outcome of cases upholds the contractual intention of the parties following the *Royal Winnipeg Ballet* decision.

4.4.1 Do Courts Uphold the Intention of the Parties?

First, we investigate whether the Tax Court upholds the intention of the parties both before and after the *Royal Winnipeg* decision using simple comparisons of the outcome of the cases to the intent of the parties. Table 4.2 shows the percentage of cases where the intention of the parties is upheld. Overall, the intention of the parties matches the outcome of the case in just 55.0 percent of cases. Before the *Royal Winnipeg* decision, courts upheld the intention of the parties in 138 of the 257 cases (52.7 percent). After the *Royal Winnipeg* decision, this increases, but only mildly. Courts upheld the intention of the parties in 151 of the 268 cases (56.3 percent) after the *Royal Winnipeg* decision. A mild increase is observed in cases where the parties intend for the relationship to be an employment relationship and in cases where the parties intend for the relationship to be an independent contractor relationship. While these percentages move in the direction that one would expect (i.e., court decisions increasingly reflect the parties' intention after the *Royal Winnipeg* decision), none of these differences is statistically significant.

We go beyond this simple structural break and illustrate the trend of courts upholding the parties' intention. The data, shown in Figure 4.2, are revealing. They indicate that lower courts were increasingly likely to uphold the parties' intention even before the *Royal Winnipeg* decision. The trend line from 1997 to 2006 is upward sloping.

From 2006 to 2010 – the five-year period following the *Royal Winnipeg* decision – the lower courts uphold the intention of the parties with greater frequency than at any other period in our dataset.[9] This period represents the high watermark of *intention* as it correlates with the outcome. In each of these five years, courts upheld the intention of the parties in between 60 percent and 80 percent of cases. Since 2011, the Tax Court has been less inclined to uphold the parties' intention. The trend line since 2011 has been sloping downward. This suggests that the effect of a higher court ruling may be eroding over time.

4.4.2   Controlling for *Wiebe Door* Factors

We now turn to multivariate regression. We include the four *Wiebe Door* factors in our analysis to see what factors may explain the decisions of the lower courts. We run a logistic regression specified as follows:

$$outcome_i = \alpha + \beta_1.\ intention_i + \beta_2.\ X_i + \varepsilon_i$$

The dependent variable *outcome* is a dichotomous variable that takes the value 1 if the court in case i decided that the worker was an employee and takes the value 0 if the court decided the worker was an independent contractor. The independent variable *intention* is a dummy variable that takes the value 1 if the parties' intended for the relationship to be an employment relationship in case i and 0 otherwise. The matrix X represents the four *Wiebe Door* factors.

We run our regression on the subset of cases before the *Royal Winnipeg* decision (specification (1)) and on the subset of cases following the decision (specification (2)). If the appeals court decision has an effect on lower court rulings, we would expect the coefficient on *intention* to be significant after the higher court decision.

Table 4.3 shows our results. The coefficient on *intention* is not significant before the *Royal Winnipeg* decision, but it is significant following the appeals court decision. The coefficient is positive. This indicates that the parties' intention is correlated with the outcome in the post-*Royal Winnipeg* era. This is suggestive of the fact that lower courts are more likely to uphold the parties' intention controlling for other relevant factors after 2006.

---

[9] The one year where this is not true is 2017, but we have only one observation included in our dataset.

Specification (3) uses all cases in our dataset, taking into account both the pre- and post-*Royal Winnipeg* cases. The intention of the parties over all cases in the 20-year period is only of marginal significance. The significance in the post-period is diluted by the insignificance in the pre-period. In specification (4) we include an interaction term between *intention* and whether the case was decided after *Royal Winnipeg*. The coefficient on this interaction term confirms that *intention* is significantly correlated with the outcome in the post-*Royal Winnipeg* era. Three of the four *Wiebe Door* factors are also significant in all of our specifications.

4.4.3   Predicting Tax Court Decisions Following *Royal Winnipeg*

Table 4.3 suggests that intention of the parties is a significant variable in our logistic regression after the appeals court decision in *Royal Winnipeg*, but not before. But how much of a difference did the appeals court decision actually make? We answer this question by examining the degree to which we can predict the outcomes of cases after *Royal*

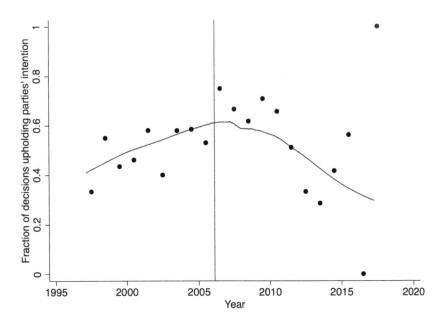

Figure 4.2   Fraction of decisions upholding parties' intention over time. Dots represent fraction of cases in each year. The continuous line represents the trend over time (Lowess). The vertical line indicates the timing of the *Royal Winnipeg* decision.

Winnipeg. We use two different models: Model 1 predicts outcomes based only the four *Wiebe Door* factors; Model 2 predicts outcomes based on the four factors *plus* the intention of the parties. Essentially, if a model that does not take intention into account (Model 1) can correctly predict the outcome of cases as well as cases that did take intention into account (Model 2) in the post-*Royal Winnipeg* period, then we take this as evidence that the lower courts are not dramatically changing the way they decide these cases even after the rule change. That is, if the intention of the parties was an important factor for the lower courts in making their determination after the *Royal Winnipeg* decision, we would expect that the predictive power of Model 2 would be much stronger than Model 1.

We generate a dynamic out-of-sample prediction model. We sort cases in chronological order and generate a predicted outcome of each case using *only* the cases that had been decided at the time of the court's decision. By the time that *Royal Winnipeg* had been handed down by the Federal Court of Appeals, 257 of the Tax Court decisions in our dataset had been decided. Thus, to predict the 258th case (the first lower court decision after *Royal Winnipeg*), we would estimate the likelihood that the court will find the worker to be an employee using a model based on the previous 257 cases. To predict the *n*th case in our dataset, we use a model based on all the previous (*n* − 1) cases. We use this dynamic out-of-sample technique to predict outcomes in both Model 1 and Model 2.

We use a logistic regression model to make predictions. We generate probabilities that the outcome of a case will be that the worker is found to be an employee for tax purposes. We then compare those probabilities to the actual outcome of the cases. We classify a prediction as being correct if the predicted probability was 50 percent or more and the actual outcome was "employee" *or* if the predicted probability was less than 50 percent and the actual outcome was "independent contractor."

We see very little difference in predictive power between Model 1 and Model 2. Both models perform extremely well. Model 1, predicting the outcome based on our measure of the four *Wiebe Door* factors, correctly predicts the outcome in 250 of the 268 cases (93.3 percent). Model 2, factoring in the intention of the parties, only marginally improves the accuracy of the prediction. Model 2 correctly predicts 251 of the 268 cases (93.7 percent). Therefore, even though the intention of the parties is

Table 4.3 *Logistic regression of outcome* (employment*) on relevant factors.*

	(1) Pre-*Royal Winnipeg*	(2) Post-*Royal Winnipeg*	(3) All Cases	(4) All Cases
	Employment			
Intention of parties	0.2526 (0.631)	6.9845** (1.409)	1.3500 (0.745)	0.6674 (0.742)
Intention * post-*Royal Winnipeg*				3.652** (1.011)
Control factors	8.5642** (1.318)	14.128** (2.576)	9.7769** (1.072)	10.0277** (1.097)
Ownership of tools and equipment	1.2876** (0.495)	2.9720** (1.008)	1.6245** (0.4393)	1.6834** (0.439)
Profit and risk factors	2.7567** (0.612)	5.1394** (1.512)	3.3411** (0.603)	3.2668** (0.590)
Integration factors	0.4147 (1.275)	0.6455 (0.945)	0.0899 (0.761)	0.1457 (0.766)
Observations	257	268	525	525

Robust standard errors in parentheses. ** $p < 0.01$ * $p < 0.05$.

statistically significant in Table 4.3, much of the variation in outcomes can be explained by reference to the variation in the four *Wiebe Door* factors. Knowing the intention of the parties adds little.

4.4.4   The Marginal Influence of Parties' Intention

Why does the intention of the parties play a largely insignificant role in predicting the outcomes of cases? We look to whether the intention of the parties may be more likely to play a role when the four *Wiebe Door* factors suggest that the case is a "close" case. We expect that the intention of the parties is less likely to matter when the four *Wiebe Door* factors provide a strong prediction of the outcome. For example, if all four *Wiebe Door* factors push in favor of a finding that the worker is an employee, the intention of the parties may not be important for a court. But if the *Wiebe Door* factors are quite inconclusive, we expect that the courts are more likely to uphold the intention of the parties.

To test this hypothesis, we look at the "error" in our predictions. As noted above, for each case we generate a predicted probability that the worker will be classified as an employee. We measure "error" here as the difference between the correct outcome and our predicted probability under Model 1, the model that predicts based on only the four *Wiebe Door* factors, but not the intention of the parties. For example, if our model had predicted that a worker would be found to be an employee with probability 90 percent and the court decided that the worker was an employee, the error would be 0.1. If the court, however, had found that the worker was an independent contractor, the error of our prediction would be 0.9.

We track the errors in prediction for each case decided after *Royal Winnipeg*. Two interesting results emerge. First, the cases where courts do depart from the intention of the parties are generally "easy" cases for the courts to decide. These are cases where the four *Wiebe Door* factors push in favor of a particular finding and the intention of the parties is not strong enough to outweigh these factors.

Figure 4.3 illustrates this point. The lighter dots represent cases where the intention of the parties was upheld. The darker dots represent cases where the courts depart from the parties' intention. The darker dots are more likely to be found in cases where the errors in prediction are low. This means that courts are more likely to depart from the intention of the parties when the *Wiebe Door* factors push strongly in the opposite direction to that intended by the parties. The lighter dots are more likely when Model 1 has higher errors of prediction. That is, the court is more likely to uphold the intention where the *Wiebe Door* factors are not conclusive.

The average "error" in cases where the courts depart from the intention of the parties (0.095) is much lower than the average "error" in prediction where courts uphold the intention of the parties (0.175). This difference is highly statistically significant ($t = 3.36$). Further, of the 18 cases that Model 1 predicts the outcome incorrectly just three were cases where the court did not uphold the parties' intentions.

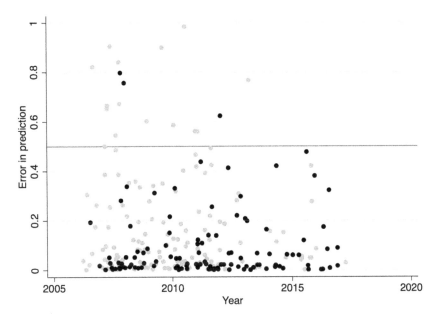

Figure 4.3 Errors in our prediction over time for each case after *Royal Winnipeg.* Lighter dots indicate that the court upheld the parties' intention. Darker dots represent the court departed from the parties' intention. Observations that lie above the dark horizontal line are those that Model 1 predicted the outcome incorrectly.

The second interesting finding is that Model 1 – based *only* on the four *Wiebe* Door factors – is getting better at predicting the outcomes of cases over time. Figure 4.4 illustrates this result with a trend line. The trend line in predicted errors is falling over time, suggesting that Model 1 is predicting the outcome of cases with greater accuracy. Indeed, our model correctly predicts the outcome of every case decided since 2013. This provides further evidence that the intention of the parties is of decreasing significance in the lower court's decisions. That is, it suggests intention is being given less weight over time.

Readers may wonder whether this improvement in prediction is attributable to our prediction being based on more cases, since we have used a dynamic out-of-sample prediction method that relies on all previous cases. The intuition for this hypothesis would be that the more data, the greater the accuracy of the prediction. But we have a similar finding even if we limit the model to predict the outcome of the case

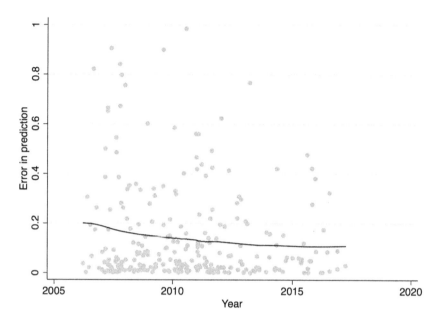

Figure 4.4   Errors in prediction over time for each case after *Royal Winnipeg*. The black line illustrates the trend in errors (Lowess).

based only on the previous 100 cases. The errors in prediction still decrease over time.

4.4.5   Limitations of our Findings

As with any empirical investigation examining written opinions in published cases, our study is not perfect. We discuss two key limitations here: (1) judicial fact discretion; and (2) selection effects.

First, consider fact discretion. While judges discuss all relevant factors – intention, control, ownership, profit and risk, integration – in each of our 525 cases, judges have enormous discretion to emphasize or de-emphasize particular facts in the written opinion. The battles in these cases may not be over how the different factors of the test are weighed, but rather about how different facts should be interpreted. For example, litigants may dispute who sets the hours of the worker, or may dispute what the most important tools and equipment are. Judges have significant discretion when writing their opinion to emphasize factors that align with the outcome they have reached (Gennaioli and Shleifer 2008). Here, this fact discretion may bias our findings by making cases appear "easier" than they actually are. In a given case, the *Wiebe Door* factors may appear to align in one direction in the *ex post* written opinion, but that alignment may not have been so obvious based on the *ex ante* arguments. Therefore, our predictive model will likely be overstating the predictive power of our simple logistic model.

Second, any study investigating the influences upon case outcomes needs to consider selection effects (Priest and Klein 1984). Here, we have attempted to control for differences in the facts across cases so that changes in the composition of cases can be adequately captured. Returning to Table 4.1, we see that the *Wiebe Door* factors do not change markedly from the pre-*Royal Winnipeg* cases to the post-*Royal Winnipeg* cases.

But the change in the law may have affected the way that litigants select disputes by litigants for trial. These selection effects may be influencing our results. In Table 4.1, for example, we observe that the percentage of cases where the parties intend the relationship to be characterized as an employment relationship drops markedly after the *Royal Winnipeg* decision (just 7.4 percent of cases, compared to 15.2 percent before the change). Further, courts in our sample are more likely to uphold the parties' intention when the parties intend to have an employment relationship (see Table 4.2). Taken together, this suggests that litigants may be more likely to settle cases where the intention was for the worker to be covered by an employment agreement after the *Royal Winnipeg* decision. This selection effect may dampen the observed impact of the rule change in our study. Parties who characterized their relationship as an independent contractor relationship are more likely to litigate after *Royal Winnipeg*, and courts are less likely to uphold that intention relative to those relationships characterized as employment relationships.

4.5   Conclusion

Our investigation into the effect of a rule change by an appellate court yields interesting results. The appellate court ordered lower courts to take into account a new factor that had previously ignored when determining whether a worker was an employee or an independent contractor. Following the rule change, lower courts were required to not only balance the four *Wiebe Door* factors, but also take into account the intention of the parties. This new fifth dimension had greatest impact in the five years following the appeals court decision in 2006. From 2006 to 2010, courts upheld the intention of the parties with greater frequency than at any other time in our dataset. The intention of the parties became a statistically significant variable in our model, correlating with the outcome of the case.

But the outcomes of cases after the rule change can be predicted with high accuracy without taking into account this new dimension. Using a model that does not include the intention of parties, our model correctly predicts the outcome in over 93 percent of our cases following the *Royal Winnipeg* decision. Adding the intention of the parties into the model improves the predictive power of the model only marginally. This suggests that the impact of the rule change has not been dramatic.

We conclude that lower courts exercise discretion in weighing the relevant factors when deciding a vague standard such as the "total relationship" test. While an appeals court may change the legal rule and emphasize the importance of a new factor to be included in the lower court's assessment, the outcomes of cases may not be greatly affected.

It may be that our chosen example is somewhat unique. The outcomes of cases appear to be highly predictable here. Changes in legal rules may have greater salience in areas of law that are less predictable or litigated less frequently than this issue. If there were fewer factors to consider, one might think that a new factor would have greater impact. One would of course expect the influence of rule change to be greater where the new law is a bright-line rule and not merely adding a new factor to a multifactor standard. Nonetheless, the expectation that lower courts will dramatically change their behavior in response to a rule change of an appellate court is not borne out by the evidence in this particular sphere.

References

Atiyah, Patrick S. 1985. *The Rise and Fall of Freedom of Contract.* Oxford, UK: Oxford University Press.

Carlson, Richard R. 2001. Why the Law Still Can't Tell an Employee When It Sees One and How It Ought to Stop Trying. *Berkeley Journal of Employment & Labor Law* 22: 295–368.

Gennaioli, Nicola, and Andrei Shleifer. 2007. The Evolution of Common Law. *Journal of Political Economy* 115: 43–68.

2008. Judicial Fact Discretion. *Journal of Legal Studies* 37: 1–35.

Gilmore, Grant. 1974. *The Death of Contract.* Columbus, OH: Ohio State University Press.

Goetz, Charles J., and Robert E. Scott. 1981. Enforcing Promises: An Examination of the Basis of Contract. *Yale Law Journal* 89: 1261–322.

Harned, Karen R., Georgine M. Kryda, and Elizabeth A. Milito. 2010. Creating a Workable Legal Standard for Defining an Independent Contractor. *Journal of Business, Entrepreneurship & Law* 4: 93–117.

Jacobi, Tonja, and Emerson H. Tiller. 2007. Legal Doctrine and Political Control. *Journal of Law, Economics, and Organization* 23: 326–45.

Kim, Pauline T. 2007. Lower Court Discretion. *New York University Law Review* 82: 283–442.

Niblett, Anthony. 2013. Tracking Inconsistent Judicial Behavior. *International Review of Law & Economics* 34: 9–20.

Niblett, Anthony, Richard A. Posner, and Andrei Shleifer. 2010. The Evolution of a Legal Rule. *Journal of Legal Studies* 39: 325–49.

Peltason, Jack W. 1961. *Fifty-Eight Lonely Men.* New York: Harcourt, Brace, & World Inc.

Ponzetto, Giacomo A. M. and Fernandez, Patricio O. 2008. Case Law versus Statute Law: An Evolutionary Comparison. *Journal of Legal Studies* 37: 370–430.

Posner, Richard A. 1973. *Economic Analysis of Law*, 1st ed. Boston: Little, Brown.

Priest, George L. 1977. The Common Law Process and the Selection of Efficient Rules. *Journal of Legal Studies* 6: 65–82.

Priest, George L., and Benjamin Klein. 1984. The Selection of Disputes for Litigation. *Journal of Legal Studies* 13: 1–55.

Read, Frank T., and Lucy S. McGough. 1978. *Let Them Be Judged: The Judicial Integration of the Deep South.* Metuchen, NJ: Scarecrow Press.

Rubin, Paul H. 1977. Why Is the Common Law Efficient? *Journal of Legal Studies* 6: 51–63.

Schwartz, Alan, and Robert E. Scott. 2003. Contract Theory and the Limits of Contract Law. *Yale Law Journal* 113: 541–619.

Trebilcock, Michael J. 1993. *The Limits of Freedom of Contract.* Cambridge, MA: Harvard University Press.

Career Judge System and Court Decision Biases

Preliminary Evidence from Japan

HATSURU MORITA AND MANABU MATSUNAKA

5.1 Introduction

Laws are made by the judiciary as well as by the legislative and the executive branches of government.[1] The courts, through their decisions, build a system of case law that complements and modifies statutes and government regulations. The case law system is important not only in common law countries such as the UK and the United States, but also in civil law countries. Japan is no exception, and the case law system plays a critical role in Japanese law. However, the behavior of judges and the characteristics of court decisions in Japan have not been thoroughly studied and hence there is a scarcity of literature on these topics.

First, the employment system for judges in Japan is career system, rather than an election or political appointment system. In the United States, most judges are elected through a ballot or politically appointed. In such an environment, we would expect judges in the United States to consider the interests of their electorates or political supporters and there is a vast body of work on their political behavior.

In contrast, Japanese judges in general do not show such political biases. It is certainly the case that until the 1970s Japanese judges had somewhat conservative bias. This was due to the fierce political conflict between the right and left during the 1960s and 1970s, in addition to the conservative Liberal Democratic Party (LDP) being in government and appointing the Supreme Court judges. However, the political conflict receded thereafter, and it has become difficult to find any consistent political biases in the court decisions. Thus, encountering a relatively

[1] This work is supported by JSPS KAKENHI grant numbers 16H03564 (Morita), and 15K03202 and 18K01360 (Matsunaka).

small variation in court decisions, many researchers turned away from empirical analyses of court decisions in Japan.

Second, the published data on Japanese court decisions are heavily biased, being neither population data nor a random sample. Journals that publish court decisions have their own editorial committees, which select only "valuable" cases for publication, namely those that contribute to the development of law in the sense that they provide solutions that differ from precedents or address new (previously unknown) issues. Thus, published data on court decisions in Japan are nonrandomly selected samples and are generally inappropriate for statistical analysis. The only way to acquire a random sample of court decisions in Japan would be to approach a court and collect all its cases during a specified period. However, such data would be too costly to construct, because case data are only supplied in paper format and photocopying is not allowed.

In addition, measuring the efficiency of court decisions is an inherently difficult task. To start with, court decisions by themselves do not indicate whether they are efficient. Most decisions just follow their precedents, and it is impossible to evaluate the efficiency of court decisions by observing only the outcomes of cases. For example, counting the number of successful lawsuits does not reveal the efficiency of court decisions. The fact that Japanese criminal courts have the conviction rate of 98 percent[2] does not tell us whether their decisions are efficient, although it may indicate the efficiency of the Japanese criminal court *system*, with its high predictability and smooth case management.

To evaluate the efficiency of Japanese court decisions, we could check whether specific changes of court decisions had any social impact. When we observe whether a change in case law improves social efficiency, we can say that the court in that case behaved in an efficient manner. By collecting many such instances, we could evaluate the general trend of efficiency of court decisions. However, it is generally difficult to evaluate the effect of changes in case law on efficiency, because Japan has a single jurisdiction and no variation in legal rules except for those revealed by the regression discontinuity design.

Thus, our contribution to the research on efficiency of court decisions based on Japanese data are twofold. First, we provide some statistics on a trend in court decisions in Japan. As noted above, published data on

---

[2] In the 2015 fiscal year, the district courts in Japan accepted 54,296 (= 74,111 − 19,815) cases, of which guilty verdicts were returned in 53,120 cases (www.courts.go.jp/app/files/toukei/616/008616.pdf, accessed May 1, 2017).

Japanese court decisions are from a nonrandom sample, and our analysis is an imperfect and preliminary one. Although we cannot make the usual causal inferences from Japanese court data, we can note some symptoms. However, as experienced researchers of Japanese law, we provide a balanced view of court decisions in Japan. Second, we provide some qualitative anecdotes that cast light on the efficiency of Japanese court decisions. In this way, our analyses remain preliminary and exploratory, but we hope they will be a starting point for future research.

The book chapter proceeds as follows. Section 5.2 describes the institutional background of the Japanese court system and proposes a hypothesis on the efficiency of court decisions. The remaining sections provide evidence for the hypothesis. Section 5.3 analyzes decisions concerning international civil jurisdiction; Section 5.4 discusses decisions on consumer protection law; and Section 5.5 provides evidence on corporate law. Finally, Section 5.6 concludes.

5.2   Institutional Background

5.2.1   The Career Judge System

Unlike in the United States, where the careers of legal professionals are more or less integrated, Japan has separated career paths for judges, prosecutors, and attorneys. After passing the national bar exam and completing studies in the Legal Training and Research Institute, a lawyer must choose a future path. If she chooses to be an attorney, she will basically remain an attorney throughout her career. If she chooses to be a judge, she will typically remain a judge until retirement age and become an attorney after retirement. If she chooses to be a prosecutor, she will typically remain a prosecutor and become an attorney after retirement. This means that Japanese judges are career judges and not recruited from attorneys, although a few exceptions exist. Like regular corporate employees, judges in Japan enjoy the tradition of "lifetime employment."

In this system,[3] judges are basically under the control of the General Secretariat of the Supreme Court, which evaluates the performance of judges and determines the career path of each,[4] Under such a unified system, we anticipate relatively little variation in judges' performance compared with their US counterparts.

---

[3] See, for example, Ramseyer and Nakazato (1999) and Ramseyer and Rasmusen (2003).
[4] There are some exceptions for the highest careers, that is, Supreme Court judges.

5.2.2   Incentives for Judges

In the United States, most judges are elected or politically appointed. It is therefore not surprising that they have an incentive to follow the views of their electorates or the political supporters, and there is an extensive literature on the political preferences of US judges.

In contrast, as noted, most Japanese judges are career judges and are neither elected nor appointed by politicians. Career judges have no incentive to heed the views of electorates, nor that of the majority party. While it is true that there was a political struggle between the leftist movement (particularly, the leftist Young Lawyers Association [*eihokyo*]) and the ruling LDP in the period immediately following World War II,[5] the ideological dispute between the left and right essentially disappeared with the end of conflicts surrounding the Japan–US Security Treaty in the 1970s. The role of Japanese judges is now universally recognized;[6] they are not politically biased but seek to follow their own "conscience" (Constitution Article 76), and ideology has no influence on the behavior of today's judges in Japan.[7]

Thus, the question is: what are the incentives for Japanese judges? Ramseyer and Rasmusen provide a possible answer.[8] They analyzed the promotion system of Japanese judges and found that a judge who makes quick and "correct" decisions – which are rarely reversed by higher courts – thereby handling more cases and improving the efficiency of the court system, is more likely to be promoted. Their observation is supported by several other witnesses.

[5] See the discussion by Ramseyer and Rasmusen (2003).
[6] See Fujita (2011). As McElwain and Winkler (2015) pointed out, the Japanese Constitution is so vague that the number of cases in which the Supreme Court has declared unconstitutionality is quite low and does not justify the argument that the Supreme Court is conservative. In addition, the constitutionality of most statutes are checked by the Cabinet Legislation Bureau before legislation in advance, which reduces the likelihood of their being ruled unconstitutional by the courts.
[7] We have interviewed several influential legal scholars from various areas of law, including contract law, property law, family law, corporate law, commercial law, constitutional law, administrative law, civil procedure law, intellectual property law, and antitrust law. Most agreed that Japanese judges are not politically biased. We have also interviewed several prominent practicing attorneys, who also shared our view. We did not interview attorneys from Japan Federation of Bar Associations because it is known to be politically biased and would not constitute a fair sample of the whole population of practicing attorneys.
[8] Ramseyer and Rasmusen (2003, p. 54).

For example, Koichi Yaguchi, who was a former Supreme Court Chief Justice and had long served in the General Secretariat of the Supreme Court, argued:

> "We evaluate judges by their performance in cases. Of course, 'performance' does not mean that outcome of each judge's cases follows the desired outcome and ideas of the evaluators."
>
> (Yaguchi 2004, p. 207)

> "My caseload was almost the same as that of the judges who criticized me. However, I handled most cases by settlement and only a few decisions were appealed. In contrast, the cases of those judges who criticized me were almost always appealed. From the viewpoint of the judicial branch as a whole, contribution to efficiency is completely different."
>
> (Yaguchi 2004, p. 130)

> "It is inappropriate that every case a judge handles is appealed and reversed."
>
> (Yaguchi 2004, p. 132)

Similarly, Shuichi Yoshikai, who was a former president of several district courts and high courts and had long served at the Administration Office of the Supreme Court, observed:

> *"There was a judge who had worked until midnight at the courthouse. ...The judge's opinions were careful and long. But the judge took a long time solving a case...*
>
> *As the president of the court, I asked whether the judge could leave earlier because staying until late had troubled staffs on duty and endangered the judge's health. The judge told me 'I'm trying.' I thought the judge had been trying hard, but the judge might have been complacent about his own work and should change his work style."*
>
> (Yoshikai 2013, p. 63)

Part of the reason why the Japanese court has adopted such a promotion system lies at the core of the career judge system, under which judges are neither appointed by the ruling party at the time nor elected through a public ballot. It would not be rational to use the political leanings of judges as criteria for promotion. Instead, the court, which is required to manage a huge caseload on a limited budget and with limited human resources, has an incentive to adopt a promotion system that encourages judges to manage cases efficiently. Here, efficiency does not refer to the efficiency of the court decisions themselves, but to the efficiency of case management by the courts. If a judge handles many cases without error, which means her decisions are not reversed by higher courts, she contributes to the efficiency of the court system. In contrast, if she handles cases slowly or her decisions are often reversed by higher courts, her performance hinders the entire court system.

While the court adopts a promotion system that encourages judges to act in an efficient manner, it is not surprising that at the same time it has an incentive to adopt rules that enable judges to manage cases efficiently. Some legal rules, such as bright-line rules, enable rapid case management, while others, such as flexible standards, require a considerable amount of effort on the part of judges and slow their case management.[9] If the court adopts a legal rule that enables judges to process many cases at a lower cost, its efficiency is improved.

Of course, the case management efficiency is not the sole or primary purpose of the court. As Calabresi (1970) posited, the efficiency goal is to minimize the sum of harm costs, precautionary costs, and administrative costs. Our hypothesis is that career judges weight the third factor too heavily, and thus fail to minimize the sum. Under some conditions, this trend is not socially harmful but may be desirable, while under other conditions it causes deviation of court decisions from the social optimum.

In the remainder of this book chapter, we explore some examples that show the biases of Japanese courts. Because courts weigh the case management efficiency against the other two factors and their biases are manifested differently depending on a number of conditions, such as the characteristics of cases the and rank of court, it is necessary to note the trade-offs made by the courts across various areas of Japanese law.

5.3   International Civil Jurisdiction

Procedural law is the most salient area where efficiency considerations in case management are important. To assess the tendency of courts to place great weight on efficiency, we examine international civil jurisdiction cases.

Under Japanese civil procedure law, international civil jurisdiction is determined by a two-step process.[10] First, the court checks whether any

---

[9] See Kaplow (1992) for a general discussion on the relationship between rules and standards.
[10] See Supreme Court decisions of October 16, 1981, *Minshu* vol. 35, no. 7, p. 1224 and November 11, 1997, *Minshu* vol. 51 no. 10 p. 4055. After April 1, 2012, the Civil Procedure Code was reformed and the case law has become invalid today.

valid inland jurisdiction can be found under the Civil Procedure Code. If the answer is no, the court declares that Japanese courts have no civil jurisdiction over the case. If the answer is yes, the court goes on to the second step, checking for any exceptional circumstances that justify denial of inland jurisdiction. It is characteristic of this two-step procedure that the first step is almost nominal. It is notoriously easy to find inland jurisdiction under the Civil Procedure Code in most cases. The core of this procedure is the second step, namely the exceptional circumstance rule[11].

Although the Supreme Court did not clarify the factors to be considered under the exceptional circumstance rule, and various factors have been taken into consideration because of the Supreme Court decision of 1981, we can empirically explore which factors are important. We examined international civil jurisdiction cases except for family law cases from 1982 to 2007, using LEX/DB and D1-Law databases[12]. The number of cases reached 46, from which we dropped three cases with jurisdiction by agreement, because the court did not need to consider the issue. Next, we split the sample into those cases where the court declared the governing law of the case and other cases where it did not (e.g., interlocutory decisions). The summary statistics is shown in Table 5.1.

To analyze the behavior of the court, we employed Fisher's exact test.[13] The key variable of interest is whether the court confirmed the existence of exceptional circumstances and denied the jurisdiction of the Japanese courts (Exceptional). We tested whether this variable is independent from the following variables: the explanatory variables are whether the governing law of the case is Japanese law or not (Governing Law JPN), whether the plaintiff is an individual (Individual Plaintiff), whether the defendant is an individual (Individual Defendant), whether the case is contract case (Contract Case), and whether the court is a district court or not (District Court). The results are shown in Table 5.2.

First, "Exceptional" is strongly correlated with the governing law decision. When the governing law of the case is Japanese law, the court

---

[11] The reason why the rule is called the "exceptional circumstance rule" is that the inland jurisdictional rule, which is also applied to international jurisdiction cases, almost always finds inland jurisdiction and that the court needs to find negating factors to achieve balanced jurisdictional rule.

[12] The data are borrowed from Kono et al. (2008). We thank the authors for their assistance.

[13] We did not employ the usual regression techniques, because the sample size is quite small. Nor did we use a chi-squared test of independence because our sample is small and some cells contained zero. When we ran a simple regression model with the dependent variable "Exceptional," we achieved a similar result.

Table 5.1 *Summary statistics*

Statistic	Obs.	Mean	St. Dev.	Min	Max
Exceptional	31	0.42	0.5	0	1
Governing Law JPN	16	0.63	0.5	0	1
Individual Plaintiff	40	0.25	0.44	0	1
Individual Defendant	40	0.28	0.45	0	1
Contract Case	40	0.45	0.5	0	1
District Court	40	0.8	0.41	0	1

Notes: JPN stands for Japan.

Table 5.2 *Exceptional circumstance rule*

	Exceptional		P-value
	No	Yes	(Fisher's exact test)
Governing Law JPN: No	0	5	0.008
: Yes	8	1	
Individual Plaintiff: No	12 (7)	6 (6)	0.412
: Yes	6 (3)	2 (1)	(0.603)
Individual Defendant: No	14 (7)	7 (3)	0.247
: Yes	4 (3)	6 (4)	(0.35)
Contract Case: No	14 (9)	4 (4)	0.013
: Yes	4 (1)	9 (3)	(0.25)
District Court: No	4 (1)	4 (2)	0.689
: Yes	14 (9)	9 (5)	(0.537)

Notes: * Numbers in parentheses are from samples without a declaration of the governing law. JPN stands for Japan.

does not find any exceptional circumstance. Other variables are not independent from "Exceptional," except for "Contract Case." However, when we limited our sample to cases with the declaration of governing law of the case, "Contract Case" became statistically insignificant. Thus, Japanese courts tend to deny inland jurisdiction when the governing law of the case is foreign law.[14]

---

[14] Note that this is not a mechanical relationship. In theory, Japanese courts have the authority to apply and interpret foreign laws, and foreign governing laws do not necessarily deny inland jurisdiction.

This tendency is contrary to current Japanese traditional international private law doctrines (see Kono et al. 2008). These doctrines argue that jurisdictional decision should be separate from governing law decisions. In contrast, the courts heavily weight the governing law factor. This is understandable from the perspective of case management efficiency. Because surveying foreign laws and writing appropriate decisions based on them require a huge amount of effort and time, judges have a strong incentive to deny the application of foreign law. It is thus not surprising that the Japanese judges want to rely only on Japanese law. At the same time, this tendency may not be socially suboptimal. Because applying foreign laws in Japanese courts requires considerable human resources of Japanese judiciary, allowing foreign courts to decide such cases would be preferable. Therefore, although we could argue that the case-handling efficiency applies here, we cannot assert the outcome is socially inefficient.

Of course, such cases alone do not provide a strong support for our hypothesis because judges in other countries without career judge systems may have similar tendencies. Therefore, we must turn to other evidence.

5.4   Consumer Law

5.4.1   Unconscionability Cases

Many countries have unconscionability doctrines for consumer contracts, and Japan is no exception. Article 10 of the Consumer Contract Act enacted in 2000 (Act No. 61 of May 12, 2000) stipulates:

> (Nullity of Clauses That Impair the Interests of Consumers Unilaterally)
>   Article 10 Any Consumer Contract clause that restricts the rights or expands the duties of the Consumer more than the application of provisions unrelated to public order in the Civil Code, the Commercial Code (Act No. 48 of 1899) and any other laws and regulations, and that unilaterally impairs the interests of the Consumer, in violation of the fundamental principle provided in the second paragraph of Article 1 of the Civil Code, is void.

The unconscionability rule has two criteria. The first criterion is whether the consumer contract clause restricts the rights or expands the duties of the consumer more than the application of the default rules of various statutes. The second criterion is whether the clause unilaterally impairs the interests of the consumer in violation of the fundamental principle of abuse of rights. The first criterion is a rather formal one, while the second is more substantive. In other words, the first criterion is a bright-line rule and the second is a vague standard.

From the viewpoint of judges, it is much easier to ascertain whether a case satisfies the first criterion because it only requires comparison of the consumer contract clause and the default rule in the statutes. In contrast, to ascertain whether a case satisfies the second criterion, a judge is required to consider the extent to which the consumer contract clause harms the consumer, which demands a huge amount of resources.

Comparing the two criteria, we expect that some judges with a heavy load of consumer law cases tend to rely on the first criterion and employ the second criterion as if it were a bright-line rule, thereby reducing the costs of managing cases, while those with relatively small caseloads tend to employ the second criterion and consider each case intensively. Under the Japanese court system, lower court (district court and high court) judges are required to handle a large number of cases, while the Supreme Court can focus on a relatively small number of cases because it can regulate permission to appeal to it.

We also expect different attitudes toward the use of the two criteria between lower courts and the Supreme Court. Note that the reason why consumers bring cases before the courts is that they believe they have been unfairly treated and their interests have suffered undue harm. Because the default rules in the statutes are usually intended to strike a balance between various parties, contract clauses in consumer cases are almost always different from the default rules: they restrict the rights or expand the duties of consumers more than the default rules. Thus, the first criterion of Article 10 of the Consumer Contract Act is almost automatically satisfied and the most important issue in consumer cases is usually the second criterion.

Considering this situation, we propose the following hypotheses: lower courts, which manage heavy caseloads, tend to employ the second criterion formally as if it were a bright-line rule and revoke consumer contract clauses, while the Supreme Court, with a lighter caseload, tends to employ the second criterion actively, examining case details, and validates consumer contract clauses. This role allotment among lower courts and the Supreme Court enhances the case-handling efficiency of the court system as a whole. We now check this prediction from the court decision data.

Table 5.3 *Breakdown of unconscionability cases*

Outcome	Lower Courts	Supreme Court	Total
Valid	33	8	41
Invalid	15	0	15
Sum	48	8	56

Notes: Lower courts include District Courts and High Courts.

As of May 1, 2017, there were 56 cases that employed Article 10 and evaluated the validity of consumer contract clauses.[15] Among the 56 cases, the court found the consumer contract clause to be valid in 41 cases and invalid in 15 cases. The breakdown of 56 cases is shown in Table 5.3.

Surprisingly, there was no case where the Supreme Court declared the consumer contract clause invalid according to Article 10. Of course, there are many cases where the Supreme Court declared a consumer contract clause invalid according to other book chapters of the act. The difference between lower courts and the Supreme Court is strongly significant: the *p*-value of the likelihood ratio test is far below 0.001. In addition, the Supreme Court reversed or modified the lower court decision in seven of the eight cases and upheld the lower court decision in only one.

As noted above, the sample here is not a nonrandom sample but a selected sample, in that only cases involving new issues and the modification of precedents are included in the published case sample. However, Table 5.3 shows a strong tendency for the Supreme Court – in contrast to lower courts – to find consumer contract clauses valid on the basis of the second criterion of Article 10 of the Consumer Contract Act.

A symbolic example can be found in the Supreme Court decision of July 12, 2011.[16] This case involved the "deduction from deposit" clause of a real estate lease contract. In the Osaka area, it is customary to include a deduction from a deposit clause, which requires tenants to pay a specified amount of money from the deposit to landlords when they leave. Some tenants sued landlords, arguing that the clause violated Article 10 of the Consumer Contract Act. The decision of the Supreme Court was not unanimous, which is rare.

---

[15] The data are acquired from the D1-Law database system (www.d1-law.com) (accessed July 19, 2019).

[16] *Saibanshu Minji* no. 237 p. 215.

The majority opinion was in favor of landlords. Mutsuo Tahara, who had long served as a business attorney, delivered a supporting opinion, arguing that people in Osaka rationally understand the clause and consider it to be part of the monthly rent. In contrast, Kiyoko Okabe, who had long served as a judge in family court (lower court), delivered a dissenting opinion, arguing that the clause was unfair. This episode shows how the background of judges has influence on court decisions. Tahara, as a business attorney, gave a socially efficient opinion. In contrast, Okabe, with long experience as a lower court judge, attempted to deliver an inefficient solution.

5.4.2   The NOVA Case

The unconscionability cases are clear examples where the Supreme Court has a socially desirable incentive to achieve efficiency, while lower courts have an incentive to deviate from the social optimum to achieve case-handling efficiency. However, when a huge number of cases are pending and the court system as a whole is required to manage them, there is an incentive to place greater importance on case-handling efficiency, thereby reaching a socially suboptimal outcome. The case of the foreign language school NOVA is one such example.

NOVA opened for business in 1981 and reached the height of its popularity around 2000. It had over 500 branches nationwide, and one of its strengths was its accessibility. However, NOVA's success was attributable (at least partly) to its business model. NOVA adopted the "lesson point system," under which a customer needed to prepurchase "lesson points" and used these to make reservations for lessons. The points were sold under a volume discount system. Suppose a single point price was 1,000 yen. When a customer bought 10 points, the price was 9,000 yen (the price per point was 900 yen); when she bought 20 points, the price was 16,000 yen (800 yen per point). This volume discount seems like a normal commercial practice.

The key to NOVA's lesson point system was its sales strategy and cancellation system. NOVA solicited huge volume purchases by providing larger discounts: when customers bought a larger volume of points, they received larger discounts and the price per point was reduced. At the same time, when customers wished to cancel their lessons and redeem prepurchased points, the remaining points were reimbursed at the normal price. For example, when a customer had purchased 20 points for 16,000 yen and decided to cancel after using 10 points, she received

7,000 yen (= 16,000 – 9,000, i.e., the volume discount price for the 10 points used), not 8,000 yen (= 16,000 * 10/20). The reimbursement rule still seems rational, because without it every customer would pre-purchase the maximum amount of points to obtain the maximum discount and then request a refund for the prepurchased points after ceasing to use NOVA's services, thereby making the volume discount scheme irrelevant.

However, the combination of soliciting of huge volume purchases and the reimbursement rule caused a serious consumer problem. Many consumers, who were subject to behavioral biases, were tempted to prepurchase too many points (more than 600), but realized that they were unable to use them all. At the same time, as the number of NOVA customers was rapidly increasing, the likelihood of customers being unable to reserve a class at their preferred time and place was decreasing. From around 2005, the number of complaints from NOVA customers reported to the National Consumer Affairs Center of Japan (NCAC) increased dramatically. On June 13, 2007, the Ministry of Economy, Trade and Industry (METI) issued a governmental order to improve business operations based on the Act on Specified Commercial Transactions (ASCT). The reasons for METI's order to NOVA were deficiencies in the contract document, deceptive advertising, and unwillingness to respond to cancellation requests, among others.[17] At about the same time, many consumers filed lawsuits against NOVA for reimbursements of prepurchased points. The reputation of NOVA deteriorated rapidly, and it filed for bankruptcy on October 26, 2007.

In the midst of the NOVA scandal, the Supreme Court delivered a decision on a dispute between NOVA and a customer, who was claiming reimbursement for prepurchased points. The decision on April 3, 2007[18] declared that the reimbursement rule of NOVA was contrary to Article 49 (2) of the ASCT and void. The court ordered NOVA to reimburse at the rate of volume discount (i.e., 8,000 yen in our example above).

Article 49 (2) of the ASCT, which is a special rule for the general penalty clause rule under the Civil Code, stipulates as follows.

[17] http://warp.da.ndl.go.jp/info:ndljp/pid/3193246/www.meti.go.jp/press/20070613004/20070613004.html (accessed May 7, 2017).
[18] *Minshu* vol. 61 no. 3 p. 967.

Article 49 (2) Where a Specified Continuous Service Contract has been rescinded pursuant to the preceding paragraph, the Service Provider may not demand that the recipient of the Specified Continuous Services pays an amount of money that exceeds the total of the amount specified in the following items according to the respective cases listed therein and the amount of the relevant delay damages based on the statutory interest rate, even when there is an agreement for liquidated damages or a provision on a penalty:

(i) if said Specified Continuous Service Contract was rescinded after the start of the offering of the Specified Continuous Services the total of the following amounts:
   (a) the amount equivalent to the consideration for the Specified Continuous Services offered and
   (b) the amount specified by the Cabinet Order referred to in Article 41, para. 2 according to the respective services specified therein as an amount of damages that are normally caused by rescission of said Specified Continuous Service Contract.
(ii) where the Specified Continuous Service Contract was canceled before the Specified Continuous Services started to be provided: the amount specified by the Cabinet Order referred to in Article 41, paragraph (2) in accordance with each of the services specified therein as the amount of costs normally required for concluding and performing a contract.

This is a similar rule to the penalty clause and a more general rule can be found in Article 9 of the Consumer Contract Act.

The fault of NOVA was obviously its sales strategy, not its cancellation system. The sales strategy violated the principle of suitability, not the penalty clause rule, and would be invalid under the Civil Code and other clauses of the ASCT. Declaring NOVA's cancellation system to be invalid would kill off many other reasonable businesses that offer volume discounts. In this regard, utilizing the ASCT had a serious side effect. Although Japan has adopted an adversarial litigation system and the plaintiff relied on the ASCT argument, the court could have exercised the discretion of clarification and let the plaintiff argue the Civil Code issues. The question is why the Supreme Court adopted such a suboptimal and inefficient solution.

A possible answer here concerns case-handling efficiency. Article 49 (2) of the ASCT is a bright-line rule, while the principle of suitability is a vague standard, which requires more efforts and time. Furthermore, unlike the United States, which has the class action system, Japanese law does not.[19] As noted above, many NOVA-related cases were pending at the time, and the court system as a whole had a strong incentive to take case-handling efficiency seriously. Efficiency consideration could have caused the Supreme Court to adopt a seemingly inefficient decision.

5.5   Corporate Law

5.5.1   Equity Offerings

5.5.1.1   Equity Offerings in Closed Firms

This section discusses cases on invalidation of equity offerings. There are three remedies for illegal and/or unfair equity offerings under the Companies Act (*hereafter* CA). Prior to the completion of an offering, a shareholder can claim for an injunction against an illegal or an extremely unfair offering (CA Article 210). After completion, a shareholder can claim for invalidation of the offering (CA Article 828, item 2) although the grounds are severely limited. In extreme cases, such as when there is only a public registration as if the issuance were completed, but no formal procedures are followed, and no money is actually paid to the company, a shareholder can request a court to confirm the nonexistence of the offering (CA Article 829) and to delete the registration.

While the injunction has been used for equity offerings by both publicly traded and closed firms, almost all the invalidation and nonexistence cases have involved offerings by closed firms. This is because share issuances by publicly traded firms are widely disclosed prior to their issuance and invalidating widely traded shares is extremely impractical. Furthermore, because closed firms often make inadequate disclosures or even hide the offering from dissatisfied shareholders, shareholders often miss the chance to seek an injunction.

5.5.1.2   Case Laws by the Supreme Courts

The Supreme Court clearly prefers rules that can be applied by looking at small numbers of simple facts over standards requiring the courts to examine the substance of cases. The Supreme Court's approach can be

[19] More precisely, Japanese law introduced a quasi-class action system on October 1, 2016 (Act on Special Measures Concerning Civil Court Proceedings for the Collective Redress for Property Damage Incurred by Consumers). However, to date, there has been no quasi-class action under this act.

viewed as substituting standards by a set of simple rules that only entails small costs.

First, the Supreme Court has denied invalidating an equity offering performed in an extremely unfair manner (Supreme Court Decision, July 14, 1994, 172 Saibanshu Minji 771; Supreme Court Decision, January 28, 1997, 51 Minshu 71). An unfair offering typically involves a share issuance by a board to secure its control over the firm in opposition to a controlling shareholder. In short, even if a board deprives the shareholder of control by issuing a large number of shares to board members, this in itself does not lead to invalidation. Nor has the Supreme Court invalidated a share issuance at a price considerably lower than a fair price without the authorization of a shareholder meeting required by the law (see CA Article 201, paragraph 1 & Article 199, paragraph 2) as a grounds for invalidation (Supreme Court Decision, July 16, 1971, 103 Saibanshu Minji 407; Supreme Court Decision, April 6, 1973, 683 Kinyu Houmu Jijou 32; Supreme Court Decision, October 11, 1977, 843 Kinyu Houmu Jijou 24).

These two scenarios both involve intensive examinations of the substances of cases. In cases of unfair issuances, the courts need to examine details of conflicts between a board and a controlling shareholder, and then judge whether the primary purpose of an issuance is unfair. Similarly, if the courts are to invalidate a low price offering without shareholder authorization, they must judge whether the issuing price is considerably lower than a fair price. Because invalidation cases involve closed firms, it is necessary to obtain and examine valuations by specialists, which clearly entails large costs in terms of both money and time.

However, the above cases do not mean that the Supreme Court has entirely neglected substantive fairness. The court has invalidated an issuance when it can find simple and clear infringements of laws.

First, an issuance without required disclosure is void unless a defendant company can show that there are no other grounds for an injunction (Supreme Court Decision, January 28, 1997, 51 Minshu 71). It is worth noting that the disclosure can be made not only by notifying each shareholder but by publishing a notice in a newspaper or even in the official gazette (CA Article 201, paragraphs 3 & 4). Accordingly, an issuance lacking disclosure is a case where the board has attempted to hide the issuance from confronting shareholders to avoid an injunction. Another situation where the Supreme Court has invalidated an equity offering is when a company issues shares against a temporary injunction order by the courts (Supreme Court Decision, December 16, 1993, 47 Minshu 5423).

These two types of illegal issuances are clearly different from unfair issuance and issuance at unfair prices without shareholder authorization in that the courts can judge only on the basis of a simple set of facts. As for the disclosure requirement, the courts only have to see whether any notices to shareholders have been made or published in newspapers or the official gazette, whether the notice is made two weeks prior to the issuance date (CA Article 201, paragraph 3), and whether the notice includes the required items (CA Article 201, paragraph 1). Whether an equity offering infringes a temporary injunction order is very easy to judge. The courts simply have to see whether a court has placed a temporarily injunction on the issuance.

A somewhat different case is an issuance lacking the necessary resolution by a board of directors. The Supreme Court has not invalidated an issuance without a board resolution (Supreme Court Decision, March 31, 1961, 15 Minshu 645). Since whether there was a necessary board resolution is obviously easy to judge, lacking a board resolution would be grounds for invalidation. However, if the courts invalidate issuances without the necessary board resolutions, it would be overkill. As noted, invalidation suits usually concern closed firms. Because these firms often do not follow the formal procedure provided by the CA, invalidating an offering without a board resolution is overinclusive. This would give shareholders frustrated with the incumbent board an incentive to claim for the invalidation of an otherwise valid issuance. In turn, if the courts attempted to invalidate an offering without a board resolution as an exceptional case, such as only when symptoms of unfairness existed, the courts would have to engage in a costly review of the substance.

As for equity offerings in closed firms, the Supreme Court has replaced substantive reviews of unfairness with a set of bright-line approaches. The Supreme Court has captured some of the unfairness in equity offerings as an infringement of the duty of disclosure or a violation of an injunction order. Because a bright-line rule is easy to circumvent, substantial fairness is sacrificed in some cases. For example, if a board places a notice in the official gazette and the controlling shareholder does not recognize it, the board will succeed in issuing a large number of shares to incumbent board members, thereby depriving the shareholder of control. However, under the current CA, this type of inefficiency occurs in only a small proportion of closed firms. Most closed firms adopt 'non-public' companies under CA (Article 2, paragraph 5). When this type of company makes equity offerings, it must be authorized by shareholder meeting (CA, Article 199, paragraphs 1 & 2). An equity offering lacking authorization is invalidated by the recent Supreme Court case (Supreme Court Decision, April 24, 2012, 66 Minshu 2908). Furthermore, when a company holds a shareholder meeting, it must notify its shareholders individually (CA Article 299). If an issuing company fails to make this notification, a resolution for issuing shares will be canceled (CA Article 831, paragraph 1, item 1), so the issuance will lack valid shareholder authorizations. Again, the lack or defects in the necessary shareholder resolution are easier to judge than substantive fairness of an issuance, which is consistent with our argument.

5.5.1.3   Lower Court Cases Prior to the Supreme Court Decision of July 14, 1994, 172 Saibanshu Minji 771

To see commonalities and differences in the preferences of the Supreme Court and the lower courts, we analyzed lower court cases on the invalidation of equity offerings prior to the formation of case laws by the Supreme Court. Our sample includes all lower court cases from July 1, 1966 to July 14, 1994.[20] Sample cases were gathered by searching in D1-Law.com and Westlaw Japan for cases referring to Article 280-15 of the Commercial Code, which provides for the invalidation suit (an equivalent of the current CA Article 828, item 2). We found 28 cases during this period. Four cases were dropped from our sample: three were not relevant to invalidation and one was mistakenly identified as a different case from another case included in our sample.

Table 5.4 shows that 11 of our sample cases that proceeded to trial invalidated equity offerings; the grounds for doing so are listed in Table 5.5. The majority involved no or insufficient disclosure of the issuance. Another two issuances were made in contravention of temporary injunction orders, which is consistent with the Supreme Court case law discussed in Section 5.5.1.1. However, we also found four cases where the lower courts invalidated equity offerings but the Supreme Court would not invalidate them; these involved one case of issuing

---

[20] We limit our sample cases to those after July 1, 1966 because the 1966 amendment of the Commercial Code greatly affected invalidations of equity offerings largely. We also limited our sample cases up to July 14, 1994 (Supreme Court Decision, July 14, 1994, 172 Saibanshu Minji 771), because, since the Supreme Court case on this date, lower courts have simply followed the set of Supreme Court cases. Therefore, we found no important differences between the Supreme Court and the lower courts thereafter.

Table 5.4 *Outcome of sample cases*

Outcomes	Number of Cases
Rejected for procedural reasons	2
Upheld as valid	11
Invalidated	11
Total	24

Table 5.5 *Grounds for invalidating equity offerings*

Invalidation Grounds	Number of Cases
Extremely unfair issuance	1
Infringement of disclosure duty	6
Issuance against a temporary injunction order	2
Issuance without a valid board resolution	3
Issuance at unfair price without a shareholder authorization	0
Others	1

Notes: the total exceeds 11 because some cases refer to more than one ground.

shares in an extremely unfair manner and three cases where the necessary board resolutions were lacking. Here, we can find signs of differences in preference between the Supreme Court and the lower courts.

To clarify the preference of the lower courts, we further classified the judgments by the grounds for invalidation claimed by plaintiffs in 22 cases that went to trial (Table 5.6). Typically, a plaintiff claims two or more grounds. The court determines whether either of the alleged grounds is sufficient for invalidation. The courts may judge that one reason is always sufficient grounds for invalidation (column (1)) but also can admit exceptions (column (2)). The court may accept exceptions in theory but not admit the exception in fact. Therefore, we counted the numbers of cases where the courts upheld the validity of issuances by admitting the exception (column (3)). In the same manner, the courts may judge that asserted grounds would not lead to invalidation without exceptions (column (6)) but can also allow for exceptional invalidations of the issuance on these grounds (column (4)). The numbers of admitted exceptions are in column (5).

The shaded cells in Table 5.6 indicate where the Supreme Court's case laws fall. It is evident that most lower court cases are consistent with the case laws formed by the Supreme Court after the sample period. The

Table 5.6 *Judgements on possible grounds for invalidating equity offerings*

Alleged Grounds for Invalidation	(1) Invalid	(2) Basically Invalid but with Exceptions	(3) Affirming the Exceptions	(4) Basically Valid but with Exceptions	(5) Affirming the Exceptions	(6) Valid
(a) Extremely unfair issuance	0	0	–	2	1	4
(b) Infringement of disclosure duty	0	11	5	0	0	0
(c) Issuance against a temporary injunction order	2	0	–	0	–	1
(d) Issuance without a valid board resolution	0	0	–	3	3	4
(e) Issuance at unfair price without a shareholder authorization	0	0	–	0	–	7

differences lie in the rows (a) and (d). Some lower courts seemed to place a higher priority on substantial efficiencies by invalidating equity offerings performed in an extremely unfair manners. However, only one case actually invalidated an issuance on these grounds. In contrast, three lower court cases invalidated issuances with the similar set of facts on the grounds that there were no valid board resolutions, as shown in row (d). Here, we can see the preference for criteria with lower case-handling costs when the court was pursuing substantial efficiencies. A remarkable point about these grounds is that the lower courts focused on the lack of board resolutions, although the Supreme Court had already declared this could not be grounds for invalidation in 1961 (Supreme Court Decision, March 31, 1961, 15 Minshu 645), that is, well before the sample period. Of the three cases, one was explicitly distinguished from the Supreme Court decision by a reference to the size of issuing companies (Oita District Court Decision, March 30, 1962, 665 Hanrei Jihou 90), but one case was distinguished without any reasoning (Urawa District Court Decision, July 23, 1984, 533 Hanrei Times 243). The remaining case did not even refer to the Supreme Court case (Nagoya District Court Decision, June 10, 1975, 26 Kaminshu 479).

In summary, the lower courts shared a preference for rules with lower case-handling costs. However, their preference for those rules is not as strong as the Supreme Court's. This may be due to a difference in procedural structures. Because there are no trials in the Supreme Court, only the lower court judges consider the raw facts of cases. Therefore, only the lower court may perceive some controlling (or large) shareholders as being unfairly deprived of control. However, even when pursuing substantial efficiencies, the lower courts still prefer to rely on rules entailing lower case-handling costs than examining substantial fairness.

The difference may simply reflect larger variations in lower court decisions because of the larger sample size than that of the Supreme Court cases.[21] While lower courts repeatedly face similar cases, the Supreme Court makes decisions on a particular legal issue on fewer occasions (usually only once). To consider this possibility, we compared seven decisions by the Supreme Court with the preceding lower courts' decisions on the same case. The result is consistent with our previous discussion. The Supreme Court and the lower courts reached the same conclusions in the majority of cases. Of seven Supreme Court cases, four

---

[21] We thank an anonymous reviewer for pointing out this perspective.

cases supported preceding decisions and held the offering to be valid (Supreme Court Decision, March 31, 1961, 15 Minshu 645; Supreme Court Decision, July 16, 1971, 103 Saibanshu Minji 407; Supreme Court Decision, April 6, 1973, 683 Kinyu Houmu Jijou 32; Supreme Court Decision, October 11, 1977, 843 Kinyu Houmu Jijou 24). One case upheld the invalidation by the preceding decision (Supreme Court Decision, December 16, 1993, 47 Minshu 5423). Furthermore, when the decision was different, the Supreme Court favored cost-efficient rules more than did lower courts. In the only case involving a reversal, the Supreme Court concluded that an unfair issuance cannot be invalidated, reversing the Osaka High Court's decision invalidating the issuance (Supreme Court Decision, July 14, 1994, 172 Saibanshu Minji 771).[22] In the remaining case, the Supreme Court maintained the invalidation by the Kanazawa branch of the Nagoya High Court, but clearly noted that an unfair issuance and fake payment for an offering are not grounds for invalidation (Supreme Court Decision, January 28, 1997, 51 Minshu 71).

5.5.2   Corporate Law Reform

Judges' preferences for rules that reduce case-handling costs or avoid costly judgments by using flexible standards can be found not only in case laws but also in lawmaking processes. During the process of the 2014 amendment of the CA (for an overview of the reform process of Japanese corporate law, see Morita 2014), there was fierce debate concerning whether to provide shareholders with the right to seek injunctions when they were dissatisfied with their merger or acquisition consideration, especially in a squeeze-out deal. The CA before the amendment had clearly provided shareholders with this injunction right in the case of short-form mergers with an extremely low consideration. However, there were no clear provisions as to the rights of shareholders squeezed out by deals that had to be authorized by shareholders (long-form mergers).

Although academic members of the Corporate Law Section of the Legislative Council favored providing shareholders with this right, it did not occur. One reason may have been the strong opposition from business associations representing managers' interests. In addition, the strong oppositions from members from the courts played a large role.

---

[22] No Supreme Court decision has overturned a preceding lower court decision to nullify an equity offering.

During the early stage of the deliberation, Yasushi Kanokogi, a member from the court[23] clearly opposed to granting the injunction right to shareholders when the consideration was "extremely unfair" for deals requiring shareholder authorization. Based on the time frame of temporary injunction order suits on equity offerings, Kanokogi said:

> "[if the right to seek an injunction is provided,] the time left to the court of the first instance is about two weeks. It takes at least ten days for both parties to make their arguments and submit their final documents, so the court judges within the remaining four days. There have already been many injunction cases on equity offerings with large financial stakes, but if we have to make judgments on injunctions on M&As, firm values of a few billion or several tens of billions of yen, or even a few hundred billion yen will be under our deliberations. If we are to discuss this topic, I want members to discuss the kinds of review that can be conducted by us within three or four days.
> ......it might be feasible enough if we review procedural issues, but if we are to review substantial issues such as considerations of M&As, whether we can review those issues in that short periods of time should be fully discussed..."
>
> (The Corporate Law Section of the Legislative Council 2010, p. 49)

Here, Kanokogi clearly refers to the time restriction. Despite its moderate tone, this is perceived as clear opposition by the courts to reviewing the fairness of consideration because members from the court do not usually speak out at the section meeting. Denying the injunction remedy meant the appraisal right would be the sole remedy for an M&A with unfair consideration. The appraisal is also a costly procedure for the court. However, providing the injunction right in addition to the appraisal remedy would increase the total case-handling costs associated with an M&A.

Furthermore, even after the idea to include extremely unfair considerations as grounds for the injunction right was abandoned and the grounds were limited to infringements of law or articles of incorporations, Kanokogi and another member from the court persistently demanded that the Ministry of Justice confirm that breach of duty of care or loyalty by directors would not be deemed 'infringements of law' (The Corporate Law Section of the Legislative Council 2011, pp. 32–33; The Corporate Law Section of the Legislative Council 2012, pp. 40–41).

---

[23] At the time, Kanokogi was a Tokyo District Court judge and a well-known specialist in corporate law issues.

Pursuing a deal with unfair considerations might well be a breach of their duties. Therefore, if a breach of directors' duty was included in the grounds for the injunction, the courts would have to examine the substantial fairness of deal including consideration.

In addition to injunction rights, another sign of avoiding costly methods of judgments is seen in an individual opinion in a well-known appraisal case regarding a share exchange deal between game developers Tecmo and Koei. The Supreme Court judged that if a deal between independent firms follow "the procedure that is regarded as generally fair," the consideration set by the shareholder meeting's resolution is basically deemed to be fair (Supreme Court Decision, February 29, 2012, 66 Minshu 1784). The Supreme Court also judged that it is under the reasonable discretion of the courts to refer to the market price on the day when a plaintiff shareholder exercised her appraisal right or an average of the market prices of periods close to the exercise date, as the fair price of the share. In supporting this court opinion, Justice Masahiko Suto noted,

> "In order to recognize firm value and an increase in it [from a merger or acquisition], various methods for valuation of share prices based on financial information or managerial policies of a target company, coupled with various simulations under different assumptions, have been proposed and in fact used. However, since these valuation methods are highly technical and far from plain and simple, demanding the courts themselves to conduct the valuation using one method is inappropriate and unrealistic considering the nature and the role of the courts. In addition, valuations by specialists entail high fees [to the parties] and require a considerable period of time. Furthermore, even these valuation methods cannot avoid being based on estimations using uncertain data, which gives them a speculative nature. Taking these points into consideration, in the appraisal procedure, at least when other appropriate methods are available, and there is no shortcoming in evaluating 'fair price' by such methods, there seems to be no use applying the above-mentioned valuation methods in addition to them."

(Supreme Court Decision, February 29, 2012, 66 Minshu 1792–93)

In addition to their reluctance to employ complicated valuation methods such as discounted cash flow (DCF) themselves, Suto's opinion is also far from eager to rely on valuations by specialists, even though the fees are paid by the parties, rather than the courts. One reason mentioned explicitly in Suto's opinion is to save time, which is consistent with our argument. Another key aspect may involve the costs for judges to understand the details of valuations. Because valuations by specialists are difficult to understand, judges would have difficulty in deciding which valuation submitted by the parties is more reliable. It may not be difficult to understand the ideas behind DCF, but understanding the presumptions used in actual valuations and their validity is difficult, as the judges found in the Tecmo/Koei case. Therefore, it is reasonable to minimize the courts' case-handling costs by avoiding technical details and by simply using market prices.

Although the preference for cost saving in appraisal procedures may not be specific to Japan (e.g., *DFC Global Co. v. Muirfield Value Partners, L.P.*, 2017 Del. LEXIS 324 [Del. 2017]), Japanese courts seem to be more eager to save costs. They do not scrutinize the procedural fairness of M&As with conflicts of interest, such as the independence of an independent committee or the effectiveness of a market check, as rigorously as do Delaware courts. Furthermore, even when the court finds an M&A to be unfair, instead of using DCF, the court discretionally adds a "fair" premium on a pre-deal price (e.g., Tokyo High Court Decision, September 12, 2008, 1301 Kinyu Shoji Hanrei 28; Osaka High Court Decision, January 31, 2012, 1390 Kinyu Shoji Hanrei 32), although it is unclear whether this trend will continue in the future.

In summary, there are signs that the courts strongly prefer easily applicable rules over flexible standards, not only on a specific topic of equity offerings in closed firms but also for M&As by listed firms. This indicates that the courts prefer cost-saving rules even if they have to sacrifice substantive efficiencies to some extent. Although we cannot definitely conclude that this preference is the result of the career judge system, the result is at least consistent with our hypothesis of judges' incentives under the system. Several factors may be involved in the preference for cost-saving rules. Judges may simply under severe time constraints, or stability and predictability may play a part, which also leads to a preference for bright-line rules. However, it is possible to argue that the career judge system produces or reinforces the effects of these factors. As we discussed in Section 5.2.2, coupled with scarce resources for the courts, the evaluation methods in the Japanese system encourage judges to increase the numbers of cases they can handle in a certain period of time. Bright-line rules decrease not only the risk to litigation parties, but also the costs for the General Secretariat of the Supreme Court in monitoring the decisions of lower courts judges. Therefore, the career judge system can be understood as the structural background of individual factors leading courts to prefer cost-saving methods.

5.6   Conclusion

This book chapter explores how the career judge system in Japan influences court decisions. We see that the system basically causes a decision bias toward case-handling efficiency, instead of toward social (or overall) efficiency. However, how the bias is realized depends on a number of factors.

First, the nature of the case is an important factor. When the case is an atypical type that rarely comes to court, the court may find no difficulty in engaging in a costly judgment and be willing to follow a rule that requires costly and detailed consideration. In contrast, when it is expected that a large number of such cases will come to court, there is a strong incentive to avoid costly case handling. In such cases, courts tend to follow clear rules instead of vague standards to save human resources. Because many equity offering cases involving closely held firms are expected to reach the courts nationwide, it is not surprising that courts follow a bright-line rule when handling such cases.

Second, the Supreme Court and lower courts have different attitudes toward case-handling efficiency. Because lower courts are confronted daily with a huge number of cases, they have an incentive to follow rules that reduce case-handling costs. In contrast, the Supreme Court with relatively abundant human resources[24] can focus on a small number of cases and tends to place more weight on substantive efficiency than case-handling efficiency.

However, this tendency of the Supreme Court has two limitations. First, when a huge number of similar cases are brought to the court at one time, the Supreme Court, which is in charge of managing the entire Japanese court system, may prefer case-handling efficiency to substantive efficiency. Second, the civil procedure rule prohibits the Supreme Court from engaging in the examination of evidence, which is left to lower courts, and the Supreme Court may not be able to examine the detail of the cases exhaustively. This limitation may restrict the Supreme Court's tendency to achieve substantive efficiency.

Our discussion up to this point may seem inconsistent with our findings with regard to the equity offering cases in closely held firms (Section 5.5.1 above). However, the inconsistency is superficial. Some

---

[24] In Japan, only the Supreme Court judges have law clerks [*saikosai chosakan*] on staff, while lower court judges do not. Lower court judges only have court clerks, who are in charge of the administration of cases at the court.

lower courts have special divisions for commercial and corporate law cases[25] and these divisions are routinely asked to handle commercial and corporate law cases, including equity offering cases. These divisions are expected to have an incentive to prefer case-handling efficiency. In contrast, other lower courts have no special divisions. Because the proportion of corporate law cases in civil cases is quite small, they are atypical cases for regular lower court judges. They may not hesitate to embark on costly considerations of case details. Not surprisingly, all of the exceptional cases presented in Table 5.6 were delivered by such regular judges, while the special division judges uniformly followed the case-law tendency of the Supreme Court.

Although we have highlighted a bias toward the case-handling efficiency under the career judge system in Japan, our analysis has several limitations. First, while we show that court decisions in Japan tend to favor case-handling efficiency, we cannot determine the overall efficiency of court decisions in Japan. It is still possible that the emphasis on case-handling efficiency is socially desirable.

Second, our analysis is methodologically constrained. As noted above, it is almost impossible to collect a nonrandom sample of court decisions in Japan. Thus, for our empirical analysis, we are forced to rely on biased samples, and the results remain preliminary ones. We hope our analysis will be a starting point for future research.

References

Calabresi, Guido. 1970. *The Cost of Accidents: A Legal and Economic Analysis.* New Haven: Yale University Press.

The Corporate Law Section of the Legislative Council. 2010. The Minute of the 7th Meeting. www.moj.go.jp/content/000060893.pdf (accessed August 1, 2018).

2011. The Minute of the 14th Meeting. www.moj.go.jp/content/000081570.pdf (accessed August 1, 2018).

2012. The Minute of the 18th Meeting. www.moj.go.jp/content/000097964.pdf (accessed August 1, 2018).

Fujita, Tokiyasu. 2011. The Supreme Court of Japan: Commentary on the Recent Work of Scholars in the United States. *Washington University Law Review* 88: 1507–26.

Kaplow, Louis. 1992. Rules versus Standards: An Economic Analysis. *Duke Law Journal* 42: 557–629.

---

[25] The best-known examples are Tokyo District Court and Osaka District Court.

Kono, Toshiyuki, Yoshihisa Hayakawa, and Hirofumi Takahata. 2008. *Kokusai Saiban Kankatsu nikansuru Hanrei no Kinouteki Bunseki: Tokudan no Jijou wo Chushin toshite* [A Functional Analysis of Case Law on International Jurisdiction: Focusing on the Special Consideration Doctrine]. *New Business Law* 890: 72–81.

McElwain, Kenneth Mori, and Christian Winkler. 2015. What's Unique about the Japanese Constitution? A Comparative and Historical Analysis. *Journal of Japanese Studies* 41: 249–80.

Morita, Hatsuru. 2014. Reforms of Japanese Corporate Law and Political Environment. *Zeitschrift füer japanisches Recht* 37: 25–38.

Ramseyer, J. Mark, and Eric B. Rasmusen. 2003. *Measuring Judicial Independence: The Political Economy of Judging in Japan.* Chicago, IL: The University of Chicago Press.

Ramseyer, J. Mark, and Minoru Nakazato. 1999. *Japanese Law: An Economic Approach.* Chicago, IL: The University of Chicago Press.

Yaguchi, Koichi. 2004. *Oraru Histori* [*Oral History*]. Tokyo: GRIPS.

Yoshikai, Shuichi. 2013. *Saibankan no Arukikata* [*Autobiography as a Judge*]. Tokyo: Shojihomu.

6

Judges Avoid Ex Post but Not Ex Ante Inefficiency

Theory and Empirical Evidence from Taiwan

YUN-CHIEN CHANG

6.1 Introduction: A New Judicial Behavioral Hypothesis

This chapter advances a new hypothesis regarding judicial behaviors: Judges tend to avoid ex post but not ex ante inefficiency.[1] Ex post inefficiency means that *substantively* inefficient outcomes arise between litigants of cases handled by judges, whereas ex ante inefficiency refers to inefficient outcomes for future (litigating and non-litigating) parties. Ex post inefficiency does *not* mean unfairness to one of the litigating parties. Rather, it refers to judgment-created net social waste borne by one or both parties. Social waste includes less effective use of resources like land and buildings and also additional transaction costs needed for one or both litigants to solve allocative inefficiency. Ex ante inefficiency, by contrast, refers to the fact that future actors will have suboptimal incentives to act. Drawing from three empirical studies of decisions by judges in Taiwan, this chapter provides preliminary evidence in support of this hypothesis. The empirical findings herein are not definitive, but the hypothesis can serve as a roadmap for future empirical studies of judicial behaviors regarding efficiency.

While economic analysis of law mostly focuses on ex ante (in)efficiency (Bebchuk 2001, p. 603; Brooks and Schwartz 2005, p. 392; Smith 2009, p. 134), ex post inefficient outcomes should not be entirely ignored. Coasean bargaining may redress ex post inefficient outcomes, but transaction costs (Chang and Lin 2017) or animosity (Farnsworth 1999) may

---

[1] Research Professor & Director of Center for Empirical Legal Studies, Institutum Iurisprudentiae, Academia Sinica, Taiwan. J.S.D., New York University School of Law. A draft of this chapter has been presented at the 1st CELS in Asia held at Academia Sinica on June 13–15, 2017. I am grateful for helpful comments by two anonymous referees, Bernie Black, Michael Heise, William Hubbard, Kate Litvak, Anthony Niblett, and Giovanni Ramello. Email: kleiber@sinica.edu.tw.

hinder such negotiations. Hence, given that judges have to render decisions allocating entitlements, institutional costs may be minimized if judges can take into account ex post inefficiency, to the extent that such accounts do not stand in the way of achieving ex ante efficiency, and are not informationally too costly.

Efficiency-minded jurists care about ex ante efficiency, but judges anywhere would care (more) about ex post efficiency. One or both parties have strong incentives to bring the ex post inefficiency (e.g., their huge economic losses qua social waste) to the judges' attention; avoiding ex post inefficient outcomes is often intuitive enough for most judges, and within the job description of judges around the world (though other terms instead of inefficiency may be used). By contrast, only certain types of judges would take into account ex ante efficiency. Several parameters that drive certain judges to care about ex ante inefficiency are worth highlighting below.

First, social science training may be important. On one end of the spectrum, no jurists in the United States now have an undergraduate degree in law; some of them major in economics or statistics and believe in the import of thinking ex ante. On the other end of the spectrum, most, if not all, judges in Germany have only doctrinal legal training and tend to believe that law is an autonomous discipline. In the middle, countries like Japan and Taiwan have both JD and LLB programs, so some judges have nonlegal training.

Second, whether judges are endowed with policy-making roles may affect the way they make decisions. While judges in common-law countries are more likely to have such roles than colleagues in civil-law countries,[2] civil-common division is a crude approximation. Constitutional courts in Germany, France, South Korea, and Taiwan (civil-law countries) are at least de facto policy-makers, while judges in ordinary courts tend to consider themselves faithful servants of the legislature.

Third, career, civil-servant judges versus appointed or elected judges may think differently. The former, in a judicial pyramid, trying to climb the ladder, will tend to follow precedents faithfully, if not single-mindedly. (For the case of Japanese judges, see Ramseyer [2015].) If the

---

[2] Traditionally, the theoretical debate on this topic falls along the line of common law (versus civil law), see Fon, Parisi, and Depoorter (2005); Garoupa and Ligüerre (2011); Niblett, Posner, and Shleifer (2010); Parisi (2004); Ponzetto and Fernandez (2008); Posner (1973); Posner (2011); Priest (1977); Rubin (1977); Rubin (1982); Zywicki and Stringham (2010).

highest court in the judicial system does not emphasize the import of thinking ex ante about the ramification of judicial decisions, lower courts will follow suit. By contrast, appointed judges who were practicing attorneys may witness the ill effect of purely ex post decisions firsthand. Appointed and elected judges will also take into account at least the political effect of their decisions – this is thinking ex ante – and may get into the habit of considering all kinds of future effects of their decisions.

The list of factors may go on, but it takes many observational studies on judges in multiple jurisdictions and perhaps field experiments with real judges to tease out which factors are the key. Theoretically, though, a typical judge in the United States is more likely to avoid ex ante inefficiency than a typical judge in, say, Germany. This chapter focuses on Taiwanese judges, whose likelihood of paying attention to ex ante inefficiency is somewhere in the middle between Germany and the United States, as more and more Taiwanese judges have nonlegal training and the desire to climb the judicial pyramid has waned in recent years in the wake of certain judicial reforms. That said, the idea that judges should not make policy is still mainstream in the judiciary in Taiwan. Empirical studies, therefore, are necessary to tease out the extent to which judges in Taiwan and elsewhere avoid creating ex ante inefficiency.

One cannot assess whether judges tend to rule in a way consistent with efficiency by studying a random legal field. Even judges in the United States are often legalistic (Epstein, Landes, and Posner 2013). Instead, one should look at legal doctrines where judges have discretion in shaping the case outcomes. For example, certain doctrines in the Taiwan Civil Code allow multiple interpretations or decisions, some of which are more efficient than others (see section 6.2). Empiricists then should analyze whether an efficient path has been followed in those court decisions.

In this book chapter, I review three of my prior empirical studies on judicial decisions in Taiwan. These prior works were not framed in terms of whether courts in Taiwan have ruled efficiently. Cast in new light, these studies of property cases offer the first research that looks into whether a civil-law court in East Asia tends to rule in favor of ex ante and/or ex post efficiency.[3]

Overall speaking, the evidence shows that judges in Taiwan tend to avoid clear ex post inefficiency while paying less or no attention to ex ante inefficiency, supporting the behavioral hypothesis. In two case

---

[3] As to whether courts in Germany rule efficiently, see Chapter 11.

studies on co-ownership partition (Section 6.3) and building encroachment (Section 6.4), this chapter observes that, from an ex post perspective, courts rule as if they prefer to maximize property values and promote valuable uses of scarce resources. In another case study on unjust enrichment for trespass (Section 6.5), however, this chapter observes that courts follow a compensation formula that clearly gives future potential trespassers suboptimal incentives to engage in ex ante negotiation. The findings thus support the judicial behavioral hypothesis above.

6.2 The Definition of (Substantive) Efficiency

The theoretical task before delving into empirical research is to spell out the definition of efficient judicial rulings concretely. As I hinted above, this chapter only explores whether judicial decisions are *substantively* efficient. Judicial decisions can be procedurally efficient but substantively inefficient. For instance, a strict and clear rule that one dollar will be awarded to every plaintiff suing for pain and suffering damages will induce pretty much every dispute to settle, minimizing litigation costs. Nonetheless, most people would agree that such under-compensation fails to force tortfeasors to internalize the social costs they create. More generally, a predictable outcome facilitated by clear court jurisprudence is often procedurally efficient,[4] though not necessarily substantively efficient. By contrast, a substantively efficient decision may take excessive resources to achieve, and thus may be procedurally inefficient (such as lengthy discovery process to get every detail right). This chapter only tests the behavioral hypothesis in the sense that judges tend to avoid ex post substantive inefficiency, but not ex ante substantive inefficiency.

In property law, economic efficiency is a joint evaluation of allocative efficiency and production efficiency (Chang 2015, pp. 507–12). Allocative efficiency prioritizes putting resources in the hands of parties who value them the most. Production efficiency, treating allocative efficiency as a product (Demsetz 2011; Fennell 2013), aims to achieve allocative

---

[4] Ramseyer (2015), in assessing the virtue of Japanese courts, emphasizes the import of predictability in torts damages. In the cases studied, Japanese courts have made very clear the level of comparative negligence and the amount of damages. Tortfeasors and victims therefore settle and there are few lawsuits over car accidents. With such a practice, judges can then devote their time to cases where their skills and experience matter more. Japanese courts are thus procedurally efficient. For the same observation, see Chapter 5.

efficiency at the lowest costs. Put differently, the highest possible level of allocative efficiency may not be desirable when its price is too steep. Transaction costs (Coase 1959, 1960) are a major component in the concern of production efficiency.

More specifically, ex ante inefficiency happens when resources in the future, according to the judge-made law, will not be assigned to parties who are more likely to value them more, and/or the transaction costs and information costs to further exchanges are so high that efficient allocation of resources that is otherwise feasible (meaning with the more efficient legal rule) cannot be achieved. By contrast, ex post inefficiency emerges when resources in question in the cases are not assigned to the party who values them more, and/or the transaction costs and information costs to move this particular resource to higher-valuers are very high. Ex post (in)efficiency may or may not lead to ex ante efficiency. In the two cases presented in the next two parts, ex post efficient decisions do not have ex ante implications. In addition, a judicial decision that creates ex ante efficiency may or may not affect the way the resource in question will be used. In the case study discussed in Section 6.5, the judicial decision that has a potentially strong ex ante effect does not change the way the landowner will use her land.

6.3   Co-ownership Partition and Anticommons

In judicial partition of co-owned land, a rule favoring partition in kind may tend to produce fragmentary land. That is, physical division of land leads to anticommons when post-partition parcels are too small to use. The costs of assembling small parcels for large-scale development may be too steep for developers. As a result, valuable development may become unattainable due to holdout from owners of tiny yet key parcels. In short, anticommons, as a source of high transaction costs, hinder allocative efficiency (Fennell 2011; Heller 1998). Partition in kind, however, has the advantage of preserving subjective value to co-owners (Miceli and Sirmans 2000). A number of civil-law countries contain stipulations in their civil codes that prefer partition in kind to partition by sale, such as Germany, France, Japan, China, and Taiwan (Chang and Fennell 2014a, p. 1). Judges, however, still have discretion and can choose partition by sale or partial partition. The question is, then, whether judges order physical division of land only when doing so does not create anticommons.

In Chang (2012, pp. 541–48), I used 404 randomly sampled district court partition decisions between 2008 and 2010 in Taiwan to examine whether judges have endeavored to avoid creating anticommons. A multinomial logistic model shows that post-partition land size is a strong predictor ($p < 0.001$) of which partition approach courts adopted. More specifically, if physical division of land would lead to fragmentary parcels, courts will order partition by sale instead. Figure 6.1 shows the distribution of (hypothetical) post-partition lot sizes if courts ordered partition in kind. The distribution of land size is broken into three groups based on which partition approach (partition in kind, partition by sale, and partial partition) the court has ordered. Cases ending in partition by sale clearly have smaller (hypothetical) lot sizes. (As shown in Figure 6.1, 50 percent of those studied here would have created a plot that is smaller than 100 square meters.) By ordering judicial auctions, judges avoid ex post inefficiency by reducing the social waste derived from fragmentary plots and the transaction costs derived from getting out of the anticommons deadlock later. Auctioning and ensuing voluntary transactions of one whole piece of land usually will transfer titles to parties who value them most, attaining allocative efficiency.[5]

Also, partial partition means mixing partition by sale, partition in kind, and owelty together to resolve the partition. The use of owelty (i.e. compensation) enables judges to assign to a co-owner a post-partition plot that is larger than what her share would create had partition in kind been adopted. Hence, one should not be surprised to find that a number of cases that could lead to fragmentary land were resolved by partial partition, as shown in Figure 6.1.

Can this decisional pattern be interpreted as avoiding ex ante inefficiency? I am inclined to say no. If co-ownership is formed voluntarily, parties can reach an ex ante solution to partition. If co-ownership is formed involuntarily, often through inheritance, judicial partition practices can hardly affect their behaviors in using resources. Judicial preference for partition by sale when a co-owner would have received tiny plots may induce co-owners to settle instead of litigating (if the judicial preference is clear enough). This would count as procedural, not substantive, efficiency, though. Moreover, this kind of preference may induce strategic behaviors, as it is very easy to transfer a tiny portion of one's share to one's spouse to set the table for partition by sale. Any co-owner

---

[5] In Chang and Fennell (2014b), we design a partial partition method that will induce co-owners to reveal their reservation values voluntarily. Our design, however, has not been implemented in Taiwan or other countries. Judges in Taiwan therefore should not be faulted for not adopting a potentially more efficiency-enhancing partition approach.

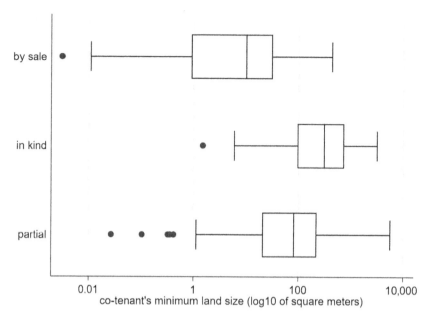

Figure 6.1   Distribution of cotenants' minimum land size by partition approaches ordered by the court.

Note: N = 477. The three vertical lines in the box show the 25 percentile, median, and 75 percentile of the data. The dots are observations that are outside the upper/lower adjacent value. This figure only includes observations that involve partition of one plot and no building. In the 93 cases of partition by sale ("by sale" in the figure), the cotenant's minimum land size represents the size of the land that the cotenant with the smallest share *would have received* if the court had ordered physical division of the co-owned plot according to cotenants' shares. In the 113 cases of partition in kind ("in kind" in the figure), the cotenant's minimum land size accurately reflects the size of the land that the cotenant with the smallest share actually received. In the 271 cases of partial partitions ("partial" in the figure; including every partition approach other than the two prototypical ones mentioned above), the cotenant's minimum land size represents the size of the land that the cotenant with the smallest share *would have received* if the court had ordered physical division of the co-owned plot *according to cotenants' shares*. Depending on the type of partial partition approach adopted by the court, the cotenant with the smallest share may receive simply compensation, remain a cotenant after partition, or receive a piece of land according to, or disproportionate to, her share.

Source: Data compiled by author, also used in Chang (2012)

could demand the lion's share by threatening judicial partition by sale, which often garners proceeds that are below fair market prices – at least in Taiwan (Chang and Fennell 2014a).

The bottom line is that the ex ante effect of the judicial preference for partition by sale when some co-owners have tiny shares is unclear. By contrast, the ex post inefficiency of ordering partition in kind is clear. I am hesitant to claim that Taiwanese judges intentionally avoid creating fragmentary shares, as I do not have systematic evidence for it. My claim is more conservative: judges I studied act as if they keep ex post efficiency in mind.

6.4   Building Encroachment and Equity Power

Building encroachment is not a stand-alone doctrine in American property law, but it is in many civil-law countries (Rizzolli 2009). Such a doctrine often imposes a duty on the encroached party to complain to the trespassing party in due course, but the prompt protest rule may not apply when the trespassers are bad faith.[6] This design prevents opportunism on the trespasser side and avoids rent-seeking on the trespassed party side. In American common law, Merrill and Smith (2012, p. 52) have identified several leading cases as dealing with continuous yet minor and good-faith encroachment of one's building on her neighbor's land. A leading case, *Pile* v. *Pedrick* (31 A. 647 [Pa.1895]), is an example of building encroachment – in short, Pedrick unintentionally built a wall that projected onto Pile's land by less than 1.5 inches. Pile demanded injunction and the court felt it had no choice under equity but to grant it (Merrill and Smith 2012, p. 58), although in a follow-up verdict, *Pile* v. *Pedrick*, (31 A. 646 [Pa.1895]), the court froze the injunction for one year.[7]

Two differences exist between the American rule and the ideal-type civil-law doctrine.[8] First, the American rule does not appear to impose a clear duty on the trespassed party to file complaints in due course, though one suspects that the estoppel doctrine may attain the same

---

[6] See German Civil Code Article 912; Swiss Civil Code Article 674; Taiwan Civil Code Article 796.

[7] Chang (2016, pp. 225–26) discusses this case as an example of the split-the-difference rule.

[8] Note that civil codes in, for example, Japan and France do not have a boundary encroachment doctrine. Moreover, such doctrines in the civil codes of, for instance, Brazil (Articles 1258 and 1259) and Austria (Article 418) are different from those in Germany, Switzerland, and Taiwan.

outcome. Second, injunctions (in the name of *rei vindicatio*) in civil law are the default when the trespassed party has fulfilled its duty. By contrast, in equity in the United States, injunctions will be issued only if the "balance of equities" test is passed – an American court will ask "whether a plaintiff who is otherwise eligible to get an injunction should not get it in light of the gross hardship to the defendant in comparison with the benefit to the plaintiff" (Merrill and Smith 2012, p. 58). Of course, even when there is no explicit authorization to civil-law courts to weigh the costs and benefits of issuing injunctions, courts can still draw on general principles such as "abuse of right" or "good faith" to rule compensation instead. As Chang and Smith (2012, 2016) argue, the differences between civil and common property laws may be more in terms of "style" than in terms of "structure."

As an empirical matter, it is worthwhile to study how civil-law judges weigh the costs and benefits of issuing injunctions, to test whether they tend to avoid ex post inefficiency when making decisions. The inquiry is more fruitful when there is an explicit proviso in the boundary encroachment doctrine that empower judges to preserve the encroaching buildings under certain conditions, as judges would be more straightforward with their considerations. Dutch Civil Code Article 5:54, for example, allows judges to weigh the harms to both parties of preserving or tearing down the encroaching building. Taiwan Civil Code Article 796-1 allows judges to preserve encroaching buildings after considering private and social interests. Analyzing relevant court cases in the Netherlands or Taiwan would shed light on whether judges use the bestowed discretion to conduct full-blown cost-benefit analysis.

In this context, courts need not worry about whether their ex post decision to preserve encroaching buildings will distort trespasser behaviors in the future. The exceptional rule in at least Taiwan and the Netherlands is designed so that trespassers have little or no room to behave strategically, as bad-faith trespassing rules out the application of judge's discretionary preservation. To the extent that judges can effectively distinguish bad-faith trespassers from good-faith ones, judges have to worry about the "to be or not to be" question for buildings in question only when they were built by persons in good faith. In other words, courts do not have to worry that avoiding ex post inefficiency will create ex ante inefficiency (according to my theory, many judges do not worry about ex ante effect anyway). In terms of avoiding ex post inefficiency, courts' standard is pretty straightforward: if trespassers value preservation of buildings more than their neighbors value demolition of buildings, courts should not grant injunctions.

Figure 6.2 Size of encroached land, culpability, and court decisions.
Note: N = 126. Jitter effects apply. Observations in which the area of the encroaching land parcel is above 100 square meters are omitted from this figure. (That is, 157–126=31 observations are not shown here.) In 51 of the 57 preservation cases, the encroaching land areas are below 100 square meters.
Source: Data compiled by Chang and also used in Chang (2014)

In Chang (2014), I find that courts in Taiwan tend to make ex post efficient decisions. The study used all 157 district court cases rendered in the first three plus years since the implementation of the Taiwan Civil Code Article 796-1 in mid-2009. The cases were used in logistic regression models in which removal (= 0) and preservation (= 1) constitute the binary decision used as the dependent variable. Regression results show that the size of the encroached land is a very important predictor of court decisions. The smaller the encroached part is, the more likely the courts are to rule for preservation. Figure 6.2 visualizes the relationship between sizes of encroached land and court decisions. When the encroached part is tiny (in many cases, smaller than 10 square meters), the economic costs of demolishing or redesigning an existing building are usually higher than the opportunity costs of neighbors' planned use (if any). Therefore, the empirical findings suggest that judges in Taiwan tend to rule efficiently in this matter.

In addition, in all cases in which the trespassers were grossly negligent, the courts ordered removal; in all cases in which the trespassers had no fault, the courts ordered preservation. Granted, the decision on culpability is endogenous within the decision. That is, judges may determine to remove buildings first and then label the trespassers as grossly negligent, and not the other way around. A more charitable reading of the culpability is that it is often a function of information costs; hence, courts are more likely to see encroachers as not at fault when the encroached part is tiny. In this sense, the size of the encroached plot drives both the decisions on culpability and those on preservation.

6.5   Trespass and Unjust Enrichment

Efficient compensation from trespassers to property owners is a harder question than it first appears. Imagine a trespasser builds a house on a parcel of an absentee landowner. (This is different from the previous case, in which buildings in question encroach over boundaries but still sit partially on building owners' land, while here buildings in question are entirely on top of others' land and building owners are often not neighbors.) In restitution lawsuits filed by landowners, how much should judges award? A first-order answer for an economist lawyer would be market rent. Had a trespasser bargained with a landowner beforehand, most likely the trespasser would have to pay market rent. Thus, by ruling that the unconsented possession unjustly enriches the trespasser by saving him the market rent, courts mimic the market (Posner 2011, p. 316). Indeed, several countries have concluded that the unjust enrichment in this context is *equivalent to rent*. For example, in the United States, according to Restatement (Third) of Restitution and Unjust Enrichment §40 comment b., a defendant's unjust enrichment may be identified with ordinary rental value.[9] Courts and scholars in Germany also use "equivalent to rent" as the standard for calculating compensation to landowners.[10] The scholarly literature in Germany and the United States does not describe in detail how courts in practice assess the

---

[9] See Illustration 3 of §40. Note also that Reporter's Note c. of §40 points out that historically, restitution is unavailable for trespass and dispossession discussed in this article.

[10] For German court cases, see BGHZ 20, 270; BGHZ 22, 395. For German scholarly literature, see Buck-Heeb (2011: 3559); Sprau (2013: 1302). For an introduction to German unjust enrichment law in English, see Dannemann (2009) and Krebs (2004).

amount of rent, though one could reasonably guess that the assessment procedure would involve appraisers who use rent value of comparable land as a basis for the assessment.[11] If courts systematically under-assess rent – failing to mimic the market – potential land users might prefer trespassing to bargaining for a property right to use land, as trespassing saves bargaining costs, prevents delays, and reduces the paid rent.

Extending the facilitate-voluntary-bargaining argument further, one could make a case for awarding above market rent to landowners. Property scholars generally prefer the property rule to the liability rule in protecting property rights (Chang 2015; Epstein 1997, 1998; Krier and Schwab 1995; Lewinsohn-Zamir 2001; Smith 2002, 2004). In the trespass context, trespassers have taken the entitlements without prior consent. Mandating usual market rent essentially transforms the property rule to the liability rule. Parchomovsky and Stein (2009), therefore, propose heightened damages, to induce potential trespassers to bargain with property owners for use rights. The compensation has to be sufficiently higher than market rent, so that even after taking into account bargaining costs, delay in using the property, the need to pay landowners earlier than later, potential trespassers would think it is in their interest to bargain rather than to trespass.

Nonetheless, a case can be made for below-market-rent compensation, too. Land is a scarce resource. Trespassers' development of the land generally makes it more valuable in the market (there are of course exceptions). The fact that trespassers develop the land and landowners do not find out the illicit use for an extended amount of time suggest that landowners are not aware of potential wealth-increasing opportunities. Below-market-rent compensation is thus a reward for trespassers who increase social value. In addition, even if we firmly believe that owners are in a better position to judge what use is most valuable, awarding incomplete compensation induces landowners to guard their properties more diligently.

I am not fully convinced by the below-market-rent argument. Unlike in the building encroachment setting, where minor infringement may arise because of reasonable surveying errors that building owners have no knowledge of, most trespassers in this scenario know or should have

---

[11] To be sure, appraisers' assessments do not always approximate market value. As Chang (2011) has empirically demonstrated in the empirical study of eminent domain compensation cases in New York City, the court-adjudicated property value is often greatly over- or under-assessed.

known that they are not entitled to use the land in question. It should be easier (particularly in a jurisdiction with advanced electronic registration and mapping systems like Taiwan) for potential trespassers to abstain from unconsented use and negotiate with the landowners than for landowners to constantly check whether there is physical invasion. Also, particularly in densely populated places (again, like Taiwan) where the opportunity costs of not developing land are clear, landowners' act of "conservation" perhaps should not be second-guessed. These landowners are in a better position than trespassers or judges to realize the best use of their plots.

I am sympathetic to the above-market-rent arguments, as I am a big believer in the advantage of voluntary transactions. My only concern is that under the current jurisprudences in the United States, Germany, Taiwan and, I suspect, many other jurisdictions, this position is untenable in courts. Therefore, I welcome above-market-rent compensation in trespass cases and certainly will not label such compensation as inefficient, though I doubt that such compensation will be common.

I am left with the option of advocating compensation equivalent to rent as the normatively tenable and efficient standard. How much have district court judges in Taiwan awarded landowners? In Chang, Chen, and Lin (2017), my coauthors and I randomly sampled 34 percent of trespass-to-land cases rendered by district courts in Taiwan between 2004 and 2012. We used hedonic regression models and nationwide authentic rents to estimate the market rent of the land under dispute in each case, and compare the market rent with the court-adjudicated rent. As Figure 6.3 shows, in 89.8 percent of the observations, courts awarded compensation that is below market rent.[12] Most of the compensation is sufficiently below our point-estimated market value that they are unlikely to fall within the reasonable range of market value. The finding is thus that judges in Taiwan have awarded suboptimally low compensation.

Under-compensation does not create ex post inefficiency, as it is only a distributional matter. That is, even if landowners were to receive no compensation, it would in no way change how the land was used and how the landowners utilize their land in the future. Under-compensation, however, will create strategic ex ante behaviors that are likely inefficient – resource users would prefer trespassing to bargaining. Judges in Taiwan, alas, fail to take this into account.

---

[12] It should be noted that the Chinese term "equivalent to rent" is ambiguous and does not necessarily imply "equivalent to *market* rent." Therefore, deviation from the market rent shall not be interpreted as judges' blatant violation of the law.

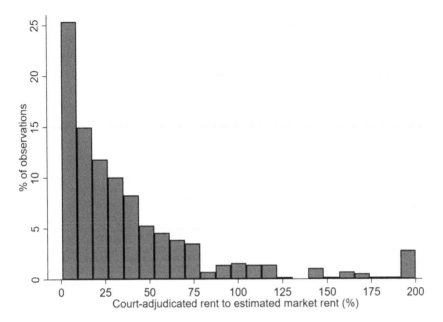

Figure 6.3 Percentages of court-adjudicated rent divided by estimated market rent.
Note: N = 568. For clarity, any percentage greater than 200% is counted as 200%, including 16 observations.
Source: Data compiled by Chang et al. and also used in Chang, Chen, and Lin (2017)

One may challenge that Chang, Chen, and Lin (2017) provide alternative explanations for the observed under-compensation: judicial precedent is one, and the anchoring effect is the other. While the formula for computing the amount of unjust enrichment does stand in the way of awarding efficient compensation, judges have room to approximate market rent, but they have failed to exploit it. Moreover, the anchoring effect contaminates judicial decisions exactly because awarding market rents is never in Taiwanese judges' mind. That is why judges are clueless about how much to award, and fall prey to the plaintiffs' claims (the anchor).

One may also challenge that the real estate sale data became available after judges studied by Chang, Chen, and Lin (2017) had already rendered their decisions. These judges may actually think that they have awarded unjust enrichment equivalent to market rent; that is, they have made honest mistakes. I beg to disagree. According to judicial precedents in Taiwan, the calculus of unjust enrichment equivalent to rent consists of two parts: land value and yield rates. The precedents and, as a result, the studied cases use tax value as land value, and everyone in Taiwan knows that the tax value of land is much lower than the market value (the former is about one-third of the latter). From the written judgments, judges do not appear to intentionally discount or inflate market yield rates in computing yield rates. Rather, it looks as if judges are trying to get a hand on market yield rates (though they fail to, and are unaware of this). It should not be very hard for Taiwanese judges to realize that the judicially determined rent is below market rent. Judges, if really wanting to awarding market rents, could inflate yield rates. At the very least, courts can limit the application of the precedent-set formula as much as possible. By contrast, as Chang, Chen, and Liu (2016) show, courts expand the application of the formula and make other doctrinally dubious moves, all making trespassing more profitable than it otherwise would be. To sum up, Taiwanese judges should be cognizant that they are awarding unjust enrichment compensation below market rent. Rather than treating the precedents that cause this as a problem, they fully and overly embrace the precedents.

6.6 Conclusion

Why did judges consistently award less than market value, while they have been inclined to make efficient decisions in other property issues? While this chapter reports only three case studies, the decisional pattern can be explained by the nature of the inefficiency involved as being ex ante or ex post. In the partition cases, the drawback of giving fragmentary parcels to co-owners is obvious to judges, and at least one co-owner has strong incentives to bring the inefficiency to judges' attention. In the building encroachment cases, the social waste of demolishing existing structures is not hard to recognize, and the encroaching parties will make sure that judges notice their costs. By contrast, in the trespass cases, future potential trespassers are not in the ex post picture. Judges cannot observe the ill effect in the future through the cases at hand. Landowners, of course, will try to convince judges of how unfair their under-compensation is. Given that courts in Taiwan have never adopted market value as the benchmark in private law matters,[13] the fairness arguments

[13] Since 2012, takings compensation for real properties should be the market value, but administrative courts in Taiwan do not have a firm grasp of the concept of market value and fail to enforce the heighted compensation standard (Chang 2017).

probably do not carry weight for judges. Hence, judges in Taiwan have not realized, and not taken into account, the ex ante inefficiency of their decisions. Put simply, judges in Taiwan care about inefficiency when they can observe it in their cases – that is, ex post inefficiency.

Taiwanese judges will not avoid ex ante inefficiency, perhaps because many of them lack the proper training in social sciences. Taiwanese judges ignores ex ante inefficiency also because they are not equipped with a formal policy-making role, which would have demanded they think beyond the parties in front of them. As a result, Taiwanese judges generally ignore the effect of judicial decisions on future transactions and future transacting parties, as they are not before the bench. The research hypothesis advanced in this chapter can be used by empiricists to measure against the judicial behaviors in their jurisdictions.

References in English

Bebchuk, Lucian Arye. 2001. Property Rights and Liability Rules: The Ex Ante View of the Cathedral. *Michigan Law Review* 100: 601–39.

Brooks, Richard R. W., and Warren F. Schwartz. 2005. Legal Uncertainty, Economic Efficiency, and the Preliminary Injunction Doctrine. *Stanford Law Review* 58: 381–410.

Chang, Yun-chien. 2011. An Empirical Study of Court-Adjudicated Takings Compensation in New York City: 1990–2003. *Journal of Empirical Legal Studies* 8 (2): 384–412.

    2012. Tenancy in "Anticommons"? A Theoretical and Empirical Analysis of Co-ownership. *Journal of Legal Analysis* 4: 515–53.

    2014. To Tear Down or Not to Tear Down? An Empirical Study of Boundary Encroachment Cases in Taiwan. Pp. 144–58 in *Empirical Legal Analysis: Assessing the Performance of Legal Institutions*, edited by Yun-chien Chang. London: Routledge.

    2015. Optional Law in Property: Theoretical Critiques. *NYU Journal of Law and Liberty* 9 (2): 459–512.

    2016. Hybrid Rule: Hidden Entitlement Protection Rule in Access to Landlocked Land Doctrine. *Tulane Law Review* 88: 217–57.

    2017. Eminent Domain Law in Taiwan: New Law, Old Practice? Pp. 93–117 in *Eminent Domain: A Comparative Perspective*, edited by Iljoong Kim, Hojun Lee and Ilya Somin. Cambridge: Cambridge University Press.

Chang, Yun-chien, and Chang-ching Lin. 2017. Do Parties Negotiate after Trespass Litigation: An Empirical Study of Coasean Bargaining. https://ssrn.com/abstract=2805063 (accessed July 9, 2019).

Chang, Yun-chien, and Henry E. Smith. 2012. An Economic Analysis of Civil versus Common Law Property. *Notre Dame Law Review* 88(1): 1–55.

2016. Structure and Style in Comparative Property Law. Pp. 131–60 in *Research Handbook on Comparative Law and Economics*, edited by Theodore Eisenberg and Giovanni B. Ramello. Northampton, MA: Edward Elgar.

Chang, Yun-chien, Kong-Pin Chen, and Chang-ching Lin. 2017. Anchoring Effect in Real Litigations. *Working Paper.*

Chang, Yun-Chien, Kong-Pin Chen, and Yu-Sheng Liu. 2016. Unlawful Possession of Land and Unjust Enrichment Equivalent to Rent: Empirical Analysis and Policy Suggestions [in Chinese]. *Chengchi Law Review* (144): 81–153.

Chang, Yun-chien, and Lee Anne Fennell. 2014a. Appendices to Partition and Revelation. *The University of Chicago Law Review Dialogue* 81(1): 1–13.

2014b. Partition and Revelation. *The University of Chicago Law Review* 81 (1): 27–51.

Coase, Ronald H. 1959. The Federal Communications Commission. *Journal of Law and Economics* 2: 1–40.

1960. The Problem of Social Cost. *Journal of Law & Economics* 3: 1–69.

Dannemann, Gerhard. 2009. *The German Law of Unjustified Enrichment and Restitution: A Comparative Introduction.* Oxford: Oxford University Press.

Demsetz, Harold. 2011. The Problem of Social Cost: What Problem? A Critique of the Reasoning of A.C. Pigou and R.H. Coase. *Review of Law & Economics* 7: 1–13.

Epstein, Lee, William M. Landes, and Richard A. Posner. 2013. *The Behavior of Federal Judges: A Theoretical and Empirical Study of Rational Choice* Cambridge, MA: Harvard University Press.

Epstein, Richard A. 1997. A Clear View of the Cathedral: The Dominance of Property Rules. *Yale Law Journal* 106: 2091–120.

1998. Protecting Property Rights with Legal Remedies: A Common Sense Reply to Professor Ayres. *Valparaiso University Law Review* 32: 833–53.

Farnsworth, Ward. 1999. Do Parties to Nuisance Cases Bargain after Judgment? A Glimpse Inside the Cathedral. *The University of Chicago Law Review* 66 (2): 373–436.

Fennell, Lee Anne. 2011. Commons, Anticommons, Semicommons. Pp. 35–56 in *Research Handbook on the Economics of Property Law*, edited by Henry E. Smith. Northampton, MA: Edward Elgar.

2013. The Problem of Resource Access. *Harvard Law Review* 126(6): 1471–531.

Fon, Vincy, Francesco Parisi, and Ben Depoorter. 2005. Litigation, Judicial Path-Dependence, and Legal Change. *European Journal of Law and Economics* 20 (1): 43–56.

Garoupa, Nuno, and Carlos Gómez Ligüerre. 2011. The Syndrome of the Efficiency of the Common Law. *Boston University International Law Journal* 29: 287–335.

Heller, Michael A. 1998. The Tragedy of the Anticommons: Property in the Transition from Marx to Markets. *Harvard Law Review* 111(3): 621–88.

Krebs, Thomas. 2004. Unrequested Benefits in German Law. Pp. 247–62 in *Understanding Unjust Enrichment*, edited by Jason W. Neyers, Mitchell McInnes and Stephen G. A. Pitel. Portland, OR: Hart.

Krier, James E., and Stewart J. Schwab. 1995. Property Rules and Liability Rules: The Cathedral in Another Light. *New York University Law Review* 70: 440–83.

Lewinsohn-Zamir, Daphna. 2001. The Choice between Property Rules and Liability Rules Revisited: Critical Observations from Behavioral Studies. *Texas Law Review* 80: 219–60.

Merrill, Thomas W., and Henry E. Smith. 2012. *Property: Principles and Policies*. 2nd ed. New York: Foundation Press.

Miceli, Thomas J., and C.F. Sirmans. 2000. Partition of Real Estate; or, Breaking Up Is (Not) Hard to Do. *Journal of Legal Studies* 29: 783–796.

Niblett, Anthony, Richard A. Posner, and Andrei Shleifer. 2010. The Evolution of a Legal Rule. *The Journal of Legal Studies* 39(2): 325–58.

Parchomovsky, Gideon, and Alex Stein. 2009. Reconceptualizing Trespass. *Northwestern University Law Review* 103: 1823–62.

Parisi, Francesco. 2004. The Efficiency of the Common Law Hypothesis. Pp. 519–22 in *The Encyclopedia of Public Choice*, edited by Charles K. Rowley and Friedrich Schneider, New York: Springer.

Ponzetto, Giacomo A. M., and Patricio A. Fernandez. 2008. Case Law versus Statute Law: An Evolutionary Comparison. *Journal of Legal Studies* 37: 379–430.

Posner, Richard A. 1973. *Economic Analysis of Law*. Boston, MA: Little, Brown. 2011. *Economic Analysis of Law*. 8th ed. New York: Aspen.

Priest, George L. 1977. The Common Law Process and the Selection of Efficient Rules. *The Journal of Legal Studies* 6: 65–82.

Ramseyer, J. Mark. 2015. *Second-Best Justice: The Virtues of Japanese Private Law*. Chicago, IL: The University of Chicago Press.

Rizzolli, Matteo. 2009. Building Encroachments. *Review of Law and Economics* 5: 661–93.

Rubin, Paul H. 1977. Why Is the Common Law Efficient? *The Journal of Legal Studies* 6(1): 51–63. 1982. Common Law and Statute Law. *Journal of Legal Studies* 11: 205–24.

Smith, Henry E. 2002. Exclusion versus Governance: Two Strategies for Delineating Property Rights. *Journal of Legal Studies* 31: S453–S87. 2004. Property and Property Rules. *New York University Law Review* 79: 1719–98. 2009. Law and Economics: Realism or Democracy? *Harvard Journal of Law & Public Policy* 32: 127–45.

Zywicki, Todd J., and Edward Peter Stringham. 2010. Common Law and Economic Efficiency, available at http://ssrn.com/abstract_id=1673968 (accessed July 9, 2019).

References in German

Buck-Heeb, Petra. 2011. Ungerechtfertigte Bereicherung - Unerlaubte Handlungen. In *Erman Bürgerliches Gesetzbuch* 3485–576. Edited by Harm Peter Westermann. 13 ed. Köln: Dr. Otto Schmidt.

Sprau, Hartwig. 2013. Werkvertrag und ähnlich Verträge - Unerlaubte Handlugen. In *Palandt Bürgerliches Gesetzbuch* 967–1438. Edited by Otto Palandt. 72 ed. Munich: C. H. Beck.

When Winning Is Not Enough

Prevailing-Party Civil Appeals in State Courts

MICHAEL HEISE

7.1 Introduction

While public and scholarly attention to the "vanishing trial" (see, for example, Galanter 2004) persists – perhaps even increasing over time (see, for example, Engstrom 2018) – civil appeals elude similar levels of empirical scrutiny and endure, to many, as something of a curious afterthought.[1] And whatever one may think about civil appeals generally, appeals launched by the party who *prevailed* at trial are typically framed as a curious and distinctively counterintuitive subset of appeals.[2] Distinctiveness notwithstanding, however, not only must legal theory account for and explain prevailing-party appeals, but a better understanding of their empirical contours is needed as well.

As many scholars note, among civil litigation's possible outcomes settlements dominate, at least empirically. One important though less frequent outcome involves those cases, having been already decided by a trial court, that pursue an appeal. Whatever legal scholars know about the small world of civil appeals, however, is dominated by an understandable focus on traditional appeals; that is, appeals initiated by the party who lost at trial. Comparatively much less is known about prevailing-party appeals.

Assessments of the objectives realized (if any) through prevailing-party appeals require a frame of reference from which to access

---

[1] Michael Heise is William G. McRoberts Professor in the Empirical Study of Law, Cornell Law School. Dawn M. Chutkow, Kevin Clermont, Jeff Rachlinski, William Hubbard, participants in the 2017 Conference on Empirical Legal Studies-Asia, in Taipei, Taiwan, and faculty workshops at the University of Toronto and the University of Chicago Law School, and anonymous referees provided helpful comments on earlier drafts of this chapter.

[2] Throughout this chapter I refer to such appeals as "prevailing-party."

prevailing-party appeals. Conventional cost-benefit analysis provides one analytical perspective and involves a general assessment of whether prevailing-party appeals' benefits match or exceed their costs to litigants and the civil justice system. Of course, the application of cost-benefit analysis necessitates clarification of prevailing-party appeals' benefits as well as their costs. One central benefit ascribed to an appellate system – and a key justification advanced for it – focuses on error correction. As a benefit and justification, error correction is both intuitive and difficult to overemphasize. Notwithstanding error correction's importance, however, other justifications for appeals exist. Alternative rationales for appellate review include a desire for lawmaking (Shavell 1995), legitimacy (Shapiro 1980), and increasing legal consistency across systems and jurisdictions.

Despite any such benefits, however, an appeal of a judgment from a concluded trial imposes various individual-level and system-wide costs. Prevailing-party appeals impose additional costs on the losing party at trial. As well, such appeals engage the courts once again and, in so doing, impose institutional-level costs. Given the potentially important costs imposed by a prevailing-party, it is important to know whether those cases appealed warrant additional litigation and to gain a better sense of what these appeals look like and how they distribute.

With the benefit of one of the largest collections of data on civil litigation in the United States, this chapter sets out to explore and describe the general empirical contours of prevailing-party civil appeals. One striking finding involves the asymmetrical distribution of prevailing-party appeals' success. While civil trial court outcomes overall typically lean in a direction favoring plaintiffs and traditional appeals favor of defendant-appellants (Eisenberg and Heise 2009; 2015), results of prevailing-party appeals favor plaintiff-appellants (where the plaintiff was prevailing-party at trial). Moreover, in terms of success with disrupting unfavorable trial court rulings, prevailing-party appeals succeeded at a rate that surpasses the success rate for traditional appeals.[3] While individual-level and system-wide costs are difficult to describe with any empirical accuracy, it is worth noting that prevailing-party appellants – similar to most appellants –internalize some portion of an appeal's costs.

---

[3] Of course, as described more fully later, it remains logically possible that rather than correct trial court error successful appeals (that upset trial court outcomes) may, in fact, *inject* new legal error. In addition, trial and appellate court outcomes vary across case types.

This chapter unfolds as follows. Section 7.2 briefly explains while civil appeals in general and prevailing-party appeals in particular warrant attention. Section 7.3 describes the data set, methodology, and basic research design. Section 7.4 presents preliminary and descriptive results. Whether the descriptive findings persist through more rigorous modeling and regression analyses is considered in Section 7.5 along with a discussion of the results and their potential implications for civil litigation.

7.2   Why Worry about Appeals?

This chapter's particular task is to assess prevailing-party civil appeals and consider what they might contribute to our general understanding of civil litigation. To these ends, one question involves whether and, if so, how prevailing-party appeals differ from traditional appeals. A related question considers what prevailing-party appeal outcomes might imply about the civil litigation system, particularly as it relates to questions relating to efficacy and efficiency.[4]

Engaging with questions about what prevailing-party appeals might imply about our litigation system, broadly construed, necessarily assumes that the appellate process itself plays a consequential role in our litigation system. The reasonableness of this predicate assumption warrants brief attention. Although few dispute the appellate process's centrality to justice systems, scholars have devoted comparatively far greater attention to trial activity (see, for example, Shavell 1995). Existing appeals scholarship reveals continued contests over rationales supporting the appellate role in our adjudicatory system. Notwithstanding competing rationales, it is difficult to overestimate error correction as a justification for an appellate system. Of course, alternative (or complementary) rationales also exist and support claims for a need for appellate review, including a desire for lawmaking (see, for example, Shavell 1995), greater legal legitimacy (see, for example, Shapiro 1980), and increasing legal consistency across systems and jurisdictions.

Much of the existing empirical scholarship on civil appeals expressly excludes prevailing-party appeals from analyses to satisfy conventional understandings of what adverse litigation means (see, for example, Clermont and Eisenberg 2001; 2002; Eisenberg and Heise 2009; 2015). By contrast, this chapter focuses on what much of the existing empirical

---

[4] For a discussion on civil court decisions and their implication for the efficiency hypothesis see generally Posner (2014).

literature expressly excludes: prevailing-party civil appeals. Despite the existing empirical literature's understandable focus on "traditional" appeals, prevailing-party appeals' seemingly counterintuitive posture alone warrants some degree of attention from scholars. As well, even though appeals in general and prevailing party appeals in particular are rare events (certainly in comparison to overall civil trial activity), prevailing-party appeals are not so rare as to justify ignoring.[5]

At first blush, the idea that a plaintiff, having "won" at trial, would pursue an appeal strikes many as anomalistic or implausible. At the procedural level, how does a prevailing plaintiff satisfy standing requirements necessary to pursue an appeal? Beyond procedural and standing questions, what might motivate a prevailing plaintiff to pursue an appeal having already won at trial?

To address these questions one must begin with basic civil procedure. After all, how can a prevailing party satisfy standing requirements for an appeal? Conventional black letter law makes clear that only a party adversely affected by a trial court judgment may appeal that judgment (see, for example, *Pub. Serv. Comm'n* v. *Brashear Freight Lines, Inc.*, 306 U.S. 204, 206 [1939]). Thus, prevailing-party appeals embody the counter-intuitive notion that the prevailing parties' interests were nonetheless *adversely* impacted by a *favorable* trial outcome. One source of prevailing-party appeals includes those cases involving crossclaims or counterclaims (permissive and compulsory).[6] While cross and counterclaims accomplish distinctly different tasks, they are similar in that they typically increase an underlying lawsuit's complexity by adding additional parties, contested legal issues, or both. Thus, the presence of either cross or counterclaims would increase the probability of a prevailing-party appeal.

How can a win at trial nonetheless harm a prevailing party's legal interests? Simply put, despite prevailing at trial a party can still *lose* something (or not win enough). For example, a prevailing party, unsatisfied with a trial court's award for damages and/or attorney fees (despite a favorable judgment), may seek appellate review on issues relating to damages or attorney fees. Similarly, a party that prevailed at trial may nonetheless elect to pursue an appeal to establish an alternative legal basis

[5] As a percentage of overall appeals in the admittedly small number of publicly available data sets, prevailing-party appeals typically range from approximately 15 to 25 percent of all appeals. See Clermont and Eisenberg (2001; 2002); Eisenberg and Heise (2009; 2015).

[6] See Fed. Rules Civ. Pro. 13(b) (2016).

for the trial court judgment. A favorable judgment's precise legal basis may be of particular interest to "repeat" litigants or litigants with potentially similar litigation opportunities. Thus, for these (and other) reasons winning at trial may *not* be enough to preclude a prevailing party from pursuing the losing party further through an appeal. Not all plaintiff trial wins are equal or, more importantly, equally satisfying for the prevailing party.

The existence of litigants who undertake appeals despite having prevailed at trial possesses potentially important implications for the civil litigation system. To the extent that (successful) prevailing-party appeals help correct trial court errors such an outcome could contribute to increased civil litigation efficacy and efficiency.

7.3   Data, Methodology, and Research Design

Four discrete, though related, data sets that span almost one decade supply the data necessary for this study and their combination forms one of the most comprehensive publicly available civil appeals data sets.

The final merged state data set used in this study draws from two separate (2001 and 2005) two-part (trial and appellate) data sets. All of the state data sets derive from the "Civil Justice Survey of State Courts," a project involving the NCSC and the BJS, which gathered data directly from state court clerks' offices on tort, contract, and property cases disposed of by trial during calendar years 2001 and 2005.

The 2001 trial data set includes state courts of general jurisdiction in a random sample of 46 of the nation's 75 most populous counties. The 75 counties from which the sample of 46 was drawn include approximately 37 percent of the 1990 US population and about one-half of all civil lawsuits filed in state courts. The 2001 trial data set includes information on 8,038 trials (U.S. Department of Justice 2004).

The second (appellate) part of the 2001 data set complements the trial data study by tracking the 1,204 cases where the trial verdict or judgment, concluded by trial during calendar 2001, was appealed to an intermediate appellate court or a state's court of last resort and concluded by April 2005 (U.S. Department of Justice 2006). Among this universe of 1,204 appeals, 47 (3.9 percent) were excluded from many of the analyses because they lacked critical information about which party prevailed at trial. Merging the trial and appellate data sets generated the 2001 data set that provides a helpful window into state court appellate activity drawn from the most representative sample of state court trial activity in the United States in 2001.

The development of the 2005 state data set closely (but not exactly) tracks the development of its predecessor, the 2001 state data set (U.S. Department of Justice 2009). The 2005 Civil Justice Survey data set includes 46 of the 75 most populous counties selected to maintain backwards compatibility with earlier Civil Justice Surveys data sets. The 2005 survey expanded coverage, however, by adding 110 counties to represent the 3,066 smaller counties not included in the country's 75 largest counties. The 2005 trial data set includes a universe of 8,872 concluded trials from 141 different counties and 40 different states.

Similar to the 2001 trial data set, the 2005 state court trials data set was complemented by a related appellate data set that tracked the 1,290 cases where the trial verdict or judgment, concluded by trial during calendar 2005, prompted an appeal to an intermediate appellate court or a state's court of last resort that was concluded by December 2009 (U.S. Department of Justice 2012). Among these 1,290 initial appeals, 20 appeals (1.6 percent) were excluded from many of the analyses because they lacked necessary information on which party prevailed at trial.

The creation of the final data set used in this study required one additional merger involving the 2001 and 2005 data sets that include both trial and appellate activity. Before merging the 2001 and 2005 data sets, however, I identified those appeals plausibly characterized as prevailing-party. Prior scholarship on appeals typically focuses on more traditional adverse appeals. The traditional "adverse" appeals include, as most would expect, those initiated by the losing party at trial. For example, if the trial court ruled for the plaintiff, most would expect that the defendant would be the appellant in any appeal. Conversely, where the trial court ruled for the defendant, one would expect the plaintiff to be the appellant. For the most part (82.1 percent of the appeals), these expectations were met. This chapter, by contrast, specifically sets out to explore the remaining 17.9 percent of appeals where conventional expectations were upset.

Merging the 2001 and 2005 data sets generates the single largest and most comprehensive source of publicly available information on state court civil appeals. The final merged data set includes 435 usable prevailing-party appeals drawn from a universe of 16,910 completed trials.[7] The appeal rate, drawn from the pool of prevailing-party appeals, is the percentage of trial court judgments that the prevailing party puts

---

[7] While the dataset makes quite clear which party "prevailed" at trial and, as well, which party initiated an appeal, given the complexities introduced by, for example, the possibility

onto the appellate docket.[8] Computing trial court disruption (and total affirmance) rates was similarly straightforward. The trial court disruption rate is the percentage of appeals that generate a formal legal conclusion that did *not* affirm *in whole* the underlying trial court decision.[9]

Despite the prevailing-party appeals data set's particular strengths, it is not without important limitations that warrant note. First, insofar as this chapter focuses on appeals – albeit unusual appeals at that – any appeal is conditioned upon litigants pursing a lawsuit to a final trial court disposition. The universe of final trial court dispositions includes only tried cases and excludes, for example, cases appealed after dispositive pretrial motions as well as cases that settled or otherwise concluded prior to any formal trial court adjudication. Second, the focus on state courts dampens any impulse to generate implications about civil appellate activity in federal courts. Third, the potential for human coding error – always a general risk in empirical studies – exists in this context. Such variables as those designed to signal the presence of cross and counter-claims, for example, are often difficult to code with precision and consistency across coders.[10]

Notwithstanding general agreement and a widespread understanding that access to appellate review is a critical component of a comprehensive judicial system, appellate courts' outcomes and how to interpret them are comparatively less well understood and developed in the research

---

of cross claims and counterclaims, which specific party actually "prevailed" at trial may not have always been clear consistently across all data coders. As such, the specter of coding error lurks in in this data set. Indeed, Clermont and Eisenberg (2002, p. 951 n.12) recognizes this complexity and its likely implications. Unlike Clermont and Eisenberg's study that involved their use of federal Administrative Office data not designed for studies such as theirs (or this study), the state civil data set used in this study has the benefit of expressly endeavoring to identify the prevailing party at trial and the party that initiated an appeal.

[8] For a similar approach to defining the appeal rate, see Clermont and Eisenberg (2001).

[9] This would include such appeals court outcomes as reversed in whole or part or remanded in whole or part.

[10] Indeed, Clermont and Eisenberg (2002) recognizes this possibility. However, it is important to note that the Clermont and Eisenberg study involved federal administrative office data not originally created for analyses that required linking trial and appellate court decisions. In contrast, the state civil data set used in this study was expressly structured in a manner to facilitate identifying the prevailing party at trial and the party that initiated an appeal. The *ex ante* commitment to merging trial and appellate court data sets was made, in part, to minimize coding complexities and errors. Finally, while the possibility of coding errors always lurks, to date no published paper has yet uncovered any systematic coding errors plaguing the NCSC data sets used in this study.

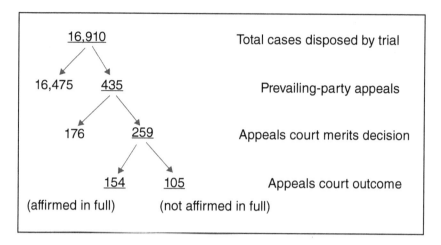

Figure 7.1   Flow of state civil trials disposed in 123 counties that were appealed to an intermediate or highest appellate state court by the party that prevailed at trial (2001–05; 2005–09).
Sources: U.S. Department of Justice (2012, 2009, 2006, 2004)

literature. In particular, basic information on how appellate outcomes distribute as well as explanations for these distributions would benefit from greater scholarly attention.

Before turning to appellate outcomes, however, information about which concluded trials initiated an appeal deserves attention. Clearly, selection effects influence the data in various and important ways. As Figure 7.1 (and Table 7.1) illustrate, the stream of cases that lead to a prevailing-party appeal encountered an array of filters as it proceeded from the civil dispute stage and through the trial and appellate processes. Notably, and as well-documented elsewhere (see, for example, Eisenberg and Heise 2009; Eisenberg and Schwab 1989; Priest and Klein 1984), as only a small fraction of civil actions filed ever reach a trial court, the subpool of tried cases may systematically differ from the larger pool of civil disputes from which they emerged.

As well, the appellate process involves its own set of litigant selections that impose additional filters. One final and important – and perhaps singularly unique – set of filters for those litigants who pursued prevailing-party appeals involve procedural requirements. To have appropriate standing to pursue an appeal, a prevailing party from trial must prove the claim that their appeal is necessary to ward off legally

Table 7.1 State civil trials, appeals, and outcomes (2001–2004, 2005–2009)

	Civil Trials	Appealed (%)	Appealed to Completion (%)	Appeal Disruption Rate (%)
(A) *Prevailing-Party Appeals:*				
All trials	16,910	2.6	1.5	40.5
Jury trials	12,592	2.4	1.5	42.4
Bench trials	4,318	3.0	1.6	35.3
Party appealing (from trial):				
Defendant	105	1.4	0.7	29.4
Plaintiff	330	3.7	2.3	43.3
N	16,910	435	259	105
(B) *Traditional Appeals:*				
All trials	16,910	11.8	7.1	31.4
Jury trials	12,592	11.2	6.9	33.3
Bench trials	4,318	13.4	7.5	26.1
Party appealing (from trial):				
Defendant	1,076	12.0	6.8	41.2
Plaintiff	916	11.8	7.5	21.3
N	16,910	1,992	1,195	375

Table 7.1 (*cont.*)

	Civil Trials	Appealed (%)	Appealed to Completion (%)	Appeal Disruption Rate (%)
(C) Trial Court				
Results:				
	Prevailing Party at Trial (%)			
Plaintiff	53.5			
Defendant	46.5			
N	16,762			

Note: "Appeal Disruption" is defined to include any appeal outcome other than "affirmed in whole." The slight discrepancy in Panel C's N (16,762) from the total N = 16,910 reflects the 0.8 percent of cases that lack critical information on which party prevailed at trial.
Sources: U.S. Department of Justice (2012, 2009, 2006, 2004).

cognizable harm. Obviously, the existence of crossclaims can increase the probability that a party who prevailed at trial satisfy the procedural requirements necessary to proceed with an appeal. The existence of prevailing-party appeals implies that, for whatever reason or reasons, for some appellants trial court victory was insufficient and that an appeal was necessary to gain something different, more, or both.

Selection effects' salience in civil litigation remains largely framed by Priest-Klein's seminal 1984 paper. While various testable hypotheses flowing from Priest-Klein's work continue to attract scholarly attention and empirical scrutiny (see, for example, Lee and Klerman 2016), two observations reside at the core of Priest-Klein's analysis. One is that the stream of legal disputes that persist through litigation and reach formal trial court adjudication (as contrasted to those disputes that settle prior to trial court adjudication) systematically differs from the larger universe of legal disputes from which tried cases emerge (Priest and Klein 1984, p. 4). A second central prediction from the Priest-Klein paper is that owing to the various and complex selection forces at work, and assuming two-sided asymmetrical information, among those cases that persist to trial court adjudication plaintiffs' success rate should approach 50 percent (Priest and Klein 1984, p. 19). That is, and at the risk of over-simplification, the Priest-Klein models predicts a 50 percent win rate for the plaintiff as objectively "obvious" cases (in terms of liability) will settle prior to a trial court adjudication. Success in the remaining sub-pool of cases where legal liability is objectively "not obvious" should distribute evenly between plaintiffs and defendants.

While it is one thing to discuss selection effect in theory and surmise about its important influence on litigation outcomes, it is quite another thing to observe it. As Figure 7.1 illustrates, from the universe of state civil cases disposed of by trial, only 2.6 percent initiated prevailing-party appeals. Far fewer still (1.5 percent) pursued an appeal to its conclusion and an appellate court decision. Of those who initiated a prevailing-party appeal, however, 59.5 percent pursued the case to an appellate court decision. Interestingly, the prevailing-party appeals' results may vindicate the appellants' persistence. If the appellant's goal is to disrupt a trial court decision, and here "disruption" is understood to mean any appellate court outcome short of a total affirmance of the trial court decision, appellants pursuing prevailing-party appeals achieved this goal in 40.5 percent of the cases that persisted to a merits decision.

There are strong theoretical, practical, and obvious reasons to expect selection effects to generate a nonrandom sample of cases that pursue a prevailing-party appeal. Assuming that litigants taking cases to trial do so partly because they can afford to pursue trial litigation and, presumably, because they sense some reasonable probability of success on the legal merits and that the case's economic value (discounted by the probability of success) exceeds the cost of litigating (Priest and Klein 1984). The sub-pool of cases that withstands settlement or withdrawal, motions for directed verdicts and summary judgments, and other dispositions more likely involves cases whose underlying merits reside somewhere in the "gray middle area" and where the legal result is somewhat uncertain. Cases where the underlying legal merits clearly favor either the plaintiff or defendant are more likely to either settle or not survive pretrial motions. Moreover, a similar set of filters arises anew during the posttrial appellate process (Priest and Klein 1984; Revesz 2000). Finally, in general one might reasonably expect, *ex ante*, that winning at trial would sub-stantially dampen the probability of a party pursuing an appeal. In all, these various selection filters influence the case stream over time and in a manner that generates a skewed subset of prevailing-party appeals. The prevailing-party appeals data set, however, permits an initial accounting of one aspect of the selection processes at work: the decision to undertake a prevailing-party appeal after trial.

7.4 Preliminary Results

Preliminary analyses identify those cases that initiated prevailing-party appeals, explore the distribution of appeal rates and appellate outcomes, and assess how these distributions vary across trial, party, and case types.

Assessing results on the raw numbers of prevailing-party appeals and their outcomes, presented in Figure 7.1, requires some context. Table 7.1 seeks to provide one point of reference by facilitating comparisons between prevailing-party appeals (panel A) and their more traditional "adverse" counterparts (panel B). What is immediately clear is that more traditional adverse appeals (1,992) numerically overwhelm prevailing-party appeals (435) by more than a factor of four-to-one. What the two sub-pools of appeals share, however, includes a similar persistence rate once an appeal has been initiated. Traditional appeals' persistence (or completion) rate[11] (60.0 percent) is remarkably close to the completion rate for prevailing-party appeals (59.5 percent). While many factors

---

[11] The persistence rate was computed by dividing the number of appeals completed by the number of appeals initiated.

account for the drop-off of those appeals initiated but not completed, notably settlement, the strikingly similar persistence rates imply that these factors influence traditional and prevailing-party appeals similarly.

Despite sharing similar persistence rates, traditional and prevailing-party appeals differ in many important ways. One notable (and critical) difference involves appellate success, with "success" defined in terms of disrupting an undesirable trial court decision. The overall success rate for prevailing-party appeals (40.5 percent) exceeds traditional appeals' success rate (31.4 percent). What might account for prevailing-party appeals' greater success in disrupting trial court decisions?

Differences in success rates for prevailing-party and traditional appeals may reflect underlying differences between prevailing-party and traditional appeals. One obvious factor that distinguishes these two distinct sub-pools of appeals involves the different barriers to pursuing an appeal these different sub-pools confront. The standard motivation for a traditional (or adverse) appeal is relatively straightforward. Specifically, a party that lost at trial but feels that a sufficient trial error in either law or fact (or both) exists to justify the added time, effort, and expense incident to pursuing an appeal. Of course, factors other than an adverse liability ruling at trial may also motivate or contribute to traditional appeals as well. Even a party that lost at trial with no objective prospect of success on appeal may nonetheless seek to externalize additional costs on the prevailing party by prolonging litigation and increasing overall legal costs by launching an appeal. Additionally, the opportunity to exercise one's right to pursue an appeal may itself supply helpful leverage in subsequent settlement negotiations. After all, even a party that lost at trial and objectively confronts a slim likelihood of appellate success may seek to exchange her right to pursue an appeal for more favorable settlement terms. Finally, an array of noneconomic factors (for example, political, social, personal, or ideological goals) may persist after a trial court loss and motivate an appeal.

Motivations for a prevailing-party appeal, by contrast, are comparatively less straightforward. After all, in the prevailing-party appellate context the appellant prevailed at trial yet, nonetheless, for some reason seeks to prolong "successful" litigation and invest additional time, energy, and resources in an appeal. Of course, as previously discussed, even parties that prevail at trial may come away with less than what they felt was warranted in terms of damages or attorney fees, for example.

Setting aside possibly different motivations for initiating appeals, perhaps more salient than *why* a party pursed an appeal is whether such an appeal – for whatever motivation – *succeeded*. As Table 7.1 makes clear, while prevailing-party appeals were far less common than traditional appeals (2.6 versus 11.8 percent) when it came to disrupting trial court outcomes prevailing-party appeals were more effective (40.5 versus 31.4 percent). That is to say, another way prevailing-party and the more conventional adverse appeals differ involves the prospect for success. The different appellate success rates imply either that prevailing-parties at trial can predict with greater accuracy than traditional appellants whether additional unrealized legal satisfaction remains after trial or that prevailing-party appellants pursue stronger appeals.

While the data will not permit a direct explanation for the different success rates, pulling various results together may provide helpful clues. For example, differences in the incidence of prevailing-party and traditional appeals and their different success rates raise the possibility that litigant filtering for prevailing-party appeals was more exacting. If so, those initiating prevailing-party appeals, having been subjected to more demanding selection obstacles, may have selected cases more prone to succeed. Even if an explanation that relies on differing litigant selections makes sense, at least one important question persists. Specifically, among the world of those contemplating pursuing a civil appeal, what explains why prevailing-party appellants systematically selected stronger cases to appeal than traditional appellants? Regrettably, existing data do not speak to this question.

Another factor distinguishing prevailing-party and traditional appeals involves the appealing party. In traditional appeals, defendants who lost at trial were only slightly more likely than disgruntled plaintiffs to initiate an appeal (12.0 versus 11.8 percent). In contrast, plaintiffs who prevailed at trial were more than two times as likely to launch a prevailing-party appeal than defendants (3.7 versus 1.4 percent). Thus, the prospect of winning at trial, but not winning "enough," is far more likely for prevailing plaintiffs than for prevailing defendants.

In addition to important party and trial type variation, as Table 7.2 illustrates, prevailing-party appeals varied across traditional case types as well. The important influence of case types on trial and appellate outcomes is well-understood (see, for example, Eisenberg and Heise 2015) and worth underscoring. That different case types interact differently with the appellate process is clear, precisely how these differences emerge, however, is less well understood. Prior research emphasizes, for example, that case type may inform a litigant's decision on whether to route a case to a judge or jury trial and that traditional appellate success

Table 7.2 *Prevailing-party appeals and disruption rates, by case category and trial type (2001–2004, 2005–2009)*

	Filed	Filed (%)	Completed	Completed (%)	App. Ct. Disrupted Tr. Ct. Decision (%)
All prevailing-party appeals	435	2.6	259	59.5	40.5
Motor vehicle	84	1.5	50	59.5	42.0
Assault, slander, libel	12	1.9	10	83.3	30.0
Product liability	12	4.1	6	50.0	50.0
Dangerous premises	31	1.7	22	71.0	27.3
Medical malpractice	47	2.6	29	61.7	41.2
Prof. malpractice	6	4.1	5	83.3	40.0
(other tort)	24	3.3	10	41.7	40.0
Employment contract	28	4.6	20	71.4	65.0
Fraud	43	4.7	28	65.1	46.4
Lease	13	3.2	6	46.2	33.3
(other contract)	100	3.1	54	54.0	38.9
Property	35	7.3	19	54.3	26.3
Tort	216	1.9	132	61.1	38.6
Contract	184	3.5	108	58.7	45.4
Property	35	7.3	19	54.3	26.3
Jury trials	307	2.4	191	62.2	42.4
Judge trials	128	3.0	68	53.1	35.3
N	435		259		105

Note: The "App. Ct. Disrupted Tr. Ct. Decision (%)" column is defined to include any appeal outcome other than "affirmed in whole."
Sources: U.S. Department of Justice (2012, 2006).

rates types vary across case (Eisenberg and Farber 2013). Moreover, case types can also influence various trial aspects differently, including case disposition time (Heise 2000). Given case types' wide-ranging influences on the civil justice system, that case types influence the appeals process should be expected. Consequently, case type controls remain essential to appeals' outcome models.[12]

Indeed, results in Table 7.2 illustrate case types' importance in the prevailing-party appeals context. Although only 2.6 percent of tried cases prompted a prevailing-party appeal, the prevailing-party appeal rate for employment contract and fraud cases exceeded 4.5 percent. More striking, perhaps, is that 7.3 percent of tried property cases led to a prevailing-party appeal. Thus, property cases were more than 2.5 times as likely generate a prevailing-party appeal. At the opposite end of the spectrum, motor vehicle and dangerous premises cases were comparatively less likely to stimulate a prevailing-party appeal (1.5 and 1.7 percent, respectively). Notably, the influence of case types in the prevailing-party appeals context is consistent with case types' influence in the more traditional, adverse appeals context (Eisenberg and Heise 2009; 2015).

While case type variations warrant careful consideration, it remains important to keep in mind that case type's labels might also mask other factors. For example, that prevailing-party appeals rates for property and professional malpractice claims exceed that of motor vehicle claims may have little to do with differences in case type labels and much more to do with likely differences in the cases' underlying financial stakes.

7.5   Selection, Rare Events, and Mixed Effects Models

Numerous, complex, and often subtle filtering processes winnow litigation from a complaint's initial filing through whatever trial and appellate litigation processes emerge. While it is clear that selection effects pose considerable methodological complexities, far less clear is whether any particular statistical model deals with selection on unobserved variables better than others (see, for example, Eisenberg 1990; Holm and Jaeger 2011). In an effort to adjust for the various selection effects, partly illustrated by Figure 7.1, and recognizing the various perspectives on how best to accomplish this task, three separate models were specified and results from those models are reported in Table 7.3. Specifically,

[12] See infra Part 7.5.

Table 7.3 *Selection and mixed effects models of state appellate outcome (disrupted trial court outcome) and decision to appeal*

	(1) Heckman	(2) Rare Events	(3) Mixed Effects
(A) Decision to Appeal:			
Trial characteristics			
Plaintiff won at trial	0.532 (0.07)**	1.29 (0.18)**	1.30 (0.13)**
Government plaintiff	−0.172 (0.33)	−0.49 (0.75)	−0.41 (0.73)
Corporate plaintiff	0.063 (0.06)	0.12 (0.14)	0.15 (0.15)
Corporate defendant	0.155 (0.05)**	0.39 (0.11)**	0.42 (0.12)**
Damages (ttl) (000,000)	0.001 (0.00)**	0.00 (0.00)**	0.00 (0.00)**
Year case filed	−0.019 (0.01)	−0.03 (0.03)	−0.03 (0.02)
State appeals rev. rate	−0.001 (0.00)	−0.00 (0.00)	−0.00 (0.00)
Case type appeals rev. rate	0.000 (0.00)	−0.00 (0.01)	−0.00 (0.01)
Case types			
Motor vehicle	(ref.)	(ref.)	(ref.)
Intentional tort	0.089 (0.17)	0.31 (0.44)	0.22 (0.35)
Product liability	0.420 (0.13)**	1.02 (0.32)**	0.96 (0.36)**
Dangerous premises	0.088 (0.08)	0.22 (0.19)	0.21 (0.23)
Medical malpractice	0.395 (0.08)**	1.02 (0.20)**	1.02 (0.20)**
Prof. malpractice	0.408 (0.21)	1.01 (0.46)*	0.79 (0.44)
Other tort	0.343 (0.11)**	0.83 (0.25)**	0.75 (0.25)**
Employment contract	0.454 (0.11)**	1.08 (0.25)**	0.91 (0.30)**
Fraud	0.462 (0.12)**	1.06 (0.26)**	0.98 (0.27)**
Lease, mortgage	0.226 (0.18)	0.50 (0.40)	0.42 (0.33)
Other contract	0.190 (0.08)*	0.49 (0.19)*	0.40 (0.22)
Property	0.628 (0.21)**	1.41 (0.42)**	1.22 (0.49)*
constant	36.169 (21.77)	54.06 (59.24)	62.43 (44.23)
N	—	16,100	16,100
(B) Appeal Outcome (Disruption)			
Trial characteristics			
Plaintiff won at trial	0.715 (0.14)**	0.74 (0.33)*	0.86 (0.36)*
Government plaintiff	−6.768 (0.30)**	0.58 (0.62)	0.83 (0.98)
Corporate plaintiff	−0.112 (0.13)	−0.29 (0.26)	−0.42 (0.36)
Corporate defendant	0.008 (0.07)	−0.25 (0.17)	−0.31 (0.28)
Damages (ttl) (000,000)	0.001 (0.00)*	0.00 (0.00)*	0.00 (0.00)

Table 7.3 (*cont.*)

	(1) Heckman	(2) Rare Events	(3) Mixed Effects
(B) Appeal Outcome (Disruption)			
Case types			
Motor vehicle	(ref.)	(ref.)	(ref.)
Intentional tort	0.042 (0.23)	0.07 (0.67)	0.01 (0.74)
Product liability	0.423 (0.20) *	0.25 (0.62)	0.26 (0.76)
Dangerous premises	−0.059 (0.23)	−0.16 (0.55)	−0.24 (0.55)
Medical malpractice	0.304 (0.14) *	−0.03 (0.35)	−0.11 (0.45)
Prof. malpractice	0.615 (0.32)	0.50 (0.76)	0.78 (0.96)
Other tort	0.200 (0.22)	−0.30 (0.56)	−0.31 (0.63)
Employment contract	0.683 (0.15) **	0.93 (0.44) *	1.33 (0.52) *
Fraud	0.690 (0.13) **	0.63 (0.36)	0.90 (0.49)
Lease, mortgage	−0.002 (0.34)	−0.12 (0.37)	−0.05 (0.87)
Other contract	0.208 (0.12)	0.02 (0.37)	0.10 (0.43)
Property	0.927 (0.27) **	−0.43 (0.54)	−0.47 (0.73)
constant	−3.174 (0.16) **	−1.84 (0.38) **	−1.82 (0.44) **
athro constant	12.534 (0.35) **	–	–
N	16,100	425	425
County-level clusters	Yes	Yes	No
State effects	No	No	Yes

Notes: Dependent variable in appeal outcome equation and model is some degree of a reversal of the trial court decision; dependent variable in decision to appeal equation and model is whether an appeal was filed. Robust standard errors are in parentheses. * $p < 0.05$, ** $p < 0.01$. I estimated the models using the "heckprob," "cloglog," and "meqrlogit" commands in Stata (v.15.0).
Sources: U.S. Department of Justice (2012, 2009, 2006, 2004).

model 1 presents results from the classic Heckman selection model. As the incidence of prevailing-party appeals are unlikely events, model 2 presents results from a rare events model specification.[13] Finally, in an effort to link results from this study with analogous studies and for

---

[13] While results from a standard rare events model ("cloglog" in Stata) are reported in model 2, results from additional supplemental models, including a multilevel mixed

robustness purposes, results from a mixed-effects model (model 3) are also reported.

7.5.1   Results

Table 7.3 is constructed to reflect the general two-stage structure of the empirical inquiry. The top panel (A) presents results from models of the threshold decision (first-stage): whether to initiate a prevailing-party appeal. The bottom panel (B) presents results from models of the prevailing-party appeal outcome (second-stage), conditioned on having decided to pursue an appeal. Both panels report results from the three separate models described above.

As an initial matter it is important to note the results' overall robustness across all three model specifications. With regard to decisions to launch a prevailing-party appeal as well as variables that correlate with a successful appeal (and, again, "success" is understood as an appeal that in some way disrupts the lower court ruling), the core substantive results in this study do not unduly pivot on model specifications or the models' associated assumptions.

7.5.1.1   Decision to Initiate a Prevailing-Party Appeal

When it came to deciding whether to pursue a prevailing-party appeal (Panel A), aside from the stable of case types (introduced into the mode to serve largely as control variables), three main trial characteristics variables of interest achieve statistical significance across all three models. First, prevailing plaintiffs were more likely to pursue a prevailing-party appeal than their prevailing defendant counterparts. Such a result does not surprise, however, insofar as it was the plaintiff who sought to vindicate her legal interests in the first instance through a trial. Moreover, while a plaintiff who prevailed at trial can appeal both the judgment (for example, any damages or injunctive relief) as well as attorney fees a prevailing defendant, by contrast, typically only appeal issues relating to attorney fees. Thus, having more issues to appeal may help explain why plaintiffs were comparatively more likely to launch prevailing-party appeals.

The remaining two main findings are similarly unsurprising. Specifically, the probability of initiating an appeal increased as the amount of damages awarded at trial increased. While admittedly an imperfect

---

effects complementary log-log model ("mecloglog" in Stata), yielded virtually identical substantive results.

measure, the size of the trial court damage awards can (however crudely) proxy for the economic "stakes" at issue. Or, to put the matter slightly differently, trial court damage awards are a plausibly rational measure of the "harm caused" by the losing defendant (see, for example, Eisenberg et al. 2002). As a case's economic stakes (as indicated by a positive sign on the damages coefficient) or the magnitude of the harm imposed on the plaintiff increases, such an increase should correspond with an increase the likelihood of litigation, including appellate litigation. Basic law and economics also comes into play as higher stakes cases more easily justify the sunk litigation costs incident to an appeal. Finally, the presence of a corporate defendant also increased the probability of launching a prevailing-party appeal. While this finding can signal many different things, some of these things flow from evidence suggesting that jurors (and, one would also assume, plaintiffs and attorneys) can systematically react differently to corporate and individual defendants. It is also intuitive to assume that the presence of insurance (or coverage with higher policy caps) or other assets is more likely for corporate defendants. Thus, to the extent that the "deep pockets" thesis has any traction, it also may help explain why corporate defendants were popular targets of prevailing-party appeals.

7.5.1.2   Successful Prevailing-Party Appeals

Deciding to launch a prevailing-party appeal is one thing, prevailing in such an appeal is another. As results in Table 7.3 (panel B) make clear, among the array of trial characteristics variables, two emerge as persistently important: plaintiffs who won at trial and, though to a slightly lesser extent, trial court damage awards. Specifically, not only were prevailing plaintiffs more likely to initiate prevailing-party appeals, but they were comparatively more likely to prevail on appeal as well. Moreover, and as one might expect, as the amount of total damages awarded at trial increased, so too did the probability of a party both initiating and prevailing in a prevailing-party appeal. Notably, however, trial court damages did not achieve statistical significance across all three specifications.

   In contrast with the prevailing plaintiff and trial court damage awards' variables, however, the influence of a corporate defendant at trial did not behave in a similar manner. That is, while the presence of a corporate defendant increased the probability of the initiation of a prevailing-party appeal, corporate defendants did not emerge as unusually easy targets for parties seeking an adjustment to a trial court "win." This potentially anomalous finding hints at an array of potential explanations. One may involve prevailing plaintiffs' overestimation of their prospects on appeal. An alternative account, however, may reflect a corporate defendant's comparative ability to successfully ward off a hostile appeal. (Of course, if any such comparative advantage exists it does not readily explain the defendant's underlying loss at trial.)

The influence of case types on trial and appellate outcomes is well-understood in the research literature (see, for example, Eisenberg and Heise 2015). As such, case type controls remain essential for case trial and appellate outcome models. As Table 7.3 reveals, however, some case types were more prone than others when it came to decisions to initiate prevailing-party appeals as well as their success. Among the array of case types correlating with a decision to launch a prevailing-party appeal, only employment contract appeals also consistently correlate with successful appellate outcomes.[14] The reduction in the number of case types that achieve statistical significance in the two alternative specifications that seek to model successful prevailing-party appeals may also reflect the substantial drop in statistical power that results after excluding cases that did not initiate a prevailing-party appeal.

7.6   Discussion

Results from efforts to model the decision to pursue prevailing-party appeals as well as their outcomes are nuanced, complex, and, on balance, somewhat mixed. Worth underscoring, however, is that prevailing-party appeals – even more so than their traditional, adverse appeal counterparts – are rare events. Indeed, prevailing-party appeals are extraordinarily unusual events. While state civil litigation during these same years generated traditional appeals in 11.8 percent of the concluded trials, prevailing-party appeals emerged from only 2.6 percent of the concluded trials. Completed traditional and prevailing-party appeals were rarer still. That is, while the universe of completed trials generated few appeals, an even small number of these appeals persisted to completion (7.1 of traditional appeals and 1.5 percent of prevailing party appeals). Accordingly, any conclusions drawn from such rare events must be done so cautiously.

What these rare events illustrate, however, is that traditional and prevailing-party appeals' outcomes share one critical trait: both types of

---

[14] Notably, a larger number of case types achieved statistical significance in the Heckman model specification.

civil appeals distribute success asymmetrically between plaintiffs and defendants. Traditional and prevailing-party appeal outcomes differ, however, when it comes to the asymmetry's direction. Specifically, while outcomes in traditional appeals tilted in a direction favoring defendants, prevailing-party appeal outcomes, in contrast, favored plaintiffs.

What to make of the asymmetrical distribution of appellate success – let alone the competing directions of the appeals' tilt – remains unclear and cannot be resolved persuasively by these data. Prior research on traditional appeals noting a tilt favoring defendants implies either a trial court preference for plaintiffs, an appeals court preference for defendants, or that plaintiffs systematically appeal weaker cases (Eisenberg and Heise 2015, p. 122). Results from this study on prevailing-party appeals' outcomes, however, suggest the reciprocal: either a trial court preference for defendants (by failing to fully satisfy plaintiffs' demands at or expectations of trial), an appellate court preference for plaintiffs pursuing prevailing-party appeals, or defendants systematically pursuing comparatively weaker prevailing-party appeals.

As data in this study will not comfortably identify the precise cause (or causes) of the uneven distribution of prevailing-party appeal outcomes broader implications for the civil litigation system persuasively drawn from these results are necessarily limited. On the one hand, the asymmetrical distribution of prevailing-party appeals' success might suggest inefficiencies at the trial court level. That is, if it is the case that trial courts systematically tilt in a direction favoring defendants (by not meeting prevailing plaintiffs' expectations), such a result would suggest some degree of trial court inefficiency. On the other hand, that our state civil litigation rules permit prevailing-party appeals provide one institutional instrument to reduce any trial court inefficiencies through appellate review. Thus, at one level, the appellate process as a whole (including traditional and prevailing-party appeals) can be understood as one institutional mechanism that reduces judicial error and, in so doing, plausibly contributes to greater efficiency and efficacy.

Such an interpretation, however, necessarily assumes that appellate courts are correct when they disrupt trial court decisions. After all, many intuitively assume that when an appellate court disrupts a lower court decision the appeals court is correcting a trial court error. And when appellate courts do so in a systematic manner this implies that "something" is going on at the trial court level which generates systematic error that, for whatever reason, many presume that appellate courts are structurally – or comparatively – better positioned to correct. After all, trial and appellate courts differ, by design, in important ways. For example, appellate courts typically do not take factual testimony from the litigating parties, including the victim, and that, where panels of judges decide appeals, the risk of an erroneous appellate court decision is spread across a number of individual appeals judges.

What this prevailing assumption ignores, however, is that the appellate court data can only empirically identify the existence of asymmetric win rates at appellate courts. How to properly understand or interpret these asymmetric win rates, however, remains beyond the reach of the data. Explanations that ascribe these different appellate court win rates to a systematic trial court "bias" that favors plaintiffs (and when corrected on appeal fuels an appellate court win rate that systematically favors defendants), however intuitively plausible, exposes itself to a similar argument that points in the opposite direction. That is, from the results it remains logically possible that the trial court decisions were, in fact, correct and that it was the appellate courts that introduced error by systematically favoring defendants on appeal (in the traditional appeals context). While logic suggests that it is likely one of the two possibilities along with, perhaps, other possible explanations, neither logic nor data necessarily suggest which explanation is the correct one.

The same logical uncertainty that confounds interpretations of traditional appellate outcomes persists in the admittedly smaller world of prevailing-party appeals. The results indicate, once again, an asymmetric distribution of successful prevailing-party appeals as between those initiated by plaintiffs and defendants. Consequently, the degree to which prevailing-party appeals provide support for an argument that appeals, on net, contribute to a more efficient or better functioning civil litigation system pivots largely on whether one interprets appellate decisions as either reducing or injecting error. While the data in this study persuasively identify important aspects of prevailing-party appeals, particularly the asymmetric distribution of prevailing-party appellate success, limitations in the data preclude imposing the analytic weight necessary to assess the competing interpretations.

References

Clermont, Kevin M., and Theodore Eisenberg. 2001. Appeal From Jury or Judge Trial: Defendants' Advantage. *American Law & Economic Review* 3: 125–64.
2002. Plaintiphobia in the Appellate Courts: Civil Rights Really Do Differ from Negotiable Instruments. *University of Illinois Law Review* 2002: 947–77.

Eisenberg, Theodore. 1990. Testing the Selection Effect: A New Theoretical Framework with Empirical Tests. *Journal of Legal Studies* 19: 337–58.

Eisenberg, Theodore, and Henry S. Farber. 2013. Why Do Plaintiffs Lose Appeals? Biased Trial Courts, Litigious Losers, or Low Trial Win Rates? *American Law & Economic Review* 15: 73–109.

Eisenberg, Theodore, and Michael Heise. 2009. Plaintiphobia in State Courts? An Empirical Study of State Court Trials on Appeal. *Journal of Legal Studies* 38: 121–55.

2015. Plaintiphobia in State Courts Redux? An Empirical Study of State Court Trials on Appeal. *Journal of Empirical Legal Studies* 12: 100–27.

Eisenberg, Theodore, Neil LaFountain, Brian Ostrom, David Rottman, and Martin T. Wells. 2002. Juries, Judges, and Punitive Damages: An Empirical Study. *Cornell Law Review* 87: 743–82.

Eisenberg, Theodore, and Stewart J, Schwab. 1989. What Shapes Perceptions of the Federal Court System? *University of Chicago Law Review* 56: 501–39.

Engstrom, Nora Freeman. 2018. *The Diminished Trial.* Unpublished manuscript. Stanford University, September.

Federal Rules of Civil Procedure, 2016. Washington, DC: U.S. Governmental Printing Office.

Galanter, Marc. 2004. The Vanishing Trial: An Examination of Trials and Related Matters in Federal and State Courts. *Journal of Empirical Legal Studies* 1(1): 459–570.

Heise, Michael. 2000. Justice Delayed?: An Empirical Analysis of Civil Case Disposition Time. *Case Western Reserve Law Review* 50: 813–49.

Holm, Anders, and Mads M. Jaeger. 2011. Dealing with Selection Bias in Educational Transition Models: The Bivariate Probit Selection Model. *Research in Social Stratification and Mobility* 29: 311–22.

Lee, Yoon-Ho, and Daniel Klerman. 2016. The Priest-Klein Hypotheses: Proofs and Generality. *International Review of Law and Economics* 48: 59–76.

Posner, Richard A. 2014. *Economic Analysis of Law* (9th ed.). New York: Wolters Kluwer.

Priest, George L., and Benjamin Klein. 1984. The Selection of Disputes for Litigation. *Journal of Legal Studies* 13: 1–55.

Revesz, Richard L. 2000. Litigation and Settlement in the Federal Appellate Courts: Impact of Panel Selection Procedures on Ideologically Divided Courts. *Journal of Legal Studies* 29: 685–710.

Shapiro, Martin. 1980. Appeal. *Law & Society Review* 14: 629–61.

Shavell, Steven. 1995. The Appeals Process as a Means of Error Correction. *Journal of Legal Studies* 24: 379–426.

U.S. Department of Justice. Bureau of Justice Statistics. 2004. *Civil Justice Survey of State Courts, 2001[United States]* (computer file). Ann Arbor, MI: Inter-University Consortium for Political and Social Research (Study No. 3957).

2006. *Supplemental Survey of Civil Appeals, 2001[United States]* (computer file). Ann Arbor, MI: Inter-University Consortium for Political and Social Research (Study No. 4539).

2009. *Civil Justice Survey of State Courts, 2005 [United States]* (computer file). Ann Arbor, MI: Inter-University Consortium for Political and Social Research (Study No. 23862).

2012. *Civil Justice Survey of Trials on Appeal, 2005 [United States]* (computer file). Ann Arbor, MI: Inter-University Consortium for Political and Social Research (Study No. 32501).

The Evolution of Case Influence in Modern Consumer Standard Form Contracts

FLORENCIA MAROTTA-WURGLER

8.1 Introduction

How does a case's influence evolve? This chapter considers the trajectory of influence for cases involving three kinds of modern standard form contracts using a hand-collected data set of all case law regarding the enforceability of shrinkwraps, browsewraps, and clickwraps. These contracts became pervasive with the rise of remote, electronic commerce, and transactions through mobile platforms. Consumers are typically presented with the terms of standard form agreements in text boxes on screens, through embedded links, or after purchase. These new contracting practices have challenged traditional contract law principles of offer and acceptance and presented courts with an opportunity to adapt such doctrines to new environments. A close look at the trajectory of influence of case influence during this dynamic period offers a number of insights into the evolution of precedent and judicial influence.

Specifically, I explore the evolution of precedent and judicial influence by examining the relative influence of each individual case in the data set introduced in Bar-Gill, Ben-Shahar, and Marotta-Wurgler (2017), which tracks cases' facts, rules, guiding rationales, and conclusions reached, as well as other information, such as court, year, and procedural details. Case influence is measured by the number of times a case has been cited or followed, with a particular focus on out-of-state citations – the standard measure of influence used in the literature, given that courts are not bound by intra-jurisdictional precedent.[1] For this work, I collected additional, granular, year-by-year counts of out-of-state citations to dive deeply into the dynamics of judicial influence.

---

[1] For federal cases, the data set tracks out-of-circuit citations, although for convenience I refer to these as "out-of-state" as well.

There is a rich literature that measures the influence of cases, judges, and courts. Landes and Posner (1976) analyze citations to measure influence and find that precedent depreciates over time. They suggest that the body of judicial decisions in earlier periods can be understood as a capital stock offering guidance to subsequent courts. As new circumstances and conditions emerge, the value of such guidance depreciates, leading courts to abandon older precedent for new precedent to replace it. Hathaway (2001) proposes a path dependence theory in which early decisions in particular areas might significantly affect the evolution of the case law in a particular area, as subsequent courts are likely to anchor on (and cite) the earlier decision.

Other studies offer empirical examinations of precedent. Farber (2005) finds that supreme court precedent fits a power law distribution. Studies by Choi and Gulati (2004a; 2004b; 2005) and Landes, Lessig, and Solomine (1998) find that influence is concentrated in very few courts and judges. Gulati and Sanchez (2002) identify a "superstar" effect, where the opinions of a handful of judges account for the vast majority of citations relative to the next-best performing judges, upon aggregating citations over many areas. Choi, Gulati, and Posner (2009) find that citation counts also display superstar, or "tournament winner," effects.

This chapter contributes by examining the relative influence of cases addressing a single issue across jurisdictions. In addition, an analysis of the relative influence of citations can also inform debates about whether cases converge or not toward a particular rule or standard, which may be the efficient one. An extensive theoretical literature in law and economics has debated whether the common law evolves toward efficiency. Posner (1973) posited that common law judges would agree on efficient rules and that, consequently, would converge toward the efficient rule across jurisdictions over time. Cooter, Kornhauser, and Lane (1979) and Kornhauser (1996) refined this by noting that, even if imperfectly informed about essential aspects of the litigants' behavior, welfare-maximizing judges will avail themselves of the mechanism of precedent to adopt positions that tend toward efficiency. Additional arguments by Priest (1977) and Rubin (1977) supported the convergence hypothesis by demonstrating that as long as transaction costs are positive, efficient rules will persist longer as controlling precedents – independent of judges' attitudes toward efficiency or their ability to distinguish efficient and inefficient outcomes – because inefficient rules are more costly than efficient ones.

Convergence and efficient outcomes can arise even when judges are biased or have self-serving motives, an account of judging most famously proposed by Justice Holmes (1897). If case law is understood from an evolutionary standpoint whereby good decisions rule out bad ones over time and experimentation, as posited by Cardozo (1921) and refined by Gennaioli and Shleifer (2007), then the common law could converge toward efficiency independent of judicial attitudes. Hadfield (1992) notes, however that bias in the cases observed by efficiency-oriented judges may prevent them from reaching to the efficient rule. Niblett, Posner, and Shleifer (2010) examine the evolution of one rule empirically but do not find convergence over time, however. Of course, there can be convergence without efficiency. "Precedential cascades," where likeminded judges who are not necessarily bound by precedent or similar facts emulate one another, can lead rulings to converge into a single outcome even if it is inefficient. Daugherty and Reinganum (1999) and Gillette (1998) discuss the potential lock-in effects that might arise regarding precedent. Kuran and Sunstein (1999) and Talley (1999) explore the conditions under which precedential cascades can arise in judicial decision making, including rule-boundedness and short tenure.

The empirical method used in this chapter is not without limitations. Highly influential cases that settle and issue and lead to convergence will likely rarely be cited and will thus not enter the analysis (Landes and Posner 1976). Relatedly, it is difficult to address the selection effects created by cases that settle (Priest and Klein 1984; Shavell 1996; Stone 1985).

The results show that, consistent with previous studies, and as documented in Issacharoff and Marotta-Wurgler (2019), a handful of opinions come to dominate a particular area of the law. Tracking granular citation patterns also yields new insights: instead of observing patterns of jurisdictional experimentation and competition, it appears that for each of the three types of contracts studied, a single case comes to dominate the field at a pivotal time and becomes deeply influential across jurisdictions and court hierarchies. Each area yields a "tournament winner" whose influence remains steady or increases during the period under study, unlike most other cases, whose influence fades. A possible explanation for this finding is that cases from prestigious courts or judges are more likely to receive attention and thus receive the benefit of an initial citation bump. Yet these only propel further citations by later courts who, facing low search costs, find cases that already cite such opinions. This continues to snowball going forward, and their influence continue to grow. These cases might continue to be cited, even as new "superstars" emerge. Like most cases, the influence of "superstars" doesn't depreciate over time. Rather, subsequent courts continue to cite them in addition to, other, more recent cases, suggesting that citation practices of "superstar" cases might experience some encrustation.

Yet the case law is also adaptable. Recent innovations in how businesses present their terms to consumers injected a new factor into the contract formation process and gave courts the opportunity to refine the conditions that would ensure a contract's enforceability. The data show how new cases emerged and case law evolved to adapt to these circumstances. Interestingly, during this new phase a leading case by a federal court becomes dominant and continues to exert influence in subsequent cases, repeating the previous pattern of legal evolution.

Section 8.2 presents the sample and summary statistics. Section 8.3 presents and discusses the results and their implications. Section 8.4 concludes.

8.2 Sample and Summary Statistics

8.2.1 Sample Overview

This chapter studies the trajectory of case influence regarding the enforcement of three relatively new types of consumer contracts, shrinkwraps, clickwraps, and browsewraps. Shrinkwraps, or "pay now, terms later" ("PNTL") contracts, involve any transaction where payment precedes the presentation of terms.[2] Clickwraps appear in online transactions where assent is sought by asking a contracting party to agree to terms by clicking an "I agree" box. Browsewraps do not require any action to manifest assent. Instead, hyperlinks to the terms, sometimes accompanied by a notice, are placed on a webpage and assent is manifested by silence, taking the benefit of the services offered, or continuing the process of completing a purchase.

Issacharoff and Marotta-Wurgler (2018) analyze the migration of cases from state to federal courts and the rise in class actions and identify the tournament-winning cases. In that chapter, and here, the sample was as in Bar-Gill, Ben-Shahar, and Marotta-Wurgler (2017). The data set includes, for each contract type, all available state and federal court opinions, including unpublished ones, reported on Lexis and Westlaw. The process of collecting cases and other data is explained in detail in Bar-Gill et al. (2017). Each case was coded on multiple dimensions,

---

[2] *See, e.g.*, Brower v. Gateway 2000, Inc., 676 N.Y.S.2d 569 (App. Div. 1998).

including court characteristics, procedural details, relevant facts (e.g., the characteristics of the transaction and the precise manner in which the terms were presented), intervening factors that might have affected the court's reasoning and final outcome, and rationales articulated by the courts. These included, among others, precedent, Uniform Commercial Code (UCC), and (Second) Restatement of Contracts sections relied upon.

Overall, there are 67 shrinkwrap cases, 32 browsewrap cases, and 110 clickwrap cases involving consumer disputes (no employment cases are included). They run from an early "terms later" case decided in 1954 through cases decided in 2016. The Bar-Gill et al. (2017) sample also includes citation-based measures of influence used in the literature. These include the number of times a case is cited by out-of-state courts and the number of times a case is followed by other courts. Citations by out-of-state courts is the traditional measure of influence. Caldeira (1985), Choi et al. (2009), and Landes et al. (1998), among others, prefer this measure because it reflects the impact of each decision beyond intrastate and intra-circuit norms. Whether other courts followed the court's treatment of the issue in question is a narrower but stronger notion of influence that helps address the concern that cases might not be cited for the issue of interest. While noisy, citation measures are a sensible proxy for influence. For this chapter, I gathered year-by-year out-of-state citations for each case. This allows for a more granular analysis of the evolution of influence.

8.2.2 Summary Statistics

Table 8.1 shows the cases and citation summary statistics. The left columns in Table 8.1 break down the cases by contract and court type. In Panel A, out of the 67 cases addressing the enforceability of PNTL cases, 50 were decided in federal court, and the vast majority of those were district court decisions. For the state cases, the opposite is true; all but two are from high courts. The dominance of federal cases is also present in browsewrap cases and clickwrap cases, reported in Panels B and C, respectively. Federal cases represent 23 out of 32 browsewrap cases and 88 out of 110 clickwrap cases. Again, the enforceability of these forms of contracts has rarely been addressed by state supreme courts, with only three such decisions for clickwraps and one for browsewraps. The high fraction of cases adjudicated in federal court is itself surprising and interesting. Issacharoff and Marotta-Wurgler

Table 8.1 *Sample cases and summary statistics*

	Number	Out-of-State Case Cites (s.d.)	Out-of-State Case Cites/Year (s.d.)	Followed (s.d.)
Panel A. Pay Now, Terms Later (PNTL) Cases				
All Courts	67	12.0 (25.0)	0.7 (1.4)	4.3 (8.6)
Federal	50	12.9 (28.1)	0.9 (1.5)	4.8 (9.9)
Appeals	8	49.4 (55.7)	3.0 (2.8)	14.4 (20.8)
District	42	5.9 (10.3)	0.4 (0.6)	2.8 (3.9)
State	17	9.5 (12.0)	0.4 (0.5)	3.0 (3.4)
Supreme	7	14.4 (13.2)	0.6 (0.4)	3.6 (3.6)
Appellate	8	6.9 (11.7)	0.4 (0.6)	2.8 (3.7)
Trial	2	3 (1.4)	0.2 (0.1)	2.0 (1.4)
Panel B. Browsewrap Cases				
All Courts	32	13.3 (31.4)	2.1 (3.1)	3.5 (5.2)
Federal	23	16.5 (36.6)	2.5 (3.4)	4.0 (5.7)
Appeals	3	72.0 (91.8)	8.5 (6.5)	9.7 (12.7)
District	20	8.2 (10.0)	1.6 (1.7)	3.1 (3.8)
State	9	5 (5.7)	0.9 (1.3)	2.4 (3.9)
Supreme	1	0	0	0 (.)
Appellate	6	7.0 (6.1)	1.3 (1.5)	3.3 (4.6)
Trial	2	1.5 (2.1)	0.3 (0.4)	1 (1.4)
Panel C. Clickwrap Cases				
All Courts	110	4.6 (7.1)	0.7 (1.3)	1.9 (2.7)
Federal	88	5.1 (7.4)	0.8 (1.4)	2.0 (2.5)
Appeals	3	22.0 (12.2)	5.3 (3.1)	3.3 (3.2)
District	85	4.5 (6.5)	0.6 (1.0)	1.9 (2.5)
State	22	3 (5.3)	0.3 (0.5)	1.6 (3.1)
Supreme	3	1.7 (1.5)	0.2 (0.2)	3.0 (5.2)
Appellate	14	3.9 (6.3)	0.3 (0.4)	1.9 (3.2)
Trial	5	1.2 (2.7)	0.4 (0.9)	0 (.)

Cases addressing the enforcement of shrinkwraps (PNTLs), browsewraps, and clickwraps. The earliest case (a PNTL) is from 1954 and the latest are from 2016. Out-of-state case citations (for federal cases, we use out-of-circuit case citations) are counted through 2017, whereas number of times followed is counted through 2014 and therefore not included in the average for cases decided in 2015 and 2016. *Source*: Issacharoff and Marotta-Wurgler (2019).

(2018) hypothesize that the prevalence of federal court opinions in addressing inherent state common law questions might in part reflect the rise in class actions and the role of the Class Action Fairness Act of 2005.

The columns on the right focus on influence as reflected by total number out-of-state and circuit citations since the case was decided; number of out-of-state and circuit citations per year (to account for the fact that older cases will have accumulated more citations, all else equal); and the number of times a case was followed. Federal cases addressing the enforceability of PNTLs have accumulated an average of 12.9 out-of-circuit citations, with circuit court cases obtaining an average of 49.4 out-of-circuit cites and district court cases receiving an average of 5.9 out-of-circuit cites. The high standard deviations in some cells indicate that high averages are driven by a few particularly influential cases –"tournament winners," as described by Issacharoff and Marotta-Wurgler (2019). Federal court opinions are more likely to be cited than other states' cases, which are cited an average of 9.5 times. Supreme court cases have more citations (14.4 on average) than state appellate and trial cases (6.9 and 3 on average, respectively), but, perhaps surprisingly, they are on average much less influential than federal circuit court cases.

The next column reports citations per year. Again, federal courts of appeals are outliers, with an average of 3 citations per year per case, while state supreme courts receive only 0.6 citations per year per case. The last column reports the average citations under the "followed" category. The pattern of citations is similar to the other two measures, except that the dominance of federal circuit court opinions is even stronger, with an average of 14.4 times followed versus 3.6 times followed for state supreme court decisions.

Panels B and C find some similar patterns in the influence of browse-wrap and clickwrap cases, respectively. Like PNTLs, circuit cases are leading in terms of average citations by remarkable margins. Circuit court opinions regarding the enforceability of browsewraps have accumulated an average of 72 out-of-circuit cites (and 8.5 cites per year), whereas the one supreme court opinion has never been cited. The three circuit court opinions involving the enforceability of clickwraps have received an average of 22 out-of-circuit citations (and 5.3 per year) versus much smaller citation numbers for the three state supreme court cases. As with PNTLs, large standard deviations indicate that these differences may be driven by one or a handful of cases.

8.3   Tracing Case Influence Over Time

Are all precedents created equal? This section explores whether precedent depreciates over time and analyzes the difference between the tournament winners and the rest.

8.3.1   Shrinkwraps

There are cases dating back to the 1950s addressing the enforceability of contracts in situations where payment preceded terms – an example is a case where warranties were stashed inside goods being purchased, such as in the glove compartment of a new car. But the practice of presenting terms after purchase became prominent with remote transactions and with sales of software in the early 1990s. Transactions involving software often involved a purchase where the terms were wrapped inside the box, and the terms could be accessed only after payment. This new form of contracting was challenging more conventional forms of contracting, where terms, even if non-negotiable, were usually at least available to review before purchase.

A number of cases addressed the enforceability of such software contracts, commonly known as End User License Agreements, though most involved business-to-business transactions. The most notable case among these is *ProCD* v. *Zeidenberg,* 86 F. 3d 1447 19, a 1996 case in which Judge Easterbrook held that a software license agreement that was shrinkwrapped inside a software box that could be accessed only after the purchaser paid for the product and opened the box was nonetheless enforceable as long as the seller gave reasonable notice of the post-purchase terms and a reasonable opportunity to return the product if they were unacceptable. The holding reversed the district court's decision, where the court refused to enforce the license after concluding that one cannot agree to hidden terms.

The *ProCD* decision, deemed controversial by many academics and commentators at the time, forged a new path in the law (Bern 2004; Braucher 2001; Petit 1998). Subsequent cases, such as *Hill* v. *Gateway,* 105 F.3d 1147 (2007), addressed the enforceability of such contracts in other contexts. In *Hill,* a consumer purchased a computer over the phone and the terms arrived inside the box when the computer was delivered. At the time when *ProCD* and *Hill* were decided, the court *hearing Klocek* v. *Gateway, Inc.,* 104 F. Supp. 2d 1332 (2000), a case with facts almost identical as those in *Hill,* declined to find that the terms in the box became part of the consumer contract, holding instead that such terms were proposed modifications by the seller and not explicitly agreed upon by the consumer under UCC 2-207. This established a seeming conflict in the treatment of these increasingly popular types of standard form contract.

Bar-Gill et al. (2017) find the logic of *ProCD* took over, as seen in Figure 8.1A. It reports the running sum of out-of-state citations to each of the 67 cases, including state supreme court cases, addressing the enforceability of PNTLs. In terms of out-of-state influence (here, out-of-circuit cases), *ProCD* and *Hill* have eclipsed all others. The granular, yearly citation patterns yield additional insights regarding the trajectory of case influence. Both cases have steadily influenced other courts since they were decided and their influence continues to grow, even over cases that are hierarchically more important, like state supreme and appellate courts. Indeed, the influence of these two dominant cases shows no sign of depreciating even after twenty years, in contrast to the patterns in Landes and Posner (1976). Similar to the patterns of influence across judges and courts, these cases (informally) exhibit a power law-like pattern in that there are a small number of clear winners that absorb much of the attention. The influence of tournament winners, at least in this setting, only increases over time, as opposed to other cases, whose influence tends to fade.

In addition, the large and steady influence of *ProCD* is consistent with the convergence hypothesis, as courts come to increasingly rely on the case when addressing the enforceability of a PNTL. Of course, this would be an interesting observation but wouldn't matter much if all cases applied the same logic and resulted in the same outcome. Yet this is not the situation. Prior to *ProCD*, and even contemporaneously, when *Klocek* was decided, there was a roughly even split between cases enforcing and refusing to enforce PNTLs (Bar-Gill et al. 2017). As time progressed, however, courts began following the logic of *ProCD* and *Hill* and enforcement of PNTLs increased as long as the requirements of reasonable notice and opportunity to return, as spelled out in those cases, were present. And as Figure 8.1A shows, by 2017, most other cases, including state supreme court cases, are rarely cited while *ProCD* and *Hill* continue their meteoric rise.

The existence of a clear leader doesn't imply that every jurisdiction has converged to a single approach. The graph reports out-of-state citations, indicating that courts are exercising discretion in their choice of precedential support. Judges must follow the doctrine of *stare decisis*, which

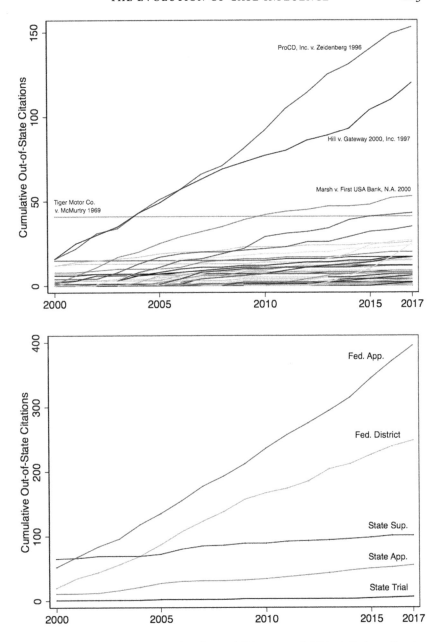

Figure 8.1 Shrinkwraps (PNTLs): influential (A) cases and (B) jurisdictions. Panel A shows the running sum of out-of-state citations (for federal cases, we use out-of-circuit citations) to each case. Leading cases are indicated. Panel B shows the running sum of out-of-state citations to all cases by court type, including Federal Appellate, Federal District, State Supreme, State Appellate, and State Trial. $N = 67$ cases.

binds them to the decisions of the higher courts in their state or circuit (if applying the same law). While *ProCD* and *Hill* are clearly the most influential, their influence might not reach across all jurisdictions because some courts might follow conflicting precedent created by the higher courts in their states. Yet this is not the case, as almost all states follow the *ProCD* approach (Bar-Gill et al. 2017). In unreported results, I find that out-of-circuit cites and intra-circuit cites for each case are highly correlated, so that the trends reported in the figure are consistent with patterns of influence within states and circuits.

Of course, while there is evidence of convergence, the findings cannot tell whether the observed convergence is consistent with an efficiency story or a "lock-in" or informational cascade story. It does appear, however, that a single case or two can be responsible for moving the entire case law in a particular direction.

Figure 8.1B explores this further by reporting the out-of-state influence of cases over time grouped by court type. The bottom three lines represent the out-of-state influence of state trial, state appellate, and state supreme courts, revealing that higher courts are more influential than lower ones, with the supreme court being cumulatively the most influential. The top two lines represent the influence of federal appellate and federal district courts, which have come to overshadow all state court precedent. Note, too, that the while the influence of state court cases fades to zero over time, federal courts, and particular federal appellate court cases, grow in influence.

8.3.2   Browsewraps

Browsewraps, too, are a relatively new form of contracting, but one that exists mostly in transactions made online. For this reason, the case law regarding their enforceability is sparser and younger. The quintessential browsewrap contract is the "Terms of Use" or "Terms of Service" that appears at the bottom of a webpage. It is only when the individual actively and voluntarily clicks on the hyperlink to the contract that the terms can be read. Litigation over these terms began around 2000 with the rise of e-commerce.

As with shrinkwraps, an early case set the framework for all that followed. In *Specht* v. *Netscape*, 306 F.3d 17 (2d Cir. 2002), an individual challenged an arbitration clause included in an End User License Agreement that was presented as a browsewrap by being hyperlinked at the bottom of a web page, and that could only be seen after scrolling down two pages. Judge Sotomayor held that the browsewrap was unenforceable because the individual was not given actual or constructive notice of the terms. The implicit holding was that acceptance by silence could constitute valid asset under such circumstances as long as the requirement of notice was satisfied.

Over the next few years, online transacting grew significantly and firms began innovating in the way in which they presented terms to consumers, thus offering courts opportunities to refine the application of the doctrine to new sets of facts. The most prominent innovations involved increased reliance on acceptance by silence, where terms would be presented as hyperlinks next to buttons saying "Purchase Now" or "Register" instead of, for example, the unambiguous "I agree" box characteristic of clickwraps, or the remotely located "Terms of Use" or "Privacy Policy" at the bottom of a webpage, like the contract at issue in *Specht*. Now the consumer was asked to take an unambiguous action to agree to the transaction (by clicking "Purchase Now," for example) but not necessarily to the terms. *Specht* had dictated that, to be enforceable, such contracts should provide sufficient notice and an opportunity to reject, yet it did not provide specifics as to how such notice could be given. A later case, *Nguyen* v. *Barnes Noble*, 763 F.3d 1171 (9th Cir. 2014), did just that by adapting the framework laid out in *Specht* to these new forms of contract presentation and explained in detail what would constitute adequate notice of the terms under the particular sets of facts in the case. Later cases, still relying on the principles of *Specht*, would also cite and rely on *Nguyen* to evaluate what types of disclosures would constitute adequate notice, so that now both cases would be cited and relied upon by subsequent courts: *Specht* for laying out the principle of notice and *Nguyen* for the proposition that a court must engage with the particulars of the website design to determine whether notice of terms was sufficient or not.

Figure 8.2A shows the running sum of out-of-state citations to each case regarding the enforceability of browsewraps. It depicts the influence of each case law regarding the enforceability of browsewraps over time and reveals a pattern similar to the shrinkwrap case law. Here, too, an early circuit court case emerged to eclipse all others. This is consistent with tournament winner pattern observed in prior studies and with PNTLs. What about the evolution of precedent? As with *ProCD*, *Specht* became the leader and its influence continued to rise as all other cases' influence subsided. Yet, uniquely, Figure 8.2A also evidences how *Nguyen*, decided twelve years later, begins building momentum and,

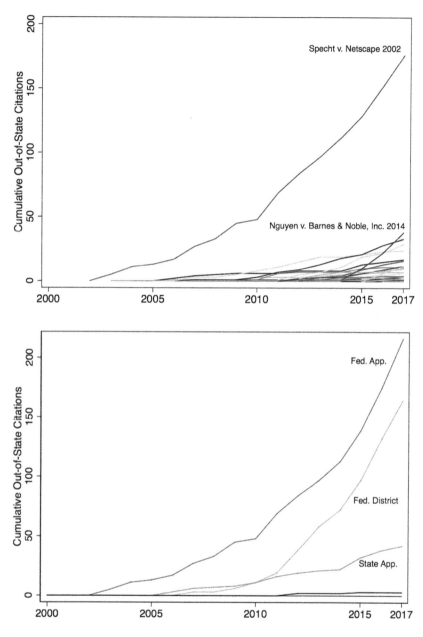

Figure 8.2 Browsewraps: influential (A) cases and (B) jurisdictions. Panel A shows the running sum of out-of-state citations (for federal cases, we use out-of-circuit citations) to each case. Leading cases are indicated. Panel B shows the running sum of out-of-state citations to all cases by court type, including Federal Appellate, Federal District, State Supreme, State Appellate, and State Trial. $N = 32$ cases.

together with *Specht*, becomes increasingly influential. Landes and Posner (1976) predict that precedent will depreciate over time and be replaced by more informative one. In the context of browsewraps, precedent has yet to depreciate over time; rather, influential decisions combine with more recent ones to work in tandem and offer a more comprehensive whole.

The findings are also consistent with the convergence and precedential cascades theories, as most cases use the framework laid out in *Specht* to determine whether a browsewrap is enforceable across jurisdictions.[3] Contrary to the precedential cascade theories, however, the rise in influence of *Nguyen* suggests that courts might not be following precedent automatically. By 2017, the top two cases in terms of influence are *Specht* and *Nguyen*. While the influence of relatively recent cases remains modest overall, the rate at which *Nguyen* is being cited over its short lifetime roughly matches *Specht*. In this area, too, "superstar" effects are apparent.

Figure 8.2B explores the relative influence of browsewrap cases at the jurisdiction level. The patterns and trends are very similar to those in the shrinkwrap space, with the difference that the influence of federal courts is not just high, but increasingly so; the growth in cumulative citations is accelerating. State supreme courts are a distant third in terms of cumulative influence.

8.3.3 Clickwraps

Clickwraps arose with online contracting. When using clickwraps, firms commonly disclose terms in a scroll box next to an "I agree" box where consumers are invited to unambiguously agree to the terms. Like with PNTLs and browsewraps, as long as terms are clearly and conspicuously disclosed, courts will deem them enforceable absent fraud or other intervening factors. When clickwraps first appeared in online transactions, courts analogized clicking "I agree" to signing on the dotted line in a paper contract. Thus, once the E-Sign Act declaring electronic signatures enforceable was passed in 2000, clickwraps did not represent decisional innovations to courts.

As noted in the previous section, firms began innovating in how they transacted with and presented terms to consumers in the mid-2000s.

---

[3] A detailed analysis of the case law across the states is reported in the Reporters' Notes of the draft Restatement of Consumer Contracts (2018).

Some of these innovations clouded the distinction between clickwraps and browsewraps. Consumers were not necessarily invited to click on "I agree" buttons. Rather, they were asked to click "Continue" or "Purchase Now" buttons and place the terms in hyperlinks nearby, thus requiring courts to determine whether the consumer had received reasonable notice of the terms. A number of cases around that time, beginning with *Fteja* v. *Facebook* 841 F. Supp. 2d 829 (S.D.N.Y. 2012), and culminating with *Berkson* v. *Gogo*, 97 F. Supp. 3d 359 (E.D.N.Y. 2015) in the period studied, laid out a framework for determining the effectiveness of disclosure in nuanced ways that engaged with the particulars of the disclosures.

Figure 8.3A depicts the running sum of out-of-state citations for all clickwrap enforcement cases. Unlike with shrinkwraps and browsewraps, where a single case or two have quickly come to dominate, the evolution of the case law in the clickwrap context doesn't reveal one superstar case from the start. A possible reason of this is that early cases may have been fairly straightforward applications of brick-and-mortar standard form contracts in terms of what constitutes adequate notice and given the signature analogy. That said, *Hotmail Corp.* v. *Van$ Money Pie, Inc.*, 47 U.S.P.Q.2d 1020, 1998 WL 388389 (N.D.Cal.), a California district court case, took a slight lead early on, only to lose its influence by 2005. *Forrest* v. *Verizon*, 805 A.2d 1007 (Dist. of Columbia Court of Appeals, 2002), which again affirmed the enforcement of clickwraps when notice was present, overtook it in terms of cumulative influence. It is more recently, when novel forms of presenting terms challenged the brick-and-mortar analogy, that saw superstars emerge. Cases like *Fteja,* which offered an in-depth analysis of the typology of contract disclosures, began to gain influence. Indeed, their influence sharpens considerably around 2015, when litigation over these novel forms of presenting terms, especially in mobile devices, increased.

Unlike the case of browsewraps, where the early winner paired up with a subsequent runner up, early leaders saw their influence depreciate over time, perhaps because they had little to contribute in the first place. Rather, it is the later cases, like *Fteja* that share the characteristic of the other tournament winners: a meteoric rise and continued influence over time.

Figure 8.3B depicts influence by court and reveals the most unusual pattern of all three contract areas. It is the federal district courts, which have absolutely no precedential authority, that have been by far the most influential beyond their own circuits. Like with shrinkwraps and

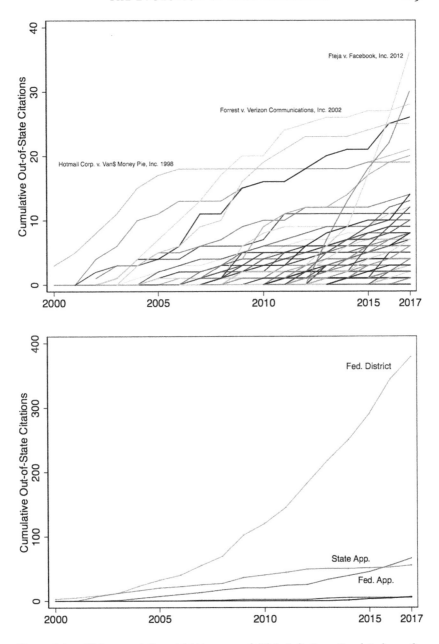

Figure 8.3   Clickwraps: influential (A) cases and (B) jurisdictions. Panel A shows the running sum of out-of-state citations (for federal cases, we use out-of-circuit citations) to each case. Leading cases are indicated. Panel B shows the running sum of out-of-state citations to all cases by court type, including Federal Appellate, Federal District, State Supreme, State Appellate, and State Trial. $N = 110$ cases.

browsewraps, this dominance is due to a handful of cases and increases over time.

8.4 Conclusion and Implications

A look at the entire case law regarding the enforcement of three different types of modern consumer standard form contracts, at a granular level using year-by-year citation rates, reveals an interesting story regarding the evolution of case influence, as well as where the law originates and how it evolves.

Consistent with other studies, I find that each area studied exhibits a tournament winner which garners much of the attention of judges deciding subsequent cases. How these superstar cases fare over time? Posner and Landes (1976) found that precedent generally depreciates over time. While this is true for most cases, this trajectory does not fit the evolution of tournament winners. These cases exhibit unique traits. First, they tend to be legally innovative. Second, their influence reaches across jurisdictions court hierarchy. Third, the influence of tournament winners tends to grow over time, in contrast with the findings of Landes and Posner (1976).

I also find that cases tend to converge toward a particular rule or standard over time, possibly due to the power law pattern in citations, where a clear winner absorbs much of the attention of subsequent judges. The results enrich our understanding of the evolution of judicial influence and help inform theories of the evolution of precedent and the common law.

References

Bar-Gill, Oren, Omri Ben-Shahar, and Florencia Marotta-Wurgler. 2017. Searching for the Common Law: An Empirical Approach to the Restatement of Consumer Contracts. *University of Chicago Law Review* 84: 7–35.

Bern, Roger C. 2004. "Terms Later" Contracting: Bad Economics, Bad Morals, and a Bad Idea for a Uniform Law, Judge Easterbrook Notwithstanding. *Journal of Law and Policy* 12: 641–796.

Braucher, Jean. 2001. UCITA and the Concept of Assent. *PLI/PAT* 673: 175–86.

Caldeira, Gregory A. 1985. The Transmission of Legal Precedent: A Study of State Supreme Courts. *American Political Science Review* 79: 178–94.

Cardozo, Benjamin N. 1921. *The Nature of the Judicial Process.* New Haven, CT: Yale University Press.

Choi, Stephen J., and G. Mitu Gulati. 2004a. A Tournament of Judges? *California Law Review* 92: 299–322.

    2004b. Choosing the Next Supreme Court Justice: An Empirical Ranking of Judge Performance. *Southern California Law Review* 78: 23–118.

    2005. Mr. Justice Posner? Unpacking the Statistics. *New York University Annual Survey of American Law* 61: 19–43.

Choi, Stephen J., G. Mitu Gulati, and Eric A. Posner, 2009. Judicial Evaluations and Information Forcing: Ranking State High Courts and Their Judges. *Duke Law Journal* 58: 1313–81.

Cooter, Robert, Lewis Kornhauser, and David Lane. 1979. Liability Rules, Limited Information, and the Role of Precedent. *Bell Journal of Economics* 10: 366–73.

Daughety, Andrew F., and Jennifer F. Reinganum. 1999. Stampede to Judgment: Persuasive Influence and Herding Behavior by Courts. *American Law and Economics Review* 1: 158–89.

Farber, Daniel A. 2005. Supreme Court Selection and Measures of Past Judicial Performance. *Florida State University Law Review* 32: 1175–96.

Gennaioli, Nicola, and Andrei Shleifer. 2007. The Evolution of Common Law. *Journal of Political Economy* 115: 43–68.

Gillette, Clayton P. 1998. Lock-In Effects in Law and Norms. *Boston University Law Review* 78: 813–42.

Gulati, Mitu, and Veronica Sanchez. 2002. Giants in a World of Pygmies? Testing the Superstar Hypothesis with Judicial Opinions in Casebooks. *Iowa Law Review* 87: 1141–212.

Hadfield, Gillian. 1992. Bias in the Evolution of Legal Rules. *Georgetown Law Journal* 80: 583–616.

Hathaway, Oona. 2001. Path Dependence in the Law: The Course and Pattern of Legal Change in a Common Law System. *Iowa Law Review* 86: 101–65.

Holmes, Oliver Wendell. 1897. The Path of the Law. *Harvard Law Review* 10: 457–78.

Issacharoff, Samuel, and Florencia Marotta-Wurgler. 2019. *The Hollowed Out Common Law*. 67 UCLA Law Review (2019).

Kornhauser, Lewis A. 1996. Notes on the Logic of Legal Change. Pp. 169–83 in *Social Rules: Origin; Character; Logic; Change*, edited by David Braybrooke. Boulder, CO: Westview.

Kuran, Timur and Cass Sunstein. 1999. Availability Cascades and Risk Regulation. *Stanford Law Review* 51: 683–768.

Landes, William M., Lessig, Lawrence, and Solimine, Michael E. 1998. Judicial Influence: A Citation Analysis of Federal Courts of Appeal Judges. *Journal of Legal Studies* 27: 271.

Landes, William M., and Richard A. Posner. 1976. Legal Precedent: A Theoretical and Empirical Analysis. *Journal of Law and Economics* 19(2): 249–307.

Niblett, Anthony, Richard A Posner, and Andrei Shleifer. 2010. The Evolution of a Legal Rule. *Journal of Legal Studies* 39: 325–58.

Petit, Christopher L. 1998. The Problem with "Money Now, Terms Later": ProCD, Inc. v. Zeidenberg and the Enforceability of "Shrinkwrap" Software Licenses. *Loyola of Los Angeles Law Review* 31: 325–52.

Posner, Richard A. 1973. *Economic Analysis of Law.* New York: Little, Brown.

Priest, George L. 1977. The Common Law Process and the Selection of Efficient Rules. *Journal of Legal Studies* 6: 65–82.

Priest, George L., and Benjamin Klein. 1984. The Selection of Disputes for Litigation. *Journal of Legal Studies* 13: 1–55.

Rubin, Paul. 1977. Why Is the Common Law Efficient? *Journal of Legal Studies* 6: 51–63.

Shavell, Steven. 1996. Any Frequency of Plaintiff Victory at Trial Is Possible. *Journal of Legal Studies* 25: 493–501.

Stone, Julius. 1985. *Precedent and Law: Dynamics of Common Law Growth.* Sydney: Butterworths.

Talley, Eric L. 1999. Precedential Cascades: A Critical Appraisal. *Southern California Law Review* 73: 87–138.

Judging Insurance Antidiscrimination Law

RONEN AVRAHAM, ALMA COHEN, AND ITY SHURTZ

9.1 Introduction

Judging insurance antidiscrimination laws is very important for efficient insurance markets.[1] Most states in the United States as well as most countries around the world prohibit insurance companies from discriminating based on various grounds, such as race, gender, etc., unless such discrimination is fair. However, courts have been struggling to understand what "fair discrimination" means.

In the absence of legal constraints, insurers can be expected to segregate policyholders into separate risk pools based on the differences in their risk profiles. Insurers can justify doing so on grounds that (i) it is fair to charge different premiums to different groups based on their differing risks and (ii) doing so incentivizes risk reduction by insureds.

The use of some policyholder characteristics that are closely tied to her driving habits, such as mileage driven, is not controversial. Identifying someone who spends more time on the road as a higher-risk policyholder, and charging a higher premium accordingly, does not raise significant policy concerns. However, insurers' use of characteristics such as gender, race, credit score, and even age does raise policy issues.

Insurers like to use characteristics such as gender, race, credit score, and age because they are correlated with risks and can thus serve as a cheap proxy for risks. Because these proxies are based on nothing but actuarial science, they are believed by some to not be problematic. This approach was echoed by one American court that postulated that "risk discrimination is not race discrimination" (National Association

---

[1] We thank Chen Fisher for excellent research assistance.

for The Advancement of Colored People 1992). On the other hand, many policy-makers would prefer to limit their use. For instance, in a landmark case the US Supreme Court once said in the context of gender and insurance: "[e]ven a true generalization about [a] class cannot justify class-based treatment" (Arizona Governing Committee v. Norris 1983).

The main argument for this approach is that making distinctions based on certain "suspect classes" such as race and gender perpetuates the notion that race or sex are legitimate grounds for differentiating between human beings in the context of insurance. Even when it is done without malicious intentions, stereotyping on the basis of suspect classes arguably can contribute to perpetuating inequality in society because it categorizes people into classes that strips them of their individuality.

This study does not aim in deciding between the two approaches. From a pure deontological perspective both approaches can be powerfully justified. But very few are pure deontologists. Most philosophers and policy-makers care about the consequences of a given policy. In this paper we provides a theoretical frameworks for thinking about the consequences of insurance antidiscrimination laws (for details see Avraham 2017). As it comes out there are three different types of costs courts and policy-makers should consider: the "distributional" cost to the protected group, the costs to the entire insurance market associated with adverse selection, and the cost to society from distortions in insureds' primary behavior. In this study we demonstrate how to estimate the hardest of all three types: the third type of costs. Specifically, we aim at estimating the consequences, in terms of traffic fatalities, that are associated with such antidiscrimination laws, with application to the case of credit score discrimination.

Credit score discrimination provides an excellent application for this issue. It is well known that (unlike gender discrimination) the price of auto insurance is quite sensitive to the insureds' credit score, which suggests insurance companies believe credit score is predictive of auto insurance risk. There are many studies that show that credit score is an effective underwriting tool (Brockett and Golden 2007), and it is widely used by insurers. The theory being that people who are irresponsible in handling their finance, might also be irresponsible drivers. Kellison et al. (2003) find that lower credit scores are associated with higher insurance prices and according to the consumer report's analysis poor credit score has a dramatic impact on auto insurance premiums, which may reach

Table 9.1 *Summary of reform states*

Year of Reform	States
1996	Montana
1997	New Hampshire
2002	Utah
2003	Alabama, Idaho, Kansas, Maine, Maryland, Minnesota, North Dakota, Rhode Island, Washington
2004	Alaska, Arkansas, Florida, Georgia, Illinois, Indiana, Louisiana, Mississippi, Missouri, Nebraska, North Carolina, Ohio, Oklahoma, Oregon, Virginia
2005	Arizona, Colorado, Iowa, Nevada, New York, Tennessee
2006	New Mexico
2008	Delaware
2011	Connecticut

Note: The table is based on hand collected data on states' credit score antidiscrimination laws.

over a $1000 per year.[2] If courts prevent insurance companies from discriminating according to the insured's credit score, automobile insurance premium will become more affordable to people with bad credit score, and by proxy – bad driving. These people, in turn, are likely to find it easier to access auto insurance market and buy better coverage for more affordable prices. As a result, in states that ban discrimination based on credit score one would expect to see more bad drivers on the road, driving more miles than in states without such ban. This in turn might have an impact of fatal car accidents.

Furthermore, while credit score discrimination has a large impact on insurance pricing, its use by insurers as an underwriting tool "remains controversial and under attack..." (Brockett and Golden 2007). Three states currently ban it completely (California, Massachusetts, and Hawaii), while in other states like Arizona or Georgia it is perfectly legitimate to make use of this information. Importantly, since the late 1990s, many states made policy changes inflicting on credit score discrimination (see Table 9.1 for details). This extensive variation provides an unusual opportunity to draw causal inference on this issue.

---

[2] www.consumerreports.org/cro/car-insurance/credit-scores-affect-auto-insurance-rates/index.htm (accessed October 22, 2015).

In this study we seek to demonstrate the importance of the distortions in primary behavior are associated with prohibiting credit score discrimination. We do so by estimating the effect of introducing laws that prohibit credit score discrimination on the number of traffic fatalities, taking a standard difference-in-differences approach and using data on traffic fatalities from the Fatality Analysis Reporting System (FARS). Eventually we find that prohibiting credit score discrimination is likely to not have an impact on insureds' primary behavior. Specifically, we find that in the first few years after the introduction of a law prohibiting credit score discrimination, there is a statistically insignificant increase in the number of traffic fatalities. Because the increase is not statistically significant we interpret the results as suggestive only.

Traffic accidents have large costs that have attracted substantial attention from economists (see, e.g., Edlin 1999; Levitt and Porter 2001). In 2013, over 33,000 people died in crash accidents the United States out of which about 31 percent were killed in alcohol-impaired driving crashes and 29 percent due to speed-related accidents. According to a study published in 2014 by the National Highway Traffic Safety Administration (NHTSA), US motor vehicle crashes cost, in 2010, almost $1 trillion in loss of productivity and loss of life.[3]

The incidence of motor vehicle crashes and traffic fatalities are likely to be significantly influenced by choices made by drivers (including choices whether to drink alcohol, how carefully to drive, which car to drive, how much to drive, and how much, if at all, insurance coverage to carry). Accordingly, economists have long been interested in evaluating the effect of different legal rules and policies on driver's behavior. In particular, studies have examined how drivers' behavior and traffic fatalities are affected by seat belt laws (see, e.g., Cohen and Einav 2003; Levitt and Porter 1999; Peltzman 1975), drunk driving laws (see, e.g., Levitt and Porter 2001; Sloan, Reilly, and Schenzler 1994), negligence standards (White 1989), taxes and insurance premiums based on miles driven (see Edlin 1999; Edlin, Karaca-Mandic, and Pinar 2006; Romem and Shurtz 2015; Vickery 1968), and automobile insurance and accident liability laws (Cohen and Dehejia 2004).

This study contributes to the large literature on the factors and policy measures that influence traffic fatalities. Our study is, to the best of our knowledge, the first to examine how drivers' behavior and traffic fatalities

---

[3] www.rmiia.org/auto/traffic_safety/Cost_of_crashes.asp

are influenced by antidiscrimination rules. There is substantial work, however, on how behavior and traffic fatalities are influenced by other legal rules. As such, this study provides useful information to policy-makers by providing some quantitative evidence on the social cost of anti-discrimination laws.

The remainder of the paper is structured as follows. Section 9.2 provides a theoretical framework for thinking about antidiscrimination laws. This part is based on Avraham (2017), Section 9.3 describes the data; Section 9.4 describes the empirical strategy; section 9.5 reports the main results; and Section 9.6 concludes.

9.2   Evaluating Insurance Antidiscriminations Laws: A Primer

Insurance is both a social and a private enterprise. When social, government-provided insurance reflects ideals of solidarity and cross-subsidization of risk among the citizens. Private insurance in contrast is profit-driven, thus requiring differential risk pricing. But risk is often correlated with characteristics that are constitutionally protected from discrimination such as race, gender, or age. States have struggled to find a middle ground between complete prohibition to complete permission of discrimination by prohibiting risk differentiation if it amounts to "unfair discrimination." The problem, however, persisted because "unfair discrimination" remained undefined. Indeed, states' constitutions and statues only provide a list of prohibited grounds for discrimination, without ever defining it.

As a result, courts' interpretation of the statutory term "unfair discrimination" is inconsistent (see Avraham, Schwarcz, and Logue 2014; 2015). Some courts permitted life insurers or homeowners' insurers to charge African American higher premiums than Caucasians since the difference was based on statistical risk, while other courts did not.[4] In the context of auto insurance, courts found that automobile insurance rates based upon sex and age are fair unless those sex-and-age-based rating factors are found to be actuarially unsound.[5] Other courts have forbidden auto insurers from discriminating based on age, sex, or zip code.[6]

---

[4] *Guidry v. Pellerin Life Ins. Co.* (364 F.Supp.2d 592 [W.D.La.2005]). And see also *Young v. Farmers' Mut. Life Ins. Co.* (1 S.W.2d 74 [Ark.1928]); *Toledo Fair Hous. Ctr. v. Nationwide Mut. Ins. Co.* (704 N.E.2d 667 [Ohio.Com.Pl.1997]).

[5] *Insurance Services Office v. Commissioner of Ins.* (381 So 2d 515 [1979]), cert den (382 So 2d 1391 [1979]).

[6] *Government Employees Ins. Co. v. Insurance Comm'r* (630 A2d 713 [1993]).

In recent decades employer and insurance companies started to discriminated based on credit scores (Clifford and Shoag 2016). Some states reacted by banning such practice. One might wonder why states bother banning discrimination based on credit score; what is wrong with such discrimination to begin with? In other words, why is it acceptable for insurance companies to discriminate based on miles driven but not based on credit score, where arguably both are good predictors of risk? Indeed, proponents of discrimination in insurance argue that the use of such proxies surmounts to rational statistical discrimination; namely, discrimination founded in business necessity with no mal intentions involved, and therefore that it should not be banned.

Philosophers and jurists are not so fast, however, to permit statistical discrimination. Moreau's view is that discrimination is wrong because it violates our deliberative freedoms, which are our "freedoms to have our decisions about how to live insulated from the effects of normatively extraneous features of us, such as our skin color or gender" (Moreau 2010). Others believe that discrimination is wrong because it disadvantages a person for no good reason, viz., that the person is a member of a certain salient social group. Hellman holds that direct discrimination is wrong because it demeans those against whom it is directed, treating them as morally inferior, not equal of moral worth (Hellman 2008). Of course, what counts as *demeaning* in the context of insurance remains to be worked out. Lippert-Rasmussen disagrees with the broad school of thought under which Hellman's approach falls, which he calls "The disrespect-based account of the badness of discrimination" (Lippert-Rasmussen 2013). Lippert-Rasmussen argues that discrimination is wrong primarily because of its *harmful effects*. Another view is that discrimination is wrong because it is based on or perpetuates inaccurate stereotypes. Some even argue that discrimination is wrong even when it relies on somewhat accurate stereotypes, which may apply to many but not all members of the group (Schaur 2003). No matter what approach one takes, clearly context matters for the determination of what fair discrimination is. For example, age discrimination in life insurance is not as bad, if it is bad at all, as age discrimination in health insurance.

In this paper we do not purport to resolve the philosophical question of whether discrimination based on credit score is unfair. Rather, we will assume it is, perhaps because as is well known credit score correlates with race, and race is a protected class in the United States. But even if discrimination based on credit score is unfair, it does not follow that banning such discrimination is desirable from an optimal policy making perspective. Costs also matter. If forbidding discrimination will unravel an entire insurance markets, or will kill hundreds of people a year, policy-makers need to pause before they allow that to happen.

For this reason, it is important to examine the social costs of allowing or prohibiting discrimination. Such costs might come in three major forms. First, in the form of higher premium to a group policy-makers purport to protect. These "distributional" costs might fall on the shoulders of the disadvantaged group, such as when gender discrimination is forbidden in life insurance, where women are the lower risks. Indeed, these costs might be high. Oxera (2011) found that after the *Test Achats* case, which required insurance companies in the EU to have unisex premiums for various lines of insurance, life insurance premiums increased for women. Similarly, Aseervatham et al. (2014) found that after that case auto insurance premium increased for young females. The trade-off in such cases is between equality and distribution: insisting on equal premiums redistribute wealth from females to males. (And compare Clifford and Shoag (2016) who report that states who ban credit score discrimination by employers have faced worse outcome for blacks).

Courts and policy-makers should also consider a second type of losses – efficiency losses in the insurance markets stemming from the fact that prohibition on discrimination causes one group to cross-subsidize another, leading to the well-known problem of adverse selection. Prohibiting insurers, for example, from discriminating between whites and blacks will causes them to charge the average of the risk posed by both races, or do a more detailed examination of each applicant to better determine the risk they pose to the pool. Each of these alternatives could pose consequences for the insurance pool. If insurers do the former, markets might unravel due to adverse selection. If they do the latter, premium might go up for everyone, driving out of the market the poorer applicants.

Interestingly, the evidence of the extent to which the theory of adverse selection accurately describes the real world is mixed. Cutler and Reber (1998) show that when Harvard University increased the premium of the most generous health plans for the policyholders regardless of the risk they imposed, the best risks in the pool (the ones with lower medical expenses) left this plan for a less generous one with a lower premium. Other evidence for adverse selection in health insurance markets exist (Cutler and ZeckJauser 2000). However, in surveying the literature, Cohen and Siegleman (2010) found that the significance of the adverse selection effect may vary by line of insurance, and the characteristic discriminated against.

The third type of costs courts and policy-makers need to incorporate is the impact of allowing and prohibiting discrimination on insureds' *primary behavior*. For example, if insurers were allowed to discriminate based on genetics, people might be deterred from having genetic tests. This, in turn, might prevent them from getting preemptive help, as well as prevent society from improving the science of genetic diseases (Hellman 2003). These costs might justify prohibiting genetic discrimination, at least in lines of insurance where people might be deterred from taking the tests, despite such discrimination being fair and despite the risk of adverse selection associated with such prohibition.

We therefore posit that courts and policy-makers should be hesitant to forbid discrimination based on credit score before they understand the empirical picture. In states that prohibit such discrimination in auto insurance (either explicitly by statute or by courts' interpretation of what "fair discrimination" is), premiums may be lower for drivers with a low credit score. But if low credit score is correlated with substance abuse, such a policy might cause more risky drivers to drive, potentially decreasing overall safety. Is it not crucial to know whether fatal accident rates rise? It might still be the case that a prohibition on credit score discrimination is not only fair but also optimal once the costs in terms of lost human lives are taken into account. Our point, however, is that the impact on primary behavior involves important empirical consideration that policy-makers should not ignore.

With this in mind, we now turn to estimating the impact of discrimination based on credit score on insureds' primary behavior on the roads.

9.3   Data

Our dataset is based on several different sources.

9.3.1   Antidiscrimination Laws

Each one of the US states has different rules with respect to the restriction of the use of policyholders' characteristics in determining insurance premiums and other underwriting decisions. We use hand collected data, previously unavailable, on credit score antidiscrimination policy – that potentially might have an effect on insurance companies' decisions to insure and the premium they charge, and that were subject to major changes over the years in several states. Table 9.1 provides further information.

9.3.2   Traffic Fatalities

We use data on the annual number traffic fatalities per year from the Fatality Analysis Reporting System (FARS). Figure 9.1 illustrates that while there are roughly 40,000 traffic fatalities per year during our sample period, since 2005 there has been a continuing decline in the number of traffic fatalities (from 41,817 in 1995 to 32,367 in 2011). These data include information on the accidents', involved vehicles, and drivers' characteristics: on average, 1.5 vehicles were involved in an accident, and about 30 percent of the accidents were associated with alcohol. Figure 9.1 shows that this rate is roughly constant over the sample period. Turning to drivers' characteristics, 73 percent of involved drivers were male and their average age was forty; the average vehicle's age was

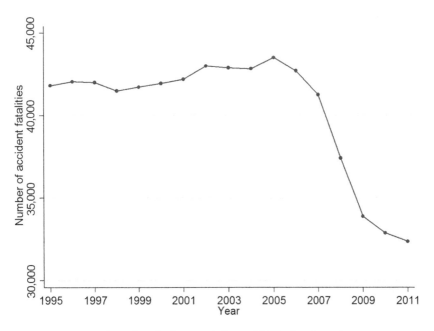

Figure 9.1   Annual accident fatalities and share of DUI related accidents 1995–2011.
Note: This figure plots the annual number of accident fatalities in the United States in the period 1995–2011.
Source: Authors' analysis of Fars data

Table 9.2 *Summary statistics of accident data*

Accident characteristics	
Mean number of vehicles involved	1.51
	(0.78)
Mean number of fatalities	1.11
	(0.41)
Driver characteristics	
Share of male drivers	0.73
	(0.45)
Mean age of drivers	40.04
	(17.96)
Vehicle characteristics	
Mean number of occupants	2.04
	(6.41)
Share of trucks	0.16
	(0.37)
Median vehicle age	7.88
	(6.18)
Number of accidents	617,428

Note: The table is based on data on all fatal accidents in the United States in the period 1995–2011. Standard deviation in parenthesis.

about eight; 16 percent of involved vehicles were trucks and there were two occupants per involved vehicle. Table 9.2 summarizes this data.

9.4   Empirical Strategy

We take advantage of the variation over time and across states in the legal regimes governing credit score discrimination in the auto insurance industry to study the consequences of prohibiting insurance providers from using such discrimination.

The past two decades have seen major changes in the policy of various states concerning this issue. Since the late 1990s many different states adopted legal reform that dramatically restricted or completely prohibited credit score discrimination. We build upon the natural experiments that are created by these reforms to causally identify the consequences of prohibiting credit score discrimination. In essence, our method is a standard differences-in-differences approach; we examine the change in various outcomes in "reform states" – states that introduced a major credit score discrimination reform – after the reform compared to the pre-reform period, relative to this change in "non-reform states" – all other states.

Econometrically we implement this identification strategy by estimating a model of the form:

$$y_{ist} = \alpha_0 + \beta_1 * year + \beta_2 * state + \beta_3 * X + \gamma * reform + \varepsilon_{ist}$$

where y_{ist} is one of the outcomes that we examine. *year* is a full set year dummies, namely a vector of year dummies for each year in the relevant time period. *state* is a vector of dummy variables for each state. X is a set of state characteristics such as GDP, unemployment rate, and the number of registered drivers. The estimates of γ capture the effect of the reform on the outcome in the "reform states" relative to the "non-reform" states.

9.5   Results and Discussion

To illustrate the results, we first show some graphical evidence on the relation between fatal accidents and prohibiting insurance providers from discriminating on the basis of an insured credit score. We use fatal accident data aggregated at the state and year levels and estimate the following version of the model in equation (1):

$$y_{ist} = \alpha_0 + \beta_1 * year + \beta_2 * state + \beta_3 * X + \gamma * years\_reform + \varepsilon_{ist}$$

where y_{ist} is the number of accident fatalities in natural log terms. The difference between equation (1) and equation (2) is that in equation (2), γ, instead of being a dummy variable indicating the post-reform period, $\gamma \in -4, \ldots 0, \ldots 3$ is a vector of dummies that capture the separate effect of the four years before and four years after the introduction of an antidiscrimination law on the outcome in the "reform states"[7] relative to the "non-reform" states in the period 1995–2011. Figure 9.2 depicts the estimates of γ's in this model. The figure shows an apparent increase of 20 percent in the number of fatalities in the first post-reform year. The effect appears to increase even more in the third post-reform year.

---

[7] See footnote 2.

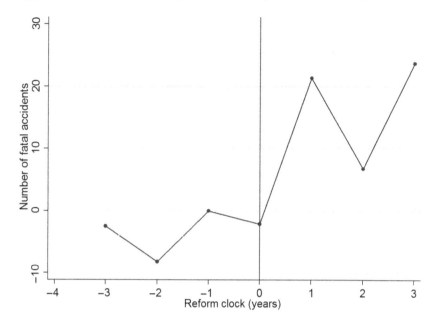

Figure 9.2   The impact of prohibiting credit score discrimination in the auto insurance market on the incidence of accident fatalities.

Note: This figure plots the reform-relative-time estimates from an OLS regression of the model in equation (2) (see Table 9.4) with the natural log of accident number as the independent variable. The data includes about 617,000 accidents spanning in the period 1995–2011. The treatment states are the states with a credit score discrimination reform and the comparison states are states that did not have a reform.

Source: Authors analysis of the Fars data

Tables 9.3 and 9.4 present the regressions estimates for equation (1) and equation (2), respectively. The difference-in-differences estimates shown in column 1 of Table 9.3, indicate an overall insignificant 3.7 percent increase in the number of traffic fatalities; adding, in columns 2, the state time-varying characteristics – GDP, unemployment rate and number of registered driver – does not change the results much; including a set of region-year dummies in column 3 increases the coefficient still remains statistically insignificant. Table 9.4 shows the year by year estimates of the effect of prohibiting credit score discrimination. Column 3, which is our preferred specification shows a statistically insignificant increase of 21.5 percent in the first year after the year the reform was introduced; an insignificant 6.9 percent increase in the following year and an insignificant 24.8 going forward.

Table 9.3 *The impact of prohibiting credit score discrimination in the auto insurance market on the incidence of fatal accidents, difference-in-differences*

	(1)	(2)	(3)
Reform	3.73	4.00	12.15
	(18.65)	(18.26)	(23.20)
State & year fixed effects	X	X	X
GDP, UI rate, & registered drivers		X	X
Interaction terms of regions and years			X
Observations	850	850	850

Note: This table reports the estimation results of the effect of incidence of accident fatalities using a regression model as in equation (1). The data include about 617,000 accidents spanning in the period 1995–2011. The treatment states are the states with a credit score discrimination reform and the comparison states are states that did not have a reform. Standard errors, in parenthesis, are clustered at the state level. One asterisk indicates significance at 5%. UI represents unemployment rate.

Table 9.4 *The impact of prohibiting credit score discrimination in the auto insurance market on the incidence of fatal accidents, difference-in-differences lags*

	(1)	(2)	(3)
Year of reform: 1st	−2.3	−1.906	−1.569
	(8.94)	(9.64)	(12.05)
Year of reform: 2nd	14.958	14.074	21.535
	(15.49)	(16.76)	(19.99)
Year of reform: 3rd	−4.772	−7.888	6.971
	(18.01)	(19.51)	(23.35)
Year of reform: ≥ 4th	6.111	3.831	24.875
	(32.77)	(32.56)	(35.10)
State & year fixed effects	X	X	X
GDP, UI rate, & registered drivers		X	X
Interaction terms of regions and years			X
Observations	850	850	850

Note: This table reports the estimation results of the effect of incidence of accident fatalities using a regression model as in equation (2). The data include about 617,000 accidents spanning in the period 1995–2011. The treatment states are the states with a credit score discrimination reform and the comparison states are states that did not have a reform. Standard errors, in parenthesis, are clustered at the state level. One asterisk indicates significance at 5%.

Because we fail to find statistically significant results, we interpret the results as only suggestive of the fact that prohibiting credit score discrimination might lead to increase in fatal accident. We have made various attempts to explore different factors related to the interaction between credit score-based discrimination and car accidents. For example, we examined accidents related to driving-under-the-influence (hereinafter DUI). Our hypothesis was that having a very low credit score may be associated with tendency to drink alcohol and therefore prohibiting the utilization of credit score would lead to more DUI-related accidents. We haven't found evidence to support this hypothesis. We also looked at the impact of prohibiting credit score discrimination on drivers' characteristics. To do so, we merged the data with zip-code level income data and assigned, for each driver involved in an accident, her income based on her zip code. We haven't found conclusive results with respect to this issue either.

Overall, our results, or the lack thereof, deserve further discussion as they reflect, we believe, inherent challenges in the empirical evaluation of this issue. The first issue is information on uninsured drivers. The primary channel through which antidiscrimination laws would affect car accidents is presumably insurance coverage. Despite considerable effort, we have not been able to find detailed data on uninsured drivers. What we could find was typically state-level aggregate data, for sporadic years. Without good data on uninsured drivers it is impossible to assess the effects of reforms on access and utilization of insurance coverage.

The second issue regards the coding of the reforms and is not inherent to our setting. Antidiscrimination reforms come in different shapes and formats and it has been quite difficult to project all this complexity into a simple discrete reform indicator. To the extent that this complexity projects on the implementation of such reforms as well, it makes it difficult for a standard estimation model, like the one we use, to capture the effects of these reforms.

Finally, an obvious limitation of our analysis is that we used data about fatal accidents. It is not unlikely that the effects of the reform are more pronounced when it comes to less severe accidents that are much more prevalent, yet good data on them is hard to find.

9.6   Conclusions

Courts in the United States engage almost entirely only in a deontological analysis of whether insurance discrimination is fair. They perceive discrimination against a protected group to be fair when they find there is correlation between risk and belonging to a group. Since there are some empirical studies showing a correlation between credit score and accident risk, discrimination based on credit score is legally fair. However, treating such correlation as a necessary and sufficient condition is problematic for various reasons among them that courts do not specify the requisite level of correlation. Neither do courts engage in a nuanced analysis that takes into account the specific line of insurance or the nature of the discrimination (increased premium, partial coverage, or outright denial of coverage). Thus, courts' determination that a specific discrimination is fair is essentially empty (Avraham 2017).

More relevant to our study here is the claim that courts should engage also in efficiency analysis, accounting for the *consequences* stemming from a prohibition on discrimination. When courts weigh the costs of antidiscrimination laws, they seldom engage in a cost-benefit analysis that considers the three types of costs discussed above. While courts sometimes look generally at the distributional impact on premiums, they rarely consider whether a prohibition of discrimination will raise the premium to the individuals in the protected group, nor whether it will incentivize insurers not to extend coverage to such individuals at all. As with respect to the second and third types of costs (adverse selection and primary behavior) courts almost never consider them

As such, failure to engage in this consequentialist analysis can lead to courts placing too much significance on whether a result fits squarely with deontological notions of fairness primarily interpreted as focused on whether there is a correlation between belonging to a group and the insured risk, and not on whether the decision will increase the premium to the protected group or reduce its coverage, introduce inefficiencies stemming from adverse selection, or otherwise alter insureds' (or third parties') primary behavior in potentially detrimental ways.

Courts obviously should not conduct the empirical research themselves but rather accept litigants' evidence on the relevant costs to society. Courts, at least in the United States, are not unaccustomed to reviewing empirical evidence on various types of costs associated with a specific reform. For example, in a recent Florida medical malpractice reform case, the Supreme Court of Florida struck down a law limiting pain and suffering damages for victims of medical malpractice, despite the legislature's determination that such caps will alleviate the medical malpractice insurance crisis (North Broward Hospital District v. Susan Kallitan 2017). Interestingly, even though the legislature's justifications for the caps were based, among other things, on a 345 pages report as well as thirteen volumes of supportive materials prepared by a special task force, the court accepts plaintiff's claim that there was no empirical evidence of a continuing medical malpractice insurance crisis justifying the caps.

To demonstrate the possible effect of prohibiting insurance providers from discriminating on the basis of insureds' credit score, we estimated the effect of introducing laws that prohibit credit score discrimination on insureds' primary behavior. Because we had no data on traffic injuries, we focused on the number of traffic fatalities. We found that introducing such laws creates a statistically insignificant increase in the number of traffic fatalities. These results may be interpreted as suggestive of the "primary costs" (or lack thereof) associated with prohibiting credit score discrimination in term of accident fatalities.

When courts do not engage in the consequentialist analysis proposed in this article, they might harm the very group policy-makers intended to help and reduce overall welfare in society. However, our failing to find that prohibition on credit score discrimination increases fatal accidents provides only very weak support for those who favor credit score discrimination. The reason is that it is still possible that such prohibition increases non-fatal accidents or increases one or both of the two other types of costs discussed above – cost associated with adverse selection and distributional costs to protected groups. Still, our empirical investigation suggests that in the context of credit score discrimination, prohibiting insurers from this practice does not carry significant primary behavior costs.

References

Arizona Governing Committee v. Norris. 1983. 463 U.S. 1073.

Aseervatham, Vijay, Christoph Lex, and Martin Spindler. 2014. How Do Unisex Rating Regulations Affect Gender Differences in Insurance Premiums? (November 7). Munich Risk and Insurance Center Working Paper 16. https://ssrn.com/abstract=2183181 or http://dx.doi.org/10.2139/ssrn.2183181 (accessed July 19, 2019).

Avraham, Ronen. 2017. Discrimination and Insurance. Pp. 335–47 in *The Routledge Handbook of the Ethics of Discrimination*, edited by Kasper Lippert-Rasmussen. London: Routledge.

Avraham, Ronen, Kyle. D. Logue, and Daniel Schwarcz. 2014. The Anatomy of Insurance Anti-discrimination Laws. *Southern California Law Review* 87: 195–274.

2015. Towards a Universal Framework for Insurance Anti-discrimination Laws. *Connecticut Insurance Law Journal* 21: 1–52.

Brockett, P. L. and Golden, L. L. 2007. Biological and Psychobehavioral Correlates of Credit Scores and Automobile Insurance Losses: Toward an Explication of Why Credit Scoring Works. *Journal of Risk and Insurance* 74(1): 23–63.

Clifford, Robert and Shoag Daniel. 2016. *No More Credit Score- Employer Credit Check Bans and Signal Substitution*. http://scholar.harvard.edu/files/shoag/files/clifford_and_shoag_2016.pdf?m=1454092507 (accessed July 9, 2019).

Cohen, Alma, and Liran Einav. 2003. The Effect of Mandatory Seat Belt Laws on Driving Behavior and Traffic Fatalities. *Review of Economics and Statistics* 85: 828–43.

Cohen, Alma, and Rajeec Dehejia. 2004. The Effects of Automobile Insurance and Accident Liability Laws on Traffic Fatalities. *Journal of Law and Economics* 47: 357–93.

Cohen, Alma, and Peter Siegelman. 2010. Testing for Adverse Selection in Insurance Markets. *Journal of Risk and Insurance* 77(1): 39–84.

Cutler, D. M., and S. J. Reber. 1998. Paying for Health Insurance: The Trade-Off between Competition and Adverse Selection. *The Quarterly Journal of Economics*, 113: 433–66.

Cutler, D. M., and Zeckhauser, A. A. 2000. The Anatomy of Health Insurance, Pp. 563–643, in: *Handbook of Health Economics*, Vol. 1, Ch. 11, edited by Anthony J. Culyer and Joseph P. Newhous. Amsterdam: Elsevier Science.

Edlin, Aaron. 1999. *Per-Mile Premiums for Auto Insurance*. National Bureau of Economic Research Working Paper No. 6934.

Edlin, Aaron. S., and Karaca-Mandic, and Pinar. 2006. The Accident Externality from Driving. *Journal of Political Economy* 114(5): 931–55.

Hellman, D. 2003. What Makes Genetic Discrimination Exception? *American Journal of Law and Medicine* 29: 77–116.

2008. *When Is Discrimination Wrong?* Cambridge: Harvard University Press.

Kellison, J. B., P. Brockett, S. H. Shin, and S. Li. 2003. *A Statistical Analysis of the Relationship between Credit History and Insurance Losses*. Bureau of Business Research. Austin: The University of Texas.

Levitt, Steven D., and Jack Porter. 2001. How Dangerous Are Drinking Drivers. *Journal of Political Economy* 109: 1198–237.

1999. *Sample Selection in the Estimation of Air Bag and Seat Belt Effectiveness*. NBER Working Paper No. 7210.

Lippert-Rasmussen, K. 2013. *Born Free and Equal?* Oxford: Oxford University Press.

Moreau, S. 2010. What Is Discrimination? *Philosophy and Public Affairs* 38(2): 143–79.

Oxera. 2011. The Impact of a Ban on the Use of Gender in Insurance. www.oxera.com/wp-content/uploads/2018/03/Oxera-report-on-gender-in-insurance-1.pdf (accessed July 19, 2019).

Peltzman, Sam. 1975. The Effects of Automobile Safety Regulation. *Journal of Political Economy* 83: 667–725.

Issi, Romem, and Ity Shurtz. 2015. *The Accident Externality of Traffic Density: Evidence from Observance of the Jewish Sabbath in Israel.* Unpublished Revision requested by the Journal of Urban Economics.

Schauer, F. 2003. *Profiles, Probabilities, and Stereotypes.* Cambridge: Harvard University Press.

Sloan A. Frank, Reilly B. A., and Schenzler, C.M.. 1994. Tort Liability versus Other Approaches for Deterring Careless Driving. *International Review of Law and Economics* 14: 53–72.

Vickery, William. 1968. Automobile Accidents, Tort Law, Externalities, and Insurance: An Economist's Critique. *Law and Contemporary Problems* 33: 464–87.

White, M. J. 1989. An Empirical Test of the Comparative and Contributory Negligence Rules in Accident Law. *Rand Journal of Economics* 20: 308–30.

Are Judges Harsher with Repeat Offenders?

Evidence from the European Court of Human Rights

ERIC LANGLAIS, ALESSANDRO MELCARNE, AND
GIOVANNI B. RAMELLO

10.1 Introduction

Only over the past two decades scholars have decided to seriously apply the customary economic analytical tools to the judiciary, namely after the path breaking article by Posner (1993) enquiring the provocative questions whether or not judges were different from the rest of humanity constrained by the incentives of the *homo oeconomicus*.[1] More precisely, the answer to the simple question "what do judges maximize?" given by Posner was the disruptive "the same as anyone else," which has represented the kick-start for a new stream of investigations trying to disentangle the judicial technology and judicial decision-making. Topics until then out of reach for the scholar of the judiciaries, such as measures of judicial performance, judicial efficiency, judicial independence, and so on, progressively became relevant both only for the academia but also for policy-making (Marciano et al. 2019; Ramello and Voigt 2012).

[1] We are greatly indebted to three anonymous referees, Dawn Chutkow, William Hubbard, and Eric Talley and to the participants to the Conference for Empirical Legal Studies in Asia participants in Taipei, of the German Law and Economics Association, of the VI International Workshop on Economics Analysis of Litigation, of the Law and Economics Workshop organized at Villa Finaly Florence by the Université Paris II, and of the AEDE Conference held in Madrid. A special thanks goes to Federica Gerbaldo that gave us help far exceeding the mere research assistance, especially in understanding the working of the ECtHR. Yun-chien Chang deserves several thanks, including one for his never-ending patience. The usual disclaimer applies.

Among others, an increasing number of researchers decided to get a glimpse in particular on the judicial decision-making process, trying to interpret the rationale and mechanisms according to which judges decide. On one hand, a number of scholars tried to understand whether cognitive biases or other emotional determinants, even minor ones such as, for instance, the anger arising from the loss of the supported sport team, were affecting the judges' decisions (Eren and Mocan 2018; Guthrie et al. 2007). Others tried to figure out whether political issues were sometime taking over the mere "ius dicere" in order to pursue political goals.

It becomes thus relevant to study judges' decisional patterns in order to understand what courts are doing and whether they are trying to convey a vicarious effect in addition to simply administering justice (Posner 1993; Sunstein et al. 2006).

It is worth reminding that for a long time, before Posner's disruptive article, judges were supposed to decide cases solely on legal grounds and merits, thus disregarding any argument that appeal to their personal viewpoint and more specifically without following a political agenda. Within judicial behaviors a number of papers have shown not only that judges indeed are follow the 'homo oeconomicus' paradigm just like anyone else and, accordingly, behave in accordance to direct on indirect monetary incentives (Ippoliti and Ramello 2018; Melcarne 2017; Melcarne and Ramello 2015), but also that they are interpreting their role in a political way, thus making their decisions sometime reflect a political orientation or strategy. In many cases they have been seen as "activist" somehow legislating from the bench. This has been intensively felt in the case of US federal judges where presidents and senators always try to nominate judges and justices sharing the same orientations on relevant topics, such as abortion, separation of church and state, environmental protection, and criminals' rights, and so on (Sunstein et al. 2006). However the hunch of a political agenda orienting judicial decision-making has been equally envisaged in many jurisdictions. For example, similar patters have been observed in several countries concerning labor courts' decisions (Desrieux and Espinosa 2019; Ichino et al. 2003).

The present research takes somewhat the same direction in as much it enters the rarely investigated field of international courts' judicial decision-making. This international setting, representing an intersection of several national politics, supplies results even more obscure to be interpreted. Although in the last decade a handful of contributions have tried to deepen the understanding of judicial decision-making and generally the working of such courts, there is still a substantial theoretical and empirical gap to be investigated (Posner and De Figuereido 2005; Romano et al. 2014; Shany 2014).

In particular, there is a lack of understanding on whether international courts' judges decide in the very same way as their national systems' piers, just shifting the usual operations to a supranational dimension that affects states rather than individuals, or if something totally different applies.

We try to have an insight on how an international court works and to supply a tentative answer by analyzing the European Court of Human Rights (ECtHR) in which the supranational settings and the possibility to exceed the traditional limits regularly existing within European countries in awarding damages might permit to shed new light on the idiosyncratic judicial decision-making.

The main research question is whether the usual theoretical pillars guiding damages awarding still applies herewith or whether a different approach should be adopted for ECtHR and other similar international courts in which for example the defendant is very often a state with a soft budget constraint or no-budget constraint at all. Furthermore, the Court is very often facing offenders, so this makes additionally the discussion more meaty vis-à-vis the usual theory of punishment, as it will be further argued in the next sections

Although we observe that the standard judicial practice here scantly applies, this per se does not supply yet a satisfying answer. The empirical investigation, however, shows patterns and regularities that might offer a reasonable explanation on how the court decides and what is the likely meaning of the peculiar damages awarding scheme that goes in the direction of performing an expressive function.

The chapter is organized as follows: Section 10.2 describes the role and the working of the ECtHR, also highlighting the just satisfaction unique tool in awarding damages that origins an interesting puzzle for observers. Section 10.3 shortly presents the main rationale used for calculating damages with specific attention to the complementary issue of aligning private incentives and public interest, since the court, by compensating victims, shifts the cost of harm on the tortfeasor thus producing deterrence. An alternative interpretation is then exposed. Section 10.4 describes the data employed and our empirical strategy, while Section 10.5 presents results and their discussion. Section 10.6 then concludes.

Table 10.1 *Yearly number of cases filed to ECtHR, 2011–2015*

Year	Number of incoming cases
2015	>40,000
2014	>56,000
2013	>65,000
2012	>65,000
2011	>64,000

Source: European Court of the Human Rights.

10.2   The ECtHR and the "Just Satisfaction" Puzzle

The European Court of Human Rights (ECtHR), albeit not directly embedded within any national judicial system, is a specialized adjudication body acting as last resort dispute resolution system within Europe. It rules on individual and state applications alleging violations of civil and political rights.

Based in Strasbourg, the Court's mandate is to monitor that the 47 member states of the Council of Europe comply with substantive provisions essentially devoted to protect individual civil and political rights as well as individual liberties. The ECtHR does it by scrutinizing allegations about breach of human rights filed by individuals against a distinct member state (Gerbaldo 2018).

According to a number of scholars, the Court is part of one of the most advanced supra-national institutional setting for protecting human rights. It was established in 1959 on the basis of the art. 19 of the European Convention of Human Rights (drafted in 1950 and entered in force in 1953) in order to protect in Europe individual, civil, and political rights and liberties. Its establishment was largely boosted as a reaction to human rights abuses occurred during the World War II. The importance of the ECtHR has increased over the years also because of the collapse of the socialist block and the subsequent transition of many eastern European countries toward market and democracy, which implied, among others, an improved respect of human rights. Since the enlargement of its jurisdiction, the number of cases filed to the ECtHR has risen dramatically in time. If in the period 1955–1982 there were, on average, 800 cases filed every year, the mass of incoming cases has recently skyrocketed, rising to several tens of thousands every year.

Table 10.1 shows the dynamics of incoming cases over time. Although the vast majority of cases are declared inadmissible (around the 90 percent), such high demand of justice has caused a constant increase in the backlog of cases that in 2015 amounted to around 65,000 cases with an estimated average disposition time of 1.6 years. On the whole this features shed new lights on the court itself and fueled a more debate on the role and functions of the ECtHR (Voeten 2008). This progressive congestion has been the target of an intense debate and several measures affecting both the supply and the demand side have been envisaged, such as respectively increase workforce (Brighton Declaration 2012)[2] or – with Protocol 11 of 1998 and then Protocol 14 of 2010 – or increasing the requirement for the case to be heard in order to avoid for example frivolous litigations.

Among other issues, one of the key elements was whether really the court was intended to pursue individual justice and, as such, was intended to redress states' violations for the benefit of each specific citizen filing a complaint or to follow a different agenda.

According to some commentators, the damages awarding scheme of the ECtHR resembles *prima facie* to a sort of random walk that can be hardly understood outside the "subjective judgments about the moral worth of the victim and the wrongdoer" (Sheldon 2015, p. 353).

Actually the picture is made more complex by the fact that the scheme, according to the art. 41 of the European Convention of Human Right and the therein asserted principle of the "just satisfaction," is not constrained by the magnitude of the harm caused but can expanded also with a so-called "non-pecuniary" component, that is to say, a top-up to the actual harm decided by the court itself. The pecuniary component in general reflects the monetary or wealth loss of the victim, and thus gives a straightforward way of how to be calculated and that the main target is harm recovery. "Non-pecuniary" stands instead for a discretionary com-ponent that might be awarded by the court as a sort of multiplier. It thus incorporates judges' moral evaluation on the harm and, what is more, it determines the final amount of damages exceeding the mere loss.

This novelty substantially differs from the general principle applied by most of the member states of the *restitutio in integrum* (in English, restoration to the original condition), required to bring victims back to their original level of welfare and that in practice obliges national courts

---

[2] www.echr.coe.int/Documents/2012_Brighton_FinalDeclaration_ENG.pdf (accessed July 19, 2019).

to awards at most damages exactly the amount of the harm suffered. It is worth noting that this Roman law principle has been widely integrated in civil law and common law systems and relates also to the economic interpretation of shifting the costs of the harm to the wrongdoer in order to provide optimal incentives, as it will be further argued.

Therefore the "just satisfaction" principle asserted by the art. 41 of the European Convention of Human Rights, gives the Court full discretion for increasing the damages and, according to a number of scholars, just translates into "allowing judges to put forward equity principle and not to award necessarily what is should be [according to the *restitutio in integrum*], but rather what they consider to be appropriate redress" (Ichim 2014 p. 22).[3]

On the whole, the particular feature of the ECtHR's damages awarding scheme makes the judicial decision-making quite opaque and it introduces substantial uncertainty in terms of expectations. This remark somehow denies one of the key roles of modern judicial systems, i.e. decreasing uncertainty in societies (Marciano et al. 2019).

One might think that in accordance to the literature asserting the political opportunities offered by the court, judges might decide to serve their own country, thus orienting their decision making in favor of their appointee. A similar orientation that would make some sense in the light of Posner (1993) would then imply a sort of random outcome in term of cases.[4]

A way out in term of finding a rationale explaining the decision-making of the ECtHR is given by the Court itself, which in a quite conspicuous number of times has defined itself as a sort of political body producing indications to its members states by means of the individual decisions. This for instance what stated in several occasions, starting from the case *Karner v. Austria* (24/10/2003 paragraph 26) when the Court clearly stresses that:

> "Although the primary purpose of the Convention system is to provide individual relief, its mission is also to determine issues on public-policy grounds in the common interest, thereby raising the general standards of

---

[3] For a detailed explanation ECtHR (2014), *Just satisfaction claims. Practice Directions* available at www.echr.coe.int/Documents/PD_satisfaction_claims_ENG.pdf (accessed July 9, 2019).

[4] Of course the process would be rather complicated because it would require alliances in order to orient the majority and obtain the expected result.

protection of human rights and extending human rights jurisprudence throughout the community of Convention States."

This viewpoint of the court about itself has then been repeatedly announced in a number of subsequent cases[5]. It might also represent an important key to interpretation in a subset of cases in which member states appear as repeat offenders. For these cases it appears quite evident that not even the minimal result of deterrence has been reached, at least in the first instance, and thus the ECtHR wants more severely conveys its disappointment for the systematic violation of the Convention.

10.3 The Role of Sanction and Damages:
Looking for a Rationale

In order to disentangle the issue, we need to refer to existing theories and tools explaining damages awarding. A quite substantial literature both in the fields of law and law and economics has tried to shed light on the role of sanctions – including damages. On one hand we have the punitive effect, as maintained by the paradigm of retributivism (White 2019). On the other, sanctions might promote equally a deterrent effect that, by shifting the social cost of the offense on the wrongdoer and promoting the victim's compensation, produces the internalization of the externality. In other terms the internalization of the social cost of the harm not only nullifies the profit of the wrongdoer (at least when the mechanism works well) but also it informs would-be wrongdoers that there will be no gain for similar offenses. This mechanism has the advantage of altering the individual choice, aligning the costs and benefits of wrongdoing. It also raises a key issue in the case of the ECtHR: if the damages awarding scheme follows the deterrence approach one should be able to detect a clear sanctioning scheme as too low damages would imply under-deterrence and too high damages would create over-deterrence, with some possible further side effects connected to the violation of the proportionality of sanctions[6].

This model dates back to the Cesaria Beccaria's work and has become the central paradigm explaining the deterrent effect of sanctions. So even when damages have compensatory and punitive purposes they should be designed in an appropriate way for restoring the utility of the victims

---

[5] For example, *Konstantin Markin* v. *Russia*, 22/02/2012 paragraph 89.
[6] For a deep discussion on this point the reader might refer to Miceli (2018).

without creating over-deterrence (Miceli 2018). A well-known tenet of the law and economics literature on the incentive effect of sanctions is that in general the proper incentive is given by the full internalization of the social cost of the harm by the wrongdoer while a too harsh punishment might reasonably discourage the undertaking of potentially risky but socially valuable actions (Cassone and Ramello 2011).

While the economic equation of aligning costs and benefits is quite straightforward, according to this viewpoint thus the "just satisfaction" principle, apparently adding a sort of random component to the final size of damages, seems to diverge from the economic rationale.

In similar situations, like for punitive damages, a way for reconciling the divergence between actual harm and amount awarded is when the social cost of an accident fairly exceeds the individual cost. This is sometime the case of treble damages in antitrust in which there are individual costs and costs affecting markets and competition (Sidak 1981). In other terms the punitive amount is simply intended to capture what otherwise would lead to miscalculations of the real social costs produced. At the end of the day, the use of such kind of damages goes always in the direction of shifting the total costs on the wrongdoer.

So far, however, this paradigm has never been clearly expressed in the case of ECtHR. At a first glimpse what appears is a different amount of damages awarded for similar violations to similar infringements. So the puzzle remains. For example, in 2013 a single country, Italy, has paid the highest amount due to just satisfaction awards to victims (€71,884,302); that is to say more than a half of the total amount paid by other countries in the same year (€135,420,274).

The picture is also blurred by the fact that in a number of cases states result as repeat offenders and accordingly the strategy of the Court might adopt an inter-temporal dimension further confusing the observer. While of course the different features attributed to the timeframe may lead to different solutions, the general framework of internalizing the externality should still apply.

However, the interpretation in this case is even more difficult as the literature so far did not produce any conclusive results. There are in fact two streams of literature. One led by Polinsky and Rubinfeld (1991) is in favor of escalating sanctions as a tool to improve deterrence when the enforcement authority is not perfectly informed about the offense propensity and thus increasing the sanctions step by step becomes a sort of "trial and error" process. Another stream goes in the opposite direction allowing, under certain circumstances, leniency toward a repeat offender and thus for sanctions declining in the number of offenses, for example, shifting the weight of sanction from the second to the first offense (Burnovski and Safra 2004). Shortly, in the latter case the intuition is that an increasing sanctioning scheme might produce over-deterrence and thus it would be better to adjust the damages' size in the first time so that the second will be only residual. However, it must be said that all these models rely upon a two-period time span and are studying individuals' criminal behavior. Moreover, they concern physical economic agents that are wealth constrained (Emons 2003; 2008).

Consequently, excluding a specific and very superficial flavor, they are ill equipped for interpreting a situation in which the wrongdoer is a state rather than individual, the number of periods is undefined if not infinite and the wrongdoer has essentially a soft budget constraint. The latter is fundamental in making sense of the internalization of cost strategy and it does only very marginally apply for countries in which the cost of paying damages would then be shifted to taxpayers. The damages would have effect only in case the value is such that the society will start to stigmatize the government and it would reasonably translate these costs in loss of votes or other relevant political currencies for politicians.

Another relevant feature affecting the incentive mechanism of sanctions can be related with the time span governments' mandates. Very often the claim in front of Court are filed and then discussed after three levels of national jurisdictions have already took place and this might increase the distance from the "real" wrongdoer.

Being governments public elected bodies, the claim and the procedure in front of the ECtHR can exceed the term of their appointment so that very often a specific government has to respond for the wrong done by the previous one. In this respect the moral message that someone envisaged to find in the ECtHR sanctioning scheme can be diluted by the fact that receivers are not always those who deserve it.[7]

Still, and despite the previous remarks, the damages awarded by the Courts are extensively using the just satisfaction mechanism in order to award non-pecuniary and thus non-compensatory damages.

---

[7] In this respect it is worth reminding that if the offense is repeat, very often the problem is systemic and not the responsibility of a unique government. For example, Italy despite its long-lasting tradition of rule of law, performs bad both in terms of effectiveness of human rights protection and in terms ancillary remedies. The number of violations is surprisingly high and steady across years. Also, claims' types are very similar to each other, thus indicating that the lack of compliance with the Convention is systematic.

All in all, except we want to believe that ECtHR judges are just following a random path, moreover, diverging from the rationality scheme identified by Posner (1993), it becomes relevant to look for a justification making sense of an apparent disorder that renders just satisfaction a rational tool for pursuing goals that cannot be easily achieved with the straight application of the *restitutio in integrum*. What is more, is the Court also following an escalating strategy for repeat offenders? If the answer is positive, since most of the theory does apply here, what might be the rationale explaining it?

The international level, the decision on repeat offenses and the fact that the sanctioned subject are states, makes the ECtHR a seminal case for these kind of courts. If one of the goals of judicial administration is to restore wrongdoing and awarding damages, in this case we have an evidence of how courts might go further, by rewarding victims even more than it would be deserved. It might be of course an emotional reaction to a specific case. But if one goes further and lets the standard paradigm fade into the background, there might be a stronger answer going in the direction of the expressive function of punishment, as theorized by Feinberg (1965):

"Punishment is a conventional device for the expression of attitudes of resentment and indignation, and of judgments of disapproval and reprobation, on the part either of the punishing authority himself or of those 'in whose name' the punishment is inflicted." (Feinberg 1965, p. 400).

This *"symbolic significance"* (Feinberg 1965, p. 400) produces what is called a *reprobative symbolism* that makes sense beyond the compensatory mechanism, since it performs the function of vindicating the law and hence it emphatically reaffirms the law. It signals its *authoritative disavowal,* that is to say, at least "moral" condemnation for the action producing the wrong and further it indicates its *symbolic nonacquiescence,* which translates in communicating without ambiguity the sense of violated justice that deserves to be condemned. It is worth noting that this kind of effect is twofold, since it communicates the symbolic significance to the wrongdoer but also to society. This might be crucial in the case of an international court based upon a convention asserting human rights and then discovering that member states recurrently are not respecting it. This symbolic role of sanctions conveys also moral norms that have been further recognized by other sciences. For example, psychology, showing that in many cases, even within societies in which wrongdoers are single individuals, although in theory the standard deterrence may be used, sometime the symbolic side is very important (Mulder 2018). It is the case for example of law and sanctions amended for discouraging illegal downloading or tax evasion. The installment of a sanctioning system, besides altering the costs/benefits ratio and thus performing deterrence, it produces a symbolic inertia. The latter can be very useful in cases in which the very low probability of being caught and the general ineffectiveness of the legal apparatus makes the detecting of the wrong very unlikely or socially very costly, as for example a system for seriously defeating downloading would hamper other important social values like, for example, privacy (Domon et al. 2019). We believe that the above on the whole can provide a likely interpretation of the ECtHR "just satisfaction" damages awarding scheme.

10.4 Data and Empirical Strategy

The dataset used for performing our empirical investigation comes from different sources. It contains figures from the Council of Europe, albeit it counts only 45 countries out of 47 because of missing data for small countries. Other data is drawn from the annual reports issued by institutional bodies related to the ECtHR. More precisely, the Registry of the ECtHR's annual reports contains data on the demand of justice (calculated as the number of filed claims per 100,000 inhabitants in a given country), while CM annual reports on the supervision and execution of ECtHR final judgments and decisions provides data on the outcomes. On the whole these reports permit the ability to gather figures on the demand of ECtHR justice for each member states, allowing comparison over time. For the control variable, data is also extracted from the World Bank and the International Monetary Fund dataset. All in all, because of some missing data we can account on a rather balanced panel of yearly observations for 45 countries between 2008 and 2014, for a total of 309 observations (we lose 6 country/year observations).

Our goal is to test whether the Court uses an increasing sanction scheme for repeat offenders and we control for a number of covariates as, for example, the gravity of violations, that might further support the thesis that the court, by awarding damages, produces general prescription, in order to perform the expressive function.

Our dependent variable is JSD, the natural logarithm[8] of the average amount of just satisfaction damages inflicted to a state for every decision in a given year. It is calculated for country i in year t, as follows:

---

[8] For a handful of countries (Andorra, Iceland, Liechtenstein, Luxemburg, and San Marino), we observe no damages awarded in some years. Accordingly, since our JSD variable is a

$$JSD_{i,t} = \ln \left(\frac{total\ sanctions\ in\ euros_{i,t} + 1}{convictions_{i,t} + settlements_{i,t}} \right)$$

One might object that the total amount of sanctions should be weighed upon filed claims. However, there is surprisingly a huge gap between filed claims and the cases declared admissible and then decided or settled. To give a glimpse on the magnitude of this gap one might consider the following: from its inception in 1959 to 2014 the Court received 700,531 claims, delivering only 25,154 decisions or settlements. Rejected claims do not undergo the scrutiny of judges and thus it would be improper to consider these figures. However, outcomes adverse to the defendant involving damages are of two different categories. The first is the usual judge-made decision. The second is the instance of settlement in which parties reach a friendly agreement involving a monetary transaction from the defendant to the plaintiff. The latter in general is smaller than the original request filed to the Court. Albeit in this case there is no analysis of the merit of the dispute, the deal amounts to an acknowledgment of responsibility and as such it must be considered a negative outcome. The average *JSD* value in our sample is €268,085.9 per year, with a maximum amount of €3,146,275.3 request Italy to pay in 2012.

The independent variable of interest is *NC*, the degree of non-compliance by a state in a given year (as assessed by the ECtHR, again in log), calculated as follows:

$$NC_{i,t} = \ln \left(\frac{assessed\ violations_{i,t}}{meritorius\ cases_{i,t}} \right)$$

The other covariates accounts for the gravity of the human rights violated (*G*), the level of demand of justice (*D*), the per capita gross domestic product (*GDP*), and an indicator for the respect of the rule of law (*ROL*). We use the *G* variable in order to account for the "gravity" of member states' human rights violation. Since the ECtHR protects a vast spectrum of rights, the damages that might be caused by different violations might be equally different in magnitude. One might suggest that a single individual violation of human physical and mental integrity through torture (art. 2, ECHR), might imply a different level of damages for a member state than the violation of the "reasonable time" of judicial

logarithmic transformation of average damages, we arbitrarily added 1 euro to every country's total amount of damages, rather than dropping these observations. In this way, for the aforementioned countries we can still compute a value of *JSD*.

proceedings (art. 6, ECHR). For this reason we coded all violations to human rights devoted to protect physical or mental integrity, lifem and safety, namely ECHR articles 2, 3, 4, and 5. Accordingly, G, measures the ratio between the number of these more "severe" violations and the overall number of assessed human rights violations as follow:

$$G_{i,t} = \frac{assessed\,"severe"\,violations_{i,t}}{assessed\,violations_{i,t}}$$

It is thus plausible to expect a positive relation between gravity and JSD. It is worth noting that even if one assumes that violations characterized by a higher gravity also causes more serious harm, we expect that judges will still differentiate violations per category in order to discourage the tendency to perpetrate violations of primary human rights. Hence, the increase in the share of more serious violations will lead to an increase of the damages awarded.

GDP is a variable including the logarithmic transformation of PPP-corrected GDP per capita. The variable controls whether there is any negative correlation either between GDP and the percentage of negative outcomes or between GDP and seriousness of violation. Indeed, it might be the case that less-economically developed countries perform worse before the Court or do not respect more basic human rights than more-economically developed ones.

The covariate D represents the demand of ECtHR's justice in a given country/year. We measure it as the as the ratio of all claims filed against a member state and that very same country's population, and then multiply it per 100,000 in order to express it as a litigation rate (figures on countries' population are extracted from the IMF's World Economic Outlook). This allows controlling for the potential influence on the percentage of negative outcomes of the bulk of incoming cases the Court has to deal with. We are not directly interested in the sign of this coefficient, but rather to avoid omitted variable biases deriving from the possible effect of this variable on NC. The number of filed claims might have a twofold influence on the percentage of unfavorable verdicts: first a large number of new applications in a given year might suggest that there has been a case of systematic violation. Alternatively, a steep increase in the number of applications might reveal a strategic behavior by specialized lawyers promoting resort to the ECtHR because of the possible gains in term of legal fees. Similarly, the chance of obtaining additional monetary relief attracts the attention of individuals not completely satisfied with the national jurisdictions' redress. Judges perceiving

Table 10.2 *Descriptive statistics*

Variable name	Description	Mean	Std. dev.	Min	Max
JSD	Average amount of just satisfaction damages inflicted to a state (Log)	8.60	3.78	0	17.91
NC	Degree of noncompliance by a state	0.04	0.13	0	1.75
G	HR violations' gravity	0.61	1.50	0	19
D	Number of claims filed per 100.000 inhabitants (Log)	1.96	1.03	−0.93	5.02
ROL	Index on rule of law	1.84	0.83	0.19	3.26
GDP	PPP-corrected GDP per capita (Log)	9.88	1.08	7.22	12.46

the opportunistic behavior might "sanction" claimants and attempt to reduce this trend awarding lower damages. Conversely, a higher number of incoming and meritorious cases indicates either the existence of a structural flaw at the national level or higher awareness of the Court authority. Furthermore, the number of new cases allows controlling for the influence, if any, of the tendency to scrutinize several similar claims all together, thus merging multiple offenses in one judgment only.

ROL is an index calculated by the World Bank and roughly captures the baseline theoretical respect of the rule of law, thus the level of human rights protection within a country.[9] Table 10.2 summarizes the variables and lists the descriptive statistics.

Our estimates are obtained via the multivariate fixed effects models that follow.[10] In particular, model (1) considers only country fixed effects, while (2) includes also year dummies. In model (3) we also add the one-year lagged value of NC in order to take into account potential inter-temporal patterns that the ECtHR might follow in awarding damages, by taking into account not only current but also past noncompliance. Our coefficient of interest, β, is expected to be positive. As we are fully aware that our identification strategy does not allow us to rule out completely all form of endogeneity issues and thus supply definitive

[9] Information can be found on: http://info.worldbank.org/governance/wgi/#home (accessed July 9, 2019).
[10] Our fixed effects strategy was supported by an Hausman test that rejected the fit of a random effects model with a 0.008 *p*-value.

Table 10.3 *Regression OLS fixed effects panel models*

Variables	(1) JSD	(2) JSD	(3) JSD
NC	4.882***	5.158***	5.754***
	(1.205)	(1.339)	(1.328)
NC_{t-1}			−1.884**
			0.825
G	0.378***	0.368***	0.399***
	(0.136)	(0.135)	(0.137)
D	0.001	−0.109	−0.379
	(0.361)	(0.393)	(0.409)
GDP	−0.133	−0.110	0.180
	(0.410)	(0.403)	(0.360)
ROL	2.173	1.359	2.784
	(1.455)	(1.646)	(2.408)
Year Fixed Effects	no	yes	yes
Country Fixed Effects	yes	yes	yes
Within-country R2	0.075	0.114	0.131
Countries	45	45	45
Observations	309	309	264

Notes: Clustered standard errors at the country level in parentheses *** $p < 0.01$, ** $p < 0.05$, * $p < 0.1$.

evidence on the causal impact of our regressors on judicial behavior, we interpret our estimates more cautiously as correlations.

$$JSD_{i,\,t} = \beta NC_{i,\,t} + \gamma G_{i,\,t} + \theta GDP_{i,\,t} + \chi ROL_{i,\,t} + \delta_i + \varepsilon_{i,\,t} \tag{1}$$

$$JSD_{i,\,t} = \beta NC_{i,\,t} + \gamma G_{i,\,t} + \theta GDP_{i,\,t} + \chi ROL_{i,\,t} + \delta_i + \mu_t + u_{i,\,t} \tag{2}$$

$$JSD_{i,\,t} = \beta NC_{i,\,t} + \xi NC_{i,\,t-1} + \gamma G_{i,\,t} + \theta GDP_{i,\,t} + \chi ROL_{i,\,t} + \delta_i + \mu_t + v_{i,t} \tag{3}$$

10.5 Results

Table 10.3 presents the result of our estimation. As it can be easily seen, NC is statistically significant and positive, thus implying that the Court employs an increasing sanction scheme for repeat offenders. Not only the ECtHR systematically diverges from a mere compensatory scheme when awarding damages, but at a given level of violations' gravity, the Court awards on average higher per case damages to less compliant states.

Our log-log model allows us to easily interpret our estimates: a 1 percent increase in the degree of noncompliance as assessed by the ECtHR correlates to a 5 percent increase of the average sanction. The implications might be manifold but the (null) hypothesis of a random outcome can be rejected. The Court not only clearly might consider costs suffered by the victim, but it seems to systematically include the social cost related to the violation of human rights and this is apparently is increasing over the number of cases.

By including the lagged value of NC as an additional regressor in model (3) we find some interesting results. Not only our main regressor of interest, NC, remains statistically significant and its coefficient increases in magnitude, but its one-year lagged variable shows an equally significant effect but with an opposing sign. In other words, from our analysis it seems to emerge that the ECtHR apparently punishes current noncompliance with higher damages, while at the same time "discounting" past-year violations. This could be interpreted as a sort of adjusting mechanism that the court might put in practice in order to avoid awarding excessive damages that would probably turn out to be ineffective in terms of fostering long-run human rights protection when punishing too harshly the wrongdoer. Furthermore, this result seems to confirm previous theoretical findings claiming that judges are adjusting damages' size in order to avoid over-deterrence in an inter-temporal perspective (Burnovski and Safra 2004). It is worth noting that if this applies for the internalization of the harm's social cost, it is even more important when the main goal is the expressive function of punishment, as a too harsh sanction would not reasonably increase the effectiveness of the signal produced, while it may be an embarrassingly too high cost for the wrongdoer. This is definitively important when defendants are States and the court's goal is simply, as previously discussed, to raise the general standards of protection of human rights within the State.

Given its attention for gravity – also confirmed by significance and positive sign of G – the ECtHR seems to care about the fact that a long-lasting number of violations might most seriously hamper the values asserted by the European Convention of Human Rights. However the increasing scheme is likely not to follow a fine-tuning of the cost-benefit ratio, as required by the internalization of the social cost of the violations. This is because several of the key features of this mechanism would not work. Reasonably the court is repeatedly exploiting the expressive feature of sanctions and trying to signal "louder" that not only a violation is a bad *per se*, but also it introduces even worse consequences when it shows a systematical possibility of non-respecting the convention.

However, it must be said that our analysis does not allow us to infer that higher damages induce higher compliance. We simply claim that the Court seems to adjust its sanctioning scheme to states' behavior. This might account that judges, when making decisions, exploit the symbolic value of their role and use the prestige of the Court to convey the political message of supporting on the whole the apparatus protecting human rights, not only in term of single violations.

10.6   Conclusions

After the path-breaking contribution by Posner (1993), courts and judicial decision-making have become an important subject matter of research. Understanding how dispute resolution systems work is a first step for making them effective institutions for society. However, if now increasing evidence is available about national judicial systems, international courts remain still an under-investigated topic far from being clearly understood. This chapter intends to advance the state of the art by studying the European Court of Human Rights, a court-making part, jointly with the Convention of Human Rights, according to many commentators of the most advance system for protecting human rights.

At a first sight what this court does is to afford a monetary relief to victims of human rights violations perpetrated by a member state and this further seems compatible with the theory explaining the role of damages. The research tries to detect whether a stable pattern of damages awarding exists or not, given that the just satisfaction doctrine actually allows judges to exert a wide discretionary power in deciding final amounts, that does not seem to emerge in cases per se. By means of a panel data analysis spanning from 2008 to 2014, the empirical investigation shows that the ECtHR tends to award higher damages when states' compliance is worse (the share of negative outcomes is higher) and the gravity is higher (the share of serious violations is larger). The above implies that the court specifically targets repeat offenders in a harsher way than single offenders. However, since the double satisfaction scheme seems not to follow the usual cost-benefit mechanism used for producing deterrence, it is reasonable to assume that, given the idiosyncratic characteristics of the environment in which ECtHR operates, this strategy responds to the necessity of satisfying an expressive function of punishment, as illustrated by Feinberg (1965). Harsher sanctions are not a fine-tuning process for making the wrongdoer pay the cost of the harm caused, that for many reasons would be weakly effective, but a "louder" voice showing that a state is deviating from the values asserted and protected by the European Convention of Human Rights.

References

Burnovski, Moshe, and Zvi Safra. 2004. Deterrence Effects of Sequential Punishment Policies: Should Repeat Offenders Be More Severely Punished? *International Review Of Law and Economics* 14(3): 341–50.

Cassone, Alberto, and Giovanni B. Ramello. 2011. The Simple Economics of Class Action: Private Provision of Club and Public Goods. *European Journal of Law and Economics* 32(2): 205–24.

Desrieux, Claudine, and Romain Espinosa. 2019. Case Selection and Judicial Decision-Making: Evidence from French Labor Courts. *European Journal of Law and Economics* 47(1): 57–88.

Domon, Koji, Alessandro Melcarne, and Giovanni B. Ramello. 2019. Digital Piracy in the Asian Countries. *Journal of Industrial and Business Economics*, DOI: 10.1007/s40812-019-00111-3.

Emons, Winand. 2003. Escalating Penalties for Repeat Offenders, *International Review of Law and Economics* 27(2): 170–78.

2003. A Note on Optimal Punishment for Repeat Offenders, *International Review of Law and Economics*, 23(3): 253–59.

Eren, Ozkan and Naci Mocan. 2018. Emotional Judges and Unlucky Juveniles. *American Economic Journal: Applied Economics* 10(3): 171–205.

Feinberg, Joel. 1965. The Expressive Function of Punishment, *The Monist* 49(3): 397–423.

Gerbaldo, Federica. 2019. Europen Court of Human Rights, in: Encyclopedia of Law and Economics, edited by, Marciano, Alain and Giovanni Battista Ramello, Springer: New York, 798–805. https://doi.org/10.1007/978-1-4614-7753-2.

Guthrie, Chris, Jeffrey J. Rachlinski, and Andrew J. Wistrich. 2007. Blinking on the Bench: How Judges Decide Cases. *Cornell Law Review* 93(1): 1–43.

Ichim Octavian. 2014. *Just Satisfaction under the European Convention on Human Rights*. Cambridge: Cambridge University Press.

Ichino, Andrea, Michele Polo, and Enrico Rettore. 2003. Are Judges Biased by Labor Market Conditions? *European Economic Review* 47(5): 913–44.

Ippoliti, Roberto and Giovanni B. Ramello. 2018. Governance of Tax Courts. *Economics of Governance* 19(4): 317–38.

Marciano, Alain, Alessandro Melcarne, and Giovanni B. Ramello. 2019. The Economic Importance of Judicial Institutions, Their Performance and the Proper Way to Measure Them. *Journal of Institutional Economics* 15(1): 81–98.

Melcarne, Alessandro. 2017. Careerism and Judicial Behavior. *European Journal of Law and Economics* 44(2): 241–64.

Melcarne, Alessandro and Giovanni B. Ramello. 2015. Judicial Independence, Judges Incentives and Efficiency. *Review of Law & Economics* 11(2): 149–69.

Miceli, Thomas. 2018. On Proportionality of Punishments and the Economic Theory of Crime. *European Journal of Law and Economics* 46(3): 303–14.

Mulder, Laetitia B. 2018. When Sanctions Convey Social Norms. *European Journal of Law and Economics* 46(3): 331–42.

Polinsky, A. Mitchell, and Daniel L. Rubinfeld. 1991. A Model of Optimal Fines for Repeat Offenders. *Journal of Public Economics* 46(3): 291–306.

Posner, Richard A. 1993. What Do Judges and Justices Maximize? The Same Thing Everyone Else Does. *Supreme Court Economic Review* 3: 1–41.

Posner Richard A., and Miguel De Figueiredo. 2005. Is the International Court of Justice Bias? *Journal of Legal Studies* 34(2): 599–630.

Ramello, Giovanni B., and Stefan Voigt. 2012. The Economics of Efficiency and the Judicial System. *International Review of Law and Economics* 32(1): 1–2.

Romano, Cesare P.R., Karen J. Alter, and Y. Shany (eds). 2014. *The Oxford Handbook of International Adjudication.* Oxford: Oxford University Press.

Shany, Yuval. 2014. *Assessing the Effectiveness of International Courts.* Oxford: Oxford University Press.

Shelton, Dinah. 2015. *Remedies in International Human Rights Law.* 3rd ed. Oxford: Oxford University Press.

Sidak, J. Gregory. 1981. Rethinking Antitrust Damages. *Stanford Law Review* 33 (2): 329–52.

Sunstein Cass R., David Schkade, Lisa M. Ellman, and Andres Sawicki. 2006. *Are Judgers Political? An Empirical Analysis of the Federal Judiciary.* New York: Brooking Institution Press.

Voeten Erik. 2008. The Impartiality of International Judges: Evidences from the European Court of Human Rights. *American Political Science Review* 102(4): 417–33.

White, Mark D. 2018. The Neglected Nuance of Beccaria's Theory of Punishment. *European Journal of Law and Economics* 46(3): 315–29.

11

Does Efficiency Trump Legality?

The Case of the German Constitutional Court

CHRISTOPH ENGEL

11.1 Research Question

Supreme courts are judicial and political bodies at a time. A visible expression of this dual role is the power of certiorari, as enjoyed by the US Supreme Court since the Judiciary Act of 1891 (26 Stat. 826). The court may pick its fights. As a beneficial side effect, the court may allocate its resources, in particular, the time and energy the justices spend on a case, to worthy causes. In economic parlance, this discretion makes the court more efficient. Efficiency comes at a political cost, though. This discretion also gives the court political power. It may direct its verdict to causes on which it wants to have a political impact, or it may put an issue on the political agenda.

Officially German constitutional law does not grant certiorari. In principle, the Constitutional Court must decide each and every case that is brought. This obligation is qualified for constitutional complaints that are directly brought by citizens. They must be accepted by the court. But officially the court does not have discretion in such cases either. It has to accept the case, "in so far as it has general constitutional significance" or "if the complainant would suffer a particularly severe disadvantage if the Court refused to decide on the complaint" (§ 93a BVerfGG). Both prescriptions bind the court. As a matter of fact, the court hears a lot of cases. In 2011,[1] 6,066 new cases have been brought. During the year, the court has issued 5,733 decisions.[2] Yet a closer look reveals that the court has crafted a whole arsenal of more subtle measures for managing

---

[1] I use 2011 since I have coded a dataset of all decisions made during the year that are electronically available on the website of the court.

[2] www.bundesverfassungsgericht.de/DE/Verfahren/Jahresstatistiken/Archiv/2011/gb2011_pdf/A-III.pdf?__blob=publicationFile&v=2 (accessed July 9, 2019).

the caseload. Only 34 rulings have been given by one of the two senates, all the remaining only by chambers of three justices. Only 76 complaints decided by the chambers have been successful. Only 467 of the dismissals have come with written reasons.[3]

From 1998 on, the court has made many of its decisions electronically available.[4] Unfortunately, this collection is incomplete. For instance for 2011, it only lists 255 decisions. The remaining decisions are not publicly available. Quite likely most of these cases have been summarily dismissed. But this is only a supposition. Strictly speaking there is an insurmountable selection problem. As this chapter shows, it is nonetheless revealing to study this incomplete evidence with quantitative methods. For multiple reasons that transcend selection and are discussed below, this evidence is inconclusive. Causal effects cannot be established. But the available information suffices to develop an index that measures how seriously the court has taken a case. This index shows pronounced variance. Apparently the court does not devote its energy randomly or uniformly, but picks cases that it considers worth the effort. While the court does not have the power of certiorari, it has found indirect ways for allocating resources to cases.

This finding triggers the obvious follow up question: does the ensuing efficiency gain come at the cost of biasing the court's jurisprudence? In the political and in the academic discourse in the United States, one concern dominates: that the Supreme Court is partisan and favors one of the political parties, or their cherished policies. In Germany, Constitutional Court justices are nominated by the political parties, which makes it possible to investigate the equivalent concern. But there are multiple other bench characteristics that might as well explain that the court, acting as a senate or chamber, takes a case more seriously. In this exercise, I find almost no signs of bias. Again, the finding has to be read with caution. I am not in a position to identify causal effects. But I at least do not find a smoking gun.

A fully worked out theory of the decision to take a case more or less seriously is beyond the scope of the present chapter. The contribution of the chapter is more modest. I first want to present evidence that, and in which ways, the German Constitutional Court exercises discretion,

---

[3] www.bundesverfassungsgericht.de/DE/Verfahren/Jahresstatistiken/Archiv/2011/gb2011_pdf/A-III.pdf?__blob=publicationFile&v=2 (accessed July 9, 2019).

[4] www.bundesverfassungsgericht.de/SiteGlobals/Forms/Suche/Entscheidungensuche_Formular.html?language_=de (accessed July 9, 2019). The website also reports select decisions from earlier years.

despite the fact that officially it does not have the power of certiorari. I second aim at finding signals of determinants of judicial discretion that may raise normative concern, or that suggest choice variables for judicial policy. Were I, for instance, to find signals that more homogeneous chambers (in terms of political orientation, professional background, tenure, gender, or age) exert more effort, the court itself or the legislator might react by using bench composition as a lever for fine tuning the allocation of resources to cases.

The remainder of this chapter is organized as follows: Section 11.2 relates the chapter to the literature. Section 11.3 introduces the German case. Section 11.4 explains how to generate the dependent variable: how seriously does the court take a case? Section 11.5 introduces bench characteristics and investigates whether they explain that the court has taken a case more seriously. Section 11.6 concludes.

11.2   Related Literature

The quantitative literature on the German Constitutional Court is still sparse. Georg Vanberg was interested in factors correlated with the decision of the court to strike down a statute. He uses all published senate decisions from 1983 to 1995 directly concerned with a statute. He finds that the court has been more likely to strike down a statute if it has held an oral hearing, and in particular if one of the parties heard claims the statute to be unconstitutional. He interprets both indicators as proxies for public scrutiny in case government were to neglect the ruling. He further finds that statutes are more likely to be struck down if the current government (after a change of majority in the elections) also claims unconstitutionality. By contrast, in policy areas that are more complex, like economic regulation or social insurance, statutes are less likely to be invalidated by the court (Vanberg 2004). I have another research question, another dependent variable, use different data, and have a different econometric approach. In one dimension, our results can be seen as complementary. While Georg Vanberg finds that the court is politically active, he too does not find that the court is active in support of one political orientation. The activity is a function of the relationship between the court on the one hand, and government and parliament on the other hand.

Shikano and Koch use dissenting votes of the justices from one of the two senates between 1970 and 2009 to identify their ideological positions. Justices selected by the Social Democrats, compared with the majority of the senate, tend to express more left-wing positions in their dissenting votes. Yet the dissenting opinions of three of these justices are fairly centrist, and one outlier even exhibits a pronounced right-wing position in his dissenting votes. Overall, the political positions expressed in the dissenting votes of justices selected by the Christian Democrats, including the one justice selected by the Liberals, are more centrist. Yet about half of them exhibit identifiable right-wing positions.

Engst et al. (2017) analyze the 20 dissenting votes that have been issued by the second senate of the German Constitutional Court between 2005 and 2016 and demonstrate that justices selected by the Social Democrats on the one hand, and the Christian Democrats on the other hand, are more likely to dissent together than with justices appointed by the respective other political party.

There is a rich quantitative literature on the jurisprudence of the US Supreme Court, and on lower US courts. Some of this literature studies the exercise of judicial discretion. In the period between 1891 and 1925, docket control was still incomplete for the US Supreme Court, which led to similar doctrinal and procedural bypasses as the ones today observed in the German Constitutional Court (for background, see Eisenberg 1974; but see Freeborn and Hartmann 2010 on sensitivity of judges to the Congressional decision to reduce discretion to reduce criminal sentences). US State Supreme Courts are much less likely to reverse cases if their jurisdiction is mandatory, indicating that they use discretion to pick the cases in which they want to intervene (Eisenberg and Miller 2009).

It has been shown that, in recent years, in its decisions to grant certiorari, the Supreme Court has been sensitive to pressure from Congress (Harvey and Friedman 2009). If the Supreme Court has requested the Solicitor General to submit a brief, this is a good predictor of the court later granting certiorari (Thompson and Wachtell 2008). The Rhode Island Supreme Court's use of its discretion in granting sentence reduction could best be explained by judge effects, indicating that the exercise of discretion is influenced by idiosyncratic predilections (Braslow and Cheit 2011). Yet what looks like a bias in exercising discretion may, at closer scrutiny, result from a selection effect. While foreign plaintiffs have been more likely to win cases in US courts, this has been shown to result from successful efforts of plaintiffs to avoid US jurisdiction if odds were low they would win (Clermont and Eisenberg 2007).

Many papers have tested for an impact of judges' political orientation on their judiciary decisions (Carroll and Tiede 2011; Schubert 1965; Segal and Spaeth 1993; 2002; Sunstein, Schkade, and Ellman 2004). In the US

Supreme Court, taking justices' ideological position with respect to civic rights into account, 60 percent of their pertinent decisions could be correctly predicted while, without this information, only 27 percent of the decisions were predicted (Segal and Spaeth 2002). In the Rehnquist court, ideological orientation predicted decisions, even if that meant for conservative justices to be activist (Solberg and Lindquist 2006). The ideology effect was particularly pronounced in judges who stood for reelection (Hall 1992; Huber and Gordon 2004; Shepherd 2009). But the ideology effect is not uncontested. Exploiting random assignment of cases for identification, one study has not found a significant effect of ideological orientation (Ashenfelter, Eisenberg, and Schwab 1995). There also is extended debate over how to measure (prenomination) political orientation (Cameron and Park 2009). In the case of the US Forest Service, only published decisions were significantly explained by political orientation (Keele et al. 2009).

An equally rich literature investigates the effect of judge gender on the decisions they make, again with very mixed outcomes (see the survey in Boyd, Epstein, and Martin 2010). In terms of judicial quality and esteem, there was practically no difference, neither in state nor in federal judges, despite the fact that female judges on average had received less prestigious training (Choi et al. 2011).

It has been shown that the professional background of justices on the US Supreme Court has considerably varied over time, but that in recent years judicial experience has been the dominant selection criterion. It has been argued that this has likely deprived the court of judicial talent, and that the criterion risks exacerbating other biases, like race or gender, that already impact on the likelihood of becoming a judge (Epstein, Knight, and Martin 2003).

11.3   The German Constitutional Court

German courts are specialized by subject matter. There are separate branches of the judiciary for criminal and private law disputes, for disputes between government and the citizens, for social security, for labor law and for tax law. Each of these branches has a specialized Supreme Court. In principle, for each dispute there can be both appeal and *Revision* (the German term for appeals for issues of law). On appeal, the case is heard again by a superior court. On *Revision*, the facts are taken for granted. Only the violation of procedural rules, and the misconstruction of substantive law, are at issue. Appeal is in the hands of

intermediate courts, while *Revision* usually goes to the respective
Supreme Court. Germany has an additional court that only decides about
constitutionality. All other courts are entitled to apply the constitution, in
particular using it for the reinterpretation of ordinary law, but they may
not declare a statute anti-constitutional. This is the prerogative of the
Constitutional Court.

There are multiple ways of bringing cases to the Constitutional Court.
The bulk of cases results from constitutional complaints by individuals.
In 2011, of 255 publicly available decisions 231, or 90.59 percent, origin-
ated in constitutional complaints. A slightly different procedure results
from complaints by individuals that provisions regarding federal elections have been violated. In 2011 the court has heard 9 such cases. If
courts deem a statutory provision anti-constitutional, they may refer the
case to the Constitutional Court. In 2011, the Constitutional Court has
received 6 such referrals. Finally there are multiple procedures for disputes between federal authorities, or between the federation and the
Laender.[5] In 2011, these procedures have led to 9 cases. One does not
need to be represented by an attorney to bring a case to the German
constitutional court. This is the most important reason why a sizable
fraction of constitutional complaints is obviously inadmissible.

The court is composed of two senates with eight justices each. Justices
are appointed by the President of the Federal Republic, but half of them
are selected by the *Bundestag* and half of them by the *Bundesrat*, that is,
by the Federation and the *Laender*, always with a majority of two-thirds.
In practice, this has led to a right of initiative for half of the justices for
the Christian Democrats, and for the other half for the Social Democrats.
At the last occasion the Christian Democrats have let their then coalition
partner, the Liberals, pick one justice, as have the Social Democrats for
their former coalition partner, the Greens. Justices are appointed for the
duration of 12 years, and may not be reappointed. The large majority of
decisions are not taken by the two senates, but by chambers of 3 justices
each. At the German constitutional court, cases are not randomly
assigned to chambers.[6]

---

[5] The complete list is to be found in § 13 Bundesverfassungsgerichtsgesetz. An English
translation is available at www.iuscomp.org/gla/statutes/BVerfGG.htm (accessed July
9, 2019).

[6] For details see www.bundesverfassungsgericht.de/DE/Verfahren/Geschaeftsverteilung/
gv2018/geschaeftsverteilung_2018.html;jsessionid=6BBFC7A10127F5887B5D2B2735C78
FE6.2_cid383 (accessed July 9, 2019).

Beginning in January 1998, the Constitutional Court has made its decisions publicly available on its website.[7] The data for this chapter covers all 255 decisions made public in 2011. I have coded the data such that both the dependent variable and explanatory variables are available in numeric form. I will explain coding as I introduce the respective variables. The main reason for limiting the data to one year is pragmatic; coding the entire year has already been quite labor intense. But the limited time span also means that I do not have reason to be concerned about changes in the court's reactions to explanatory variables over time.

11.4   How Seriously Does the Court Take a Case?

The German Constitutional Court is obliged to decide all cases that are brought. Nonetheless, the court does not devote the same amount of effort to all cases. In this more subtle way it allocates scarce judicial resources to cases, and eases the caseload. While it seems plain that the court makes such choices, they are difficult to trace. In this section, I introduce the multiple observable indicators. I next show that they are highly correlated. This observation invites the aggregation of information from individual indicators. Using exploratory factor analysis, it turns out that a single factor best captures the information. Loadings from the individual indicators have an intuitive interpretation.

The first indicator comes from the decision itself. Doctrinally, whether a reference to the Constitutional Court is admissible or not is a question of law, not of discretion. Yet with tongue in cheek, observers of court practice have said: if the Court wants to hear a case, it'll find reasons why it is admissible; if the Court does not want to hear the case, it'll find ways to declare it inadmissible. There is one procedure that supports this view. In 2011, the Court has received six references from lower courts for preliminary ruling. The Court has declared all of them inadmissible, usually with lengthy reasons that do not only cover procedural issues, but substance. The obvious explanation stems from the fact that, in this procedure, chambers may only declare the reference inadmissible, and do not have jurisdiction to decide on the merits.[8] If chambers did not want to burden the senate with cases they deem less relevant, declaring them inadmissible is the way out.

---

[7] www.bundesverfassungsgericht.de/entscheidungen.html (accessed July 9, 2019).
[8] § 81a Bundesverfassungsgerichtsgesetz (accessed July 9, 2019).

For sure, for some cases, admissibility is patently out of the question. The fact that the court declares the case inadmissible need therefore not follow from discretion but may only indicate that the court follows the procedural rules given to it by the legislator. Yet there is enough room at the margin to make the fact that the case is declared (in)admissible a potential indicator of how seriously the court has taken that particular case. Over all procedures, the court has declared 72 cases, or 28.24 percent of all cases, inadmissible, or has confined its decision to preliminary procedural issues. Since the court has avoided to decide on the merits of the case, one might argue that it has taken the case less seriously.

The second indicator is the body that has taken the decision. Constitutional complaints are screened by chambers of three justices. The chamber may refer the case to the senate. But it may also unanimously decide that the case is inadmissible, admissible but unwarranted, or even admissible and warranted. As mentioned, if lower courts referred the case to the Constitutional Court, the chamber may only screen for admissibility. Over all procedures, in 2011, 219 decisions, or 85.88 percent, have been taken by a chamber. Propelling the case to the senate is certainly a way of taking a case more seriously.

The third indicator is a procedural choice. Chambers sit *in camera* by design, while senates may choose to have an oral hearing with the parties, and if the Court deems fit also with other stakeholders and experts. Arguably if there is a hearing, this indicates that the Court takes the case particularly seriously. Of the 36 senate decisions, this happened in four cases.

The fourth indicator is also only available for decisions taken by a senate. The only decision chambers may take if they are not unanimous is to refer the case to the senate. These intermediary decisions are not made publicly available. Senates are free to decide by majority. If they do, the size of the majority is reported. In 2011, 2 cases have been decided by a majority of 5, one case by a majority of 6, and 4 cases by a majority of 7. To make the size of the majority comparable across court composition, I translate these numbers into a fraction of the respective bench.[9] Anecdotal evidence from conversations with justices makes it clear that almost

---

[9] Occasionally, senates decide with less than 8 justices, for example, since the successor to a justice who has left the court has not yet been appointed. In 2011, one decision was taken by a senate of 6, and 3 were taken by a senate of 7. All these four decisions were unanimous.

no case decided by a senate is uncontroversial. The senate always has to work hard to achieve a compromise. Yet in the self-understanding of the court, such a jointly agreed decision is highly desirable. It strengthens the authority of the court as an institution. In the light of this, if the court decides by majority, this implies dissent that was so powerful that it could not be removed by debate or by striving for a compromise. Consequently, majority decisions indicate that the court had to struggle with the case more than with others, which one may interpret as a signal that the court has taken the case particularly seriously.

The fifth indicator results from the way how the court deals with the case. In principle, it is for the complainant to inform the Constitutional Court about the facts of the underlying conflict and, if necessary, to provide background information. Yet the court is entitled to give other stakeholders, and experts, the opportunity to submit the equivalent of an *amicus brief*.[10] However, unlike the law in the United States, in Germany outsiders may only address the court if the court solicits their view. If it does, this is reported in the final decision. In 2011, the court has exercised this option in 75 cases, or in 29.41 percent of all cases. Asking for *amicus briefs* indicates that the court either deems its decision particularly relevant for one stakeholder, or that it wants to further clarify the issue. Both suggest that the Court takes this case more seriously than others.

The sixth indicator is a straightforward measure of the energy the court devotes to a case: the length of the decision. In the electronic version of its decisions, the court numbers paragraphs, the mean being 25.44 paragraphs. But variance is pronounced, with many decisions being fairly short. Unsurprisingly, the very lengthy decisions are all taken by senates. But chamber decisions may be remarkably extended as well, the longest of them having 76 paragraphs.

A seventh indicator is taken from the way how the court writes. It sometimes formulates a few sentences akin to black letter rules (*ratio decidendi*). These sentences precede the official decision and are mainly directed to the legal community, telling them how the court sees the current decision contribute to the evolution of constitutional law, but they are of course also noted by the wider public. The court only does so if the decision has been taken by a senate. In 2011, 15 of 36 senate decisions, or 41.67 percent of them, have such rules. Arguably, black

---

[10] § 27a Bundesverfassungsgerichtsgesetz (accessed July 9, 2019).

letter rules indicate that the Court takes the case seriously since it envisions that the decision will have ramifications for future cases.

An eighth indicator results from the way how the court communicates its decision. Whenever the Court formulated black letter rules, it also issued a press release. But press releases are also made available in 33 more cases. Twenty-seven cases decided by chambers are accompanied by a press release. All in all, they are issued in 18.82 percent of all cases. A press release indicates that, in the Court's perception, the wider public has an interest in this particular case, or in the reasons for deciding it.

A more ambiguous ninth indicator for the effort the court devotes to the case is the time it takes for deciding. The indicator is weak, since the court might also procrastinate on cases it deems less relevant or interesting. The *rubrum* informs about the year when the case has reached the court. Ninety-four cases have been decided in the same year of 2011, 89 are from 2010, 30 are from 2009, 25 are from 2008, 8 are from 2007, 3 are from 2006, and 6 are from 2005.

The tenth indicator exploits a feature of German constitutional doctrine. In its jurisprudence, the German Constitutional Court has shaped the German constitution in a way similar to the *Lochner*[11] era in US constitutional law. Any intervention into freedom or property, and any public act that might treat comparable cases differently, come under the scrutiny of the Constitution. If one of the specific guarantees of freedom or equality is applicable, it provides the constitutional standard. But if not, the general clauses of freedom (Art. 2 I Basic Law) or of equality (Art. 3 I Basic Law) may be invoked.[12] The fact that any exercise of sovereign powers comes under constitutional scrutiny is, however, not tantamount to constitutional verdict. In principle, any interference with a fundamental right may be justified if only it turns out proportional, given the aim pursued by government. One should therefore expect that all cases, if they are not declared inadmissible, have a section on proportionality. Actually, this is not true. The court applies the proportionality test only in 110, or in 43.14 percent, of all cases. That practice makes discussion of the proportionality test a good indicator of how seriously the court took the case. If the test is applied, this means that the court

---

[11] *Lochner* v. *New York* (198 U.S. 45 [1905]); it is often said that the era came to an end with *West Coast Hotel Co.* v. *Parrish* (300 U.S. 379 [1937]).

[12] Leading case German Constitutional Court Jun 6, 1989, BVerfGE 80, 137 – Reiten im Walde.

discusses the merits of the case.[13] Conversely, if the court decides without discussing proportionality, this is an indication for it summarily dismissing the case.

As a first analytic step, Table 11.1 shows that these 10 indicators are highly correlated. Correlations are weakest, both in terms of the size of the correlation and of significance levels, between declaring a case inadmissible and the remaining indicators. Duration is not significantly correlated with having an oral hearing, and with not deciding unanimously. Applying the proportionality test is not significantly correlated with the decision being taken by a chamber. All remaining correlations are significant, and mostly strong.

While these correlations suggest that these 10 indicators have something in common, it is still unclear what constitutes the common denominator, and how much and in which way the individual indicators contribute to the underlying construct. In the presentation of the indicators, I have already explained why one has reason to believe that all of them measure different dimensions of the court taking a case seriously. That invites a statistical procedure that is able to construct this underlying latent (unobserved) variable, and to investigate whether these indicators are manifestations of the court taking a case more or less seriously. The appropriate procedure to do this is (exploratory) factor analysis.[14]

Arguably, the 15 percent of cases not resulting from constitutional complaints are less comparable. To be on the safe side, I therefore confine

---

[13] Except if it is one of the rare cases where fundamental freedoms are irrelevant for legality. Since for estimation I confine the dataset to cases resulting from constitutional complaints, for my statistical models this is not an issue.

[14] More technically, (exploratory) factor analysis is a method to reduce the dimensionality of the dataset. As with all statistical analysis, the goal is to explain the observed variance of one or more variables. The more two variables are correlated, the more they explain the same difference from the respective mean. If factor analysis, as in the case of this dataset, results in a single factor with explanatory power (Eigenvalue > 1), the loading on each factor measures the relevance of variance in one variable for explaining variance in all variables. A variable has a high loading if differences in this one variable are particularly predictive for differences in other variables. If only one factor has an Eigenvalue > 1, this implies that all the relevant information is enshrined in this factor. For each datapoint (for each ruling, in the present dataset), this information can be expressed by one number. Technically, it is the length of a vector in a multidimensional space constituted by all variables. The purpose of factor analysis is defining the location of this vector in the multidimensional space. Once this location is found, for each datapoint the length of the vector can be calculated by adding up the factor loadings, multiplied by the expression of the respective variable for the respective datapoint.

Table 11.1 Correlation of indicators for taking cases seriously

	Proc	Chamber	Oral	Majority	Brief	Length	Black	Press	Duration	Proportionality
Proc	1	-0.021	-0.009	0.066	-0.309***	-0.161*	-0.046	-0.079	-0.188**	-0.265***
Chamber		1	-0.311***	0.368***	-0.233***	-0.438***	-0.617***	-0.410***	-0.202**	-0.011
Oral			1	-0.581***	0.196***	0.491***	0.505***	0.262***	0.096	0.145*
Majority				1	-0.231***	-0.426***	-0.543***	-0.309***	-0.068	-0.146*
Brief					1	0.520***	0.387***	0.284***	0.242***	0.289***
Length						1	0.761***	0.525***	0.308***	0.361***
Black							1	0.519***	0.229***	0.186**
Press								1	0.322***	0.290***
Duration									1	0.187**
Proportionality										1

Notes: proc: court has not taken a decision on the merits; chamber: decision has been taken by a chamber (not a senate). oral: (senate) has held an oral hearing; majority: (senate) has decided by majority; brief: court has solicited briefs. length: number of paragraphs, in the official electronic version; black: (senate) has formulated black letter rules. press: court has made a press release; duration: years that the case takes before decision; proportionality: proportionality test is applied. standardized correlations, $N = 255$. *** $p < .001$, ** $p < .01$, * $p < .05$

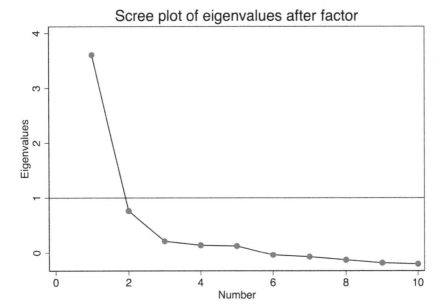

Figure 11.1   Factor analysis finds unique measure.

the statistical analysis to the 231 decisions on constitutional complaints.[15] The procedure finds 10 separate factors. But only the first factor has an Eigenvalue > 1,[16] and therefore above the explanatory power of individual observed variables. This implies that the 10 indicators can be aggregated to a unique latent variable.

Table 11.2 shows that the first factor has an intuitive interpretation. Three indicators have a negative loading: if they are high, the court has taken the case less seriously. Results suggest that a decision by a chamber, and a decision only on procedural grounds, indicate that the court has taken the case less seriously. The variable "size of majority" is 1 except if there was a majority vote. It thus is a measure of the fraction of the bench that was in support of the decision. Hence it must be interpreted in the reverse: if the court decides by majority, it has taken the case more seriously. This also holds if it has applied the proportionality test, if it has taken longer to decide, if it has solicited briefs, if it has held an oral

---

[15] Results look similar if I keep these cases in. The additional estimates are available upon request.
[16] The Eigenvalue of the first factor is 3.602.

Table 11.2 *Relative weight of indicators that court takes a case seriously*

	Loading
Chamber	−0.774
Size of majority	−0.539
No decision on the merits	−0.215
Proportionality test	0.376
Duration	0.400
Briefs solicited	0.491
Oral hearing	0.504
Press release	0.601
Length	0.845
Black letter rules	0.891

Notes: factor loadings for first factor.

hearing, if it has made a press release, and if it has written a longer decision. The (positive or negative) size of the coefficient can be interpreted as a measure for the relative importance of the respective indicator. Hence a decision by a chamber is the strongest indicator that the court has not taken the case seriously, and black letter rules are the strongest indicator that the court has taken the case seriously.

Figure 11.2 collects the seriousness scores of individual cases that are recovered from this statistical model. The distribution is heavily right-skewed. The court has taken the mass of all constitutional complaints not very seriously on which is has decided in 2011. Most of them do even have a negative score, indicating that the court has allocated very few resources to them.

11.5   Has the Court Been Biased?

As pointed out in the introduction, the fact that the court discriminates between cases when deciding how much effort to devote to one of them is not per se normatively problematic. To the contrary: if the court allocates its limited resources to the cases that deserve it, it does a better job. Or in the language used in the introduction: such discrimination would be efficient. But efficiency might come at the price of bias. In this section, I want to explore whether there is reason for suspicion. Let me repeat what I had already pointed out in the introduction: this paper does not pretend to offer a fully worked out theory for the motives of the court to

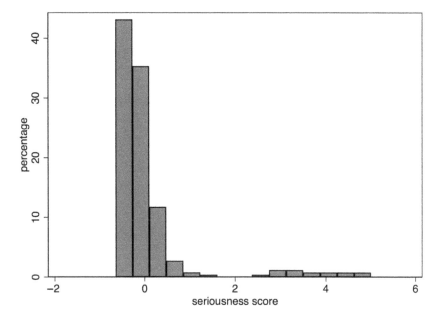

Figure 11.2 Seriousness scores.
Predicted values from factor analysis (loadings reported in Table 11.2).

take some cases more seriously than others. The following analysis merely checks whether bench characteristics explain how seriously the court has taken a case. As there are no obvious normative reasons why they should, significant effects signal that the court might be biased. Such effects deserve closer scrutiny in future work.

The international literature on supreme courts has been most interested in interpreting them as political actors or political arenas, and testing how the political procedure for selecting judges, their measurable political attitudes, demographic characteristics of individual judges or panels impact on case outcomes. The following section contributes the German case to this literature. It is limited in one way, but fairly information rich in another. The limitation results from the fact that (the rare case where justices write a dissenting opinion notwithstanding) votes of individual justices are not reported. More importantly, the large majority of all decisions are taken unanimously in the first place. Therefore, the data does not allow to identify choices of individual judges. Yet the fact that more than 85 percent of all decisions are taken by chambers, and that chamber composition varies widely, provides a rich dataset for measuring the effect of various indicators of bench composition on the degree by which the court takes the concrete case seriously.

The court always reports which justices have been on the bench. Justices differ in seven observed dimensions. Consequently, in each of these dimensions, the composition of the bench may be characterized. In so doing I always follow the same procedure. I first record or generate the respective measure for each justice. For the bench in question, I then calculate the average. Take the example of gender. If two members of a chamber of three have been female, my indicator for the fraction of females on that bench is at 0.66. Note that this procedure is not vulnerable to the identification problems known as ecological inference (King, Rosen, and Tanner 2004). For I do not aim at inferring from the behavior of the bench how seriously female justices take cases. All I investigate is in which way entire benches behave differently if the fraction of females on the bench goes up.

Table 11.3 summarizes in which ways the 18 justices who have been on the court in 2011 differ in observable ways. During the year, three justices have left the court (Bryde, Hohmann-Dennhardt, and Mellinghoff), and two justices have joined the court (Baer and Britz). The third open position has only been filled in 2012. The first column lists the number of months a justice has been on the court in January 2011. For decisions taken later in the year I add the pertinent number of months. The next column reports the age of the justice, calculated as 2011 minus the year of birth. The following two columns are dummies that are 1 if the justice is a woman or a law professor, respectively. Note that more than half of the justices are professors of law. They keep their university positions, with the right to return once they have completed their term at the Constitutional Court.

As mentioned, effectively the political parties have fixed slots at the court. The next column lists the party that has nominated the respective justice. Individual justices have heard differently many cases throughout the year. Those who have been on the court for the entire year have heard between 39 and 87 cases.

The final column reports a measure for the variance of bench composition. For each case, I calculate the fraction of cases the deciding justices have heard in this composition throughout the year. The theoretical maximum of this measure is 1. That would imply that the same justices have been together for every case they have heard in the year. For the purposes of Table 11.3 only, for each justice I average this number over all cases she has heard. The measure shows that most of the time

Table 11.3 *Bench characteristics*

	Tenure	Age	Female	Professor	Party	Cases	Joint
Baer	−2	47	1	1	Green	45	0.827
Britz	−2	43	1	1	SPD	53	0.906
Bryde	119	68	0	1	Green	9	0.566
di Fabio	132	57	0	1	CDU	41	0.746
Eichberger	68	58	0	0	CDU	39	0.770
Gaier	73	57	0	0	SPD	63	0.868
Gerhardt	89	63	0	0	SPD	56	0.782
Hermanns	0	52	1	0	SPD	41	0.743
Hohmann-Dennhardt	143	61	1	0	SPD	11	0.655
Huber	0	52	0	1	CDU	87	0.849
Kirchhof	38	61	0	1	CDU	80	0.822
Landau	62	63	0	0	CDU	54	0.759
Lübbe-Wolff	104	58	1	1	SPD	87	0.849
Masing	32	52	0	1	SPD	38	0.774
Mellinghoff	119	57	0	0	CDU	78	0.855
Paulus	9	43	0	1	FDP	63	0.868
Schluckebier	50	62	0	0	CDU	51	0.797
Voßkuhle	31	48	0	1	SPD	44	0.749

Notes: tenure: number of months a justice has been on the court in January 2011. joint: fraction of cases this justice has decided with the same colleagues (see text for detail).

most justices have decided jointly with colleagues with whom they have taken many other decisions throughout the year. Yet not so rarely they also had to come to terms with colleagues with whom they interacted less frequently. And there was variance between justices in this respect. Some of them faced an unusual bench composition considerably more often than others.

As I have pointed out, I only observe benches (and their composition), not individual justices. Therefore, for the following analysis, for each case I average each characteristic over the justices that have been sitting on the bench. As shown in Table 11.4, some of these characteristics are highly correlated. If the fraction of justices nominated by the Social Democrats or the Greens was high, on average the justices have had shorter tenure on the bench, have decided fewer cases during the year, have been less

Table 11.4 *Correlation of bench characteristics*

	Left	Joint	Tenure	Workload	Professor	Female	Age
Left	1	-0.033	-0.190**	-0.487***	-0.476***	-0.461***	-0.554***
Joint		1	-0.115+	0.386***	0.285***	-0.072	-0.309***
Tenure			1	0.369***	-0.448***	-0.009	0.547***
Workload				1	0.440***	0.227***	-0.024
Professor					1	0.135*	-0.316***
Female						1	0.375***
Age							1

Notes: all decisions, i.e., chamber and senate rulings. left: fraction of justices on the decision body that have been nominated by the SPD or the Greens. joint: mean of fraction of decisions taken jointly by justices on the decision body. tenure: mean number of months justices on the decision body have been on the court. workload: mean of number of cases decided by justices on the decision body. professor: fraction of justices on the decision body who are professors. female: fraction of justices on the decision body who are female. age: mean age of justices on the decision body. *** $p < .001$, ** $p < .01$, * $p < .05$, + $p < .1$

likely to be professors or female,[17] and were younger. Conversely, the judges who have been most frequently together on the same bench have dealt with more cases, were more likely to be professors, and were younger. If the judges on a bench had longer tenure, they dealt with more cases, were older and less likely to be professors. Those who dealt with more cases were more likely to be professors and female. Professors were more likely to be female, and female justices were elder.

If explanatory variables are highly correlated, multivariate regression can be misleading. The fact that one explanatory variable turns out insignificant when controlling for the other, and vice versa, may only imply that too much of the variance in the dependent variable is already explained by the respective other independent variable. I therefore first check whether each bench characteristic in isolation significantly explains how seriously the court takes a case, but thereafter also present multivariate regressions that control for all other bench characteristics.

Bench characteristics are not the only possible determinant of the court taking a case seriously. Arguably, case characteristics matter as well. Since this chapter is interested in the effect of bench characteristics, I only check, however, whether the effect of the respective bench characteristic changes if I control for observable case characteristics, namely: whether the constitutional complaint is directed against a statute or the decision by the highest court with jurisdiction about the respective subject matter, rather than the decision of a lower court or an administrative agency;[18] whether the complainant has been represented by a lawyer, or even by one of the highly visible big law firms or a professor;[19] how many briefs by third parties the court has received (as an indicator for the interest of outsiders in the outcome of the case); which subject matter was at stake.[20]

In these estimations, the dependent variable is constructed. It is the predicted value from exploratory factor analysis: how seriously did the court take the case in question. Bench characteristics are also specific for

---

[17] Readers may wonder why this correlation is negative, although all female justices have been nominated by the Social Democrats or the Greens. Yet most chambers with two justices nominated by these parties were all male.

[18] Both explanatory variables are dummies.

[19] Both explanatory variables are dummies.

[20] Dummy variables for cases that have a business context, concern social security or welfare, family relations, disputes between private parties, concern democratic institutions, disputes between citizens and the state, or tax law. The residual category is cases that fall in none of these case categories.

Table 11.5 Bench characteristics as explanations for cases being taken more seriously

	All complaints univariate		Chamber only univariate		All complaints multivariate		Chamber only multivariate		All complaints SEM		Chamber only SEM	
	Model 1	Model 2	Model 3	Model 4	Model 5	Model 6	Model 7	Model 8	Model 9	Model 10	Model 11	Model 12
left	0.454	-0.016	0.118	0.014	-0.306	0.014	-0.146	-0.066	0.018	0.001	0.125	0.063
	(0.386)	(0.258)	(0.120)	(0.120)	(0.693)	(0.511)	(0.286)	(0.268)	(0.046)	(0.034)	(0.184)	(0.161)
joint	-5.414***	-2.712***	-0.205	-0.155	-06.046***	-3.374***	0.197	-0.125	0.452*	0.278*	-0.174	0.036
	(0.423)	(0.364)	(0.271)	(0.259)	(0.493)	(0.413)	(0.335)	(0.319)	(0.208)	(0.123)	(0.218)	(0.191)
tenure	0.005	0.002	-0.001	0.001	0.005	0.000	0.001	0.001	-0.001	0.000	-0.001	-0.000
	(0.003)	(0.002)	(0.001)	(0.001)	(0.005)	(0.004)	(0.002)	(0.002)	(0.000)	(0.001)	(0.001)	(0.001)
workload	-0.015**	-0.001	-0.004**	-0.002	0.005	0.012+	-0.006+	-0.001	-0.001	-0.001	0.004+	0.000
	(0.005)	(0.004)	(0.0015)	(0.002)	(0.008)	(0.006)	(0.003)	(0.003)	(0.001)	(0.001)	(0.002)	(0.002)
professor	-01.312***	-0.122	-0.173	-0.123	-0.417	-0.260	0.064	-0.033	0.036	0.025	0.028	0.107
	(0.488)	(0.319)	(0.157)	(0.149)	(0.777)	(0.578)	(0.003)	(0.306)	(0.053)	(0.039)	(0.209)	(0.185)
female	-0.251	0.008	-0.118	-0.149+	-0.287	-0.244	-0.077	-0.195+	0.019	0.016	0.057	0.134
	(0.260)	(0.179)	(0.080)	(0.083)	(0.250)	(0.195)	(0.103)	(0.103)	(0.019)	(0.015)	(0.067)	(0.066)
age	0.025	0.008	0.001	0.004	-0.050	-0.016	-0.001	0.005	0.004	0.001	-0.001	-0.005
	(0.016)	(0.011)	(0.005)	(0.005)	(0.030)	(0.023)	(0.013)	(0.012)	(0.003)	(0.002)	(0.008)	(0.007)
case controls	no	yes	no	yes	no	yes	no	yes	no	yes	no	yes
cons	suppressed	suppressed	suppressed	suppressed	7.931**	2.942+	.046	-.404				
					(2.283)	(1.762)	(1.007)	(.971)				
N	231	231	212	212	231	231	212	212	231	231	212	212

Notes: Models 1–8: OLS, dv: predicted value from factor analysis (Table 11.2). Models 9–12: structural equations models that simultaneously generate seriousness index and explain it with the list of bench characteristics (and case characteristics, if applicable), component generating the seriousness score not reported. variable names for bench characteristics as in Table 11.3. models 1–4 are actually a series of regressions that only have a constant (not reported) and a single explanatory variable. models 5–8 report a single regression each that controls for all explanatory variables. Models 2, 4, 6, 8, 10, 12: regression additionally controls for case characteristics (see text for detail). Models 1–2, 5–6, 9–10 include constitutional complaints decided by a senate; Models 3–4, 7–8, 11–12 only cover decisions by chambers. *** $p < .001$, ** $p < .01$, * $p < .05$, + $p < .1$.

individual cases. The analysis therefore twice looks at characteristics of each case: first for constructing the dependent variable, and then for explaining it with bench characteristics. One may be concerned that this procedure puts too much stress on the reliability of the constructed seriousness score. As a safeguard, I therefore also estimate structural equation models that simultaneously generate and explain the dependent variable.[21] To the extent that I exclusively look at decisions taken by chambers, this alternative procedure has an additional advantage. As explained in the previous section, numerous indicators for the court taking the case seriously are by design only available if the decision has been taken by a senate. In the structural model that exclusively looks at decisions taken by chambers, I do not use these indicators for generating the dependent variable.

Table 11.5 shows that, irrespective of in the specification of the regression, there is very little sign of any bias in the court's decision to take a case more seriously. In the international discourse the one characteristic of the bench that has attracted most interest and effort is political orientation. Across all specifications, I never find a significant effect. This also holds for tenure and age. If the justices have been longer on the court, or if they are elder, this does not matter for how seriously the court takes a case. In two specifications that control for case characteristics (Models 4 and 8), I find a weakly significant negative gender effect. But the effect disappears if I simultaneously generate and explain the dependent variable (Models 10 and 12). If I use no other explanatory variable and all constitutional complaints, I find a significant negative effect of professors being on the bench (Model 1). But the effect already disappears if I control for case characteristics (Model 2). In two specifications I find a significant negative effect of workload: if the justices on the specific bench see more cases throughout the year, they take the individual case less seriously (Models 1 and 3). But the effect turns positive in the structural equation models for chambers only (Model 11) and, most importantly, it is always insignificant if I add case controls.

---

[21] Identification is not a reason for concern since the structural model has a single latent variable (the seriousness score). Stata syntax is sem (ernst -> $ser) (ernst <- $bench) if cc, latent(ernst) nocapslatent, where "ernst" is the latent variable. The term in the first bracket generates it, exploiting all the seriousness indicators (captured by vector $ser). The term in the second bracket explains this latent variable with bench characteristics (captured by vector $bench).

The most surprising finding is for the measure of joint experience. If I also consider constitutional complaints on which a senate has decided, I find a highly significant, negative effect, both if I only use this one bench characteristic for explanation (Models 1 and 2) and in multiple regression (Models 5 and 6). This suggests that, the more the bench is homogeneous in terms of having joint decision experience, the less effort they allocate to the individual case. However, if I simultaneously generate the dependent variable and explain it in a structural equation model, the effect reverses (Models 9 and 10). And, most importantly, it disappears whenever I exclusively consider the cases decided by chambers. The seeming effect of joint experience is an artifact. It just captures the fact that, by design, justices have much less joint experience if they decide as a senate. This follows from the fact that the great majority of decisions are taken by chambers, and that chamber composition is fairly stable over time.

11.6   Conclusions

While there is an extensive quantitative literature on the US Supreme Court (see e.g., Benjamin and Vanberg 2016; Black and Spriggs 2013), and growing interest in the quantitative analysis of the jurisprudence of Supreme Courts in countries like Israel (see e.g., Eisenberg, Fisher, and Rosen-Zvi 2011; Weinshall-Margel 2011), Taiwan (see e.g., Eisenberg and Huang 2012), Spain (see e.g., Garoupa, Gili, and Gómez-Pomar 2012), or India (see e.g., Robinson 2013), the jurisprudence of the German Constitutional Court thus far has hardly been touched by quantitative scrutiny. This chapter is an attempt at helping close this gap in the literature.

The German case is interesting for multiple reasons. The court decides more than 85 percent of all cases in chambers of three, rather than in senates of eight justices. Consequently in a single year there is already considerable variation with respect to a multitude of bench characteristics. These characteristics include by which political party the justice has been selected, gender, age, and whether the justice is a law professor. Moreover, several measures for the composition of the respective bench may be calculated: how long have the justices on average been on the court, how many cases have they on average heard throughout the year, and how frequently have they together been on the bench? The German case is also interesting since the court legally must hear all cases that are referred to it.

While the German Constitutional Court may not refuse to decide a case, it has found multiple ways to take a case more or less seriously. For the scientific analyst, this provides an opportunity to observe judicial discretion, and to generate a continuous measure of how seriously the court has taken the individual case. This index is generated using factor analysis. The following indicators contribute to the generation of a measure for taking a case more or less seriously: whether the court has referred the case to a senate, whether the court has formulated the implications of the case for the evolution of constitutional law in the form of black letter rules, whether the court has solicited amicus briefs, whether it has held an oral hearing, whether the court has issued a press release, how many paragraphs the decision is long, and whether the court has applied the proportionality test. Generating predicted values from this statistical model, one sees that there is considerable variance. While the court devotes little effort to most cases, there are quite a few cases it takes more seriously. This not only holds for cases referred to the senate, but encompasses a considerable number of chamber decisions.

Is this good or bad news? The resources of the court are limited. The most severe limit is the number of justices. The statute defines that the court is composed of two senates with eight justices each. If the court devotes most energy to the cases that deserve most attention, this is normatively desirable. But the court's decision to take a case seriously might also be determined by factors that are normatively less desirable. This decision of the court might be biased. The literature has been most concerned about bias originating in bench characteristics. For the German constitutional court, multiple bench characteristics are observed. Yet I find virtually no sign of any of these characteristics influencing the courts decision how seriously to take a case.

In terms of statistical techniques, my analysis is limited. I can only use data from cases the court itself has decided to make public on its website. These cases are only a small fraction of the total of cases decided in my year of observation. I cannot exclude that the decision how much effort to devote to the remaining cases has been biased. Moreover I only observe bench characteristics. They are not randomly assigned. I can therefore not exclude that other characteristics of the bench that I cannot observe do actually have an effect. Finally frequentist statistics are problematic in the first place. Arguably the decision how much energy to devote on one case is not independent from the decision to devote energy on other cases. Arguably this also holds across chambers from the same senate (the justices must decide how much energy to reserve for choices taken by the plenum) and also for decisions taken by the respective other senate (the institutional culture of the court is strong, and the court quite openly cares about its reputation with government and the public at large). Essentially I therefore have a single observation. I acknowledge all these limitations. For the purposes of my analysis they are insurmountable. But I do not therefore consider the exercise pointless. Readers should be aware that the evidence is only suggestive. I could at most have found a smoking gun. But I find it remarkable that there is virtually no sign of smoke. My evidence suggests that, when the German constitutional court decides how much energy to devote to a single case, it is not biased by bench characteristics.

References

Ashenfelter, Orley, Theodore Eisenberg, and Stewart J. Schwab. 1995. Politics and the Judiciary: The Influence of Judicial Background on Case Outcomes. *Journal of Legal Studies* 24: 257–81.

Benjamin, Stuart Minor, and Georg Vanberg. 2016. Judicial Retirements and the Staying Power of US Supreme Court Decisions. *Journal of Empirical Legal Studies* 13(1): 5–26.

Black, Ryan C., and James F Spriggs. 2013. The Citation and Depreciation of US Supreme Court Precedent. *Journal of Empirical Legal Studies* 10(2): 325–58.

Boyd, Christina L., Lee Epstein, and Andrew D. Martin. 2010. Untangling the Causal Effects of Sex on Judging. *American Journal of Political Science* 54(2): 389–411.

Braslow, Laura, and Ross E. Cheit. 2011. Judicial Discretion and (Un) equal Access: A Systematic Study of Motions to Reduce Criminal Sentences in Rhode Island Superior Court (1998–2003). *Journal of Empirical Legal Studies* 8(1): 24–47.

Cameron, Charles M., and Jee-Kwang Park. 2009. How Will They Vote? Predicting the Future Behavior of Supreme Court Nominees, 1937–2006. *Journal of Empirical Legal Studies* 6: 485–511.

Carroll, Royce, and Lydia Tiede. 2011. Judicial Behavior on the Chilean Constitutional Tribunal. *Journal of Empirical Legal Studies* 8: 856–77.

Choi, Stephen J., G. Mitu Gulati, Mirya Holman, and Eric A. Posner. 2011. Judging Women. *Journal of Empirical Legal Studies* 8: 504–32.

Clermont, Kevin M., and Theodore Eisenberg. 2007. Xenophilia or Xenophobia in US Courts? Before and After 9/11. *Journal of Empirical Legal Studies* 4(2): 441–64.

Eisenberg, Theodore. 1974. Congressional Authority to Restrict Lower Federal Court Jurisdiction. *Yale Law Journal* 83: 498–533.

Eisenberg, Theodore, and Geoffrey P. Miller. 2009. Reversal, Dissent, and Variability in State Supreme Courts: The Centrality of Jurisdictional Source. *Boston University Law Review* 89: 1451–504.

Eisenberg, Theodore, and Kuo-Chang Huang. 2012. The Effect of Rules Shifting Supreme Court Jurisdiction from Mandatory to Discretionary: An Empirical Lesson from Taiwan. *International Review of Law and Economics* 32(1): 3–18.

Eisenberg, Theodore, Talia Fisher, and Issi Rosen-Zvi. 2011. Does the Judge Matter? Exploiting Random Assignment on a Court of Last Resort to Assess Judge and Case Selection Effects. *Journal of Empirical Legal Studies* 9: 246–90.

Engst, Benjamin G, Thomas Gschwend, Nils Schaks, Sebastian Sternberg, and Caroline Wittig. 2017. Zum Einfluss der Parteinähe auf das Abstimmungsverhalten der Bundesverfassungsrichter–eine quantitative Untersuchung. *JuristenZeitung* 72(17): 816–26.

Epstein, Lee, Jack Knight, and Andrew D. Martin. 2003. The Norm of Judicial Experience and Its Consequences for Career Diversity on the U.S. Supreme Court. *California Law Review* 91: 903–66.

Freeborn, Beth A., and Monica E. Hartmann. 2010. Judicial Discretion and Sentencing Behavior: Did the Feeney Amendment Rein in District Judges? *Journal of Empirical Legal Studies* 7(2): 355–78.

Garoupa, Nuno, Marian Gili, and Fernando Gómez-Pomar. 2012. Political Influence and Career Judges: An Empirical Analysis of Administrative Review by the Spanish Supreme Court. *Journal of Empirical Legal Studies* 9(4): 795–826.

Hall, Melinda Gann. 1992. Electoral Politics and Strategic Voting in State Supreme Courts. *Journal of Politics* 54: 427–46.

Harvey, Anna, and Barry Friedman. 2009. Ducking Trouble: Congressionally Induced Selection Bias in the Supreme Court's Agenda. *Journal of Politics* 71(2): 574–92.

Huber, Gregory A., and Sanford C. Gordon. 2004. Accountability and Coercion: Is Justice Blind When It Runs for Office? *American Journal of Political Science* 48: 247–63.

Keele, Denise M., Robert W. Malmsheimer, Donald W. Floyd, and Lianjun Zhang. 2009: An Analysis of Ideological Effects in Published versus Unpublished Judicial Opinions. *Journal of Empirical Legal Studies* 6(1): 213–39.

King, Gary, Ori Rosen, and Martin A. Tanner. 2004. *Ecological Inference: New Methodological Strategies*. New York: Cambridge University Press.

Robinson, Nick. 2013. A Quantitative Analysis of the Indian Supreme Court's Workload. *Journal of Empirical Legal Studies* 10(3): 570–601.

Schubert, Glendon. 1965. *The Judicial Mind: The Attitudes and Ideologies of Supreme Court Justices 1946–1963*. Evanston: Northwestern University Press.

Segal, Jeffrey A., and Harold J. Spaeth. 1993. *The Supreme Court and the Attitu-dinal Model.* New York: Cambridge University Press.

  2002. *The Supreme Court and the Attitudinal Model Revisited.* New York: Cambridge University Press.

Shepherd, Joanna M. 2009. The Influence of Retention Politics on Judges' Voting. *Journal of Legal Studies* 38: 169–206.

Solberg, Rorie Spill, and Stefanie A. Lindquist. 2006. Activism, Ideology, and Federalism: Judicial Behavior in Constitutional Challenges before the Rehnquist Court, 1986–2000. *Journal of Empirical Legal Studies* 3: 237–61.

Sunstein, Cass R., David Schkade, and Lisa Michelle Ellman. 2004. Ideological Voting on Federal Courts of Appeals: A Preliminary Investigation. *Virginia Law Review* 90: 301–54.

Thompson, David C., and Melanie F. Wachtell. 2008. An Empirical Analysis of Supreme Court Certiorari Petition Procedures: The Call for Response and the Call for the Views of the Solicitor General. *George Mason Law Review* 16: 237–302.

Vanberg, Georg. 2004. *The Politics of Constitutional Review in Germany.* New York: Cambridge University Press.

Weinshall-Margel, Keren. 2011. Attitudinal and Neo-Institutional Models of Supreme Court Decision Making: An Empirical and Comparative Perspec-tive from Israel. *Journal of Empirical Legal Studies* 8: 556–86.

INDEX

Act on Specified Commercial
    Transactions, Japan (ASCT),
    144–46
adverse selection, insurance
    antidiscrimination law, U.S.,
    and, 229–30
agreed judgments, ODR and,
    57
allocative efficiency, property law,
    Taiwan, and, 163–64
America Invents Act, 20, 27
amicus briefs, German Constitutional
    Court and, 269
anticommons, 164–65
appeals. *See also* Federal Court of
    Appeals, Canada;
    prevailing-party appeals, U.S.
    career judge system, Japan, and,
        135–37
    civil, 179–201
    civil litigation, Taiwan, and,
        77–79, 86–94, 97–100, 104–8
    civil litigation, U.S., and,
        86–94, 97–99
    error correction and,
        180–81
    Germany and, 265–66
    motivations for, 191
Art Unit in Patent Office, 13
ASCT. *See* Act on Specified
    Commercial Transactions,
    Japan
assessments, unjust enrichment and,
    170–71
attorney fees, civil litigation, Taiwan,
    and, 76
attorneys, Japan, 134

Berkson v. Gogo, 218
black letter rules (*ratio decidendi*),
    German Constitutional Court
    and, 269–70
board resolutions for equity offerings,
    148–52
Brown v. Board of Education, 112
browsewraps, 207, 214–17
    citations and, 208–10
    Nguyen v. Barnes Noble and, 215–17
    out-of-state citations and, 215–17
    Specht v. Netscape and, 214–17
building encroachment
    Japan and, 167
    Netherlands and, 168
    Pile v. Pedrick and, 167
    Taiwan and, 168–70
    U.S. and, 167–68

Canada. *See also* Federal Court of Appeals,
    Canada; Tax Court of Canada
    lower courts in, 110–13
    Wolf v. Canada in, 115
career judge system, Japan, 132–42
    appeals and, 135–37
    attorneys separate from, 134
    case management efficiency and,
        135–42, 156–58
career judges, ex ante inefficiency and,
    161–62
case duration, 49
    civil litigation, Taiwan, and, 88–94,
        96–100
    civil litigation, U.S., and, 88–94, 96–100
    jury trials and, 93–94
    litigant welfare and, 58–60
    ODR and, 33, 49–62, 64, 70

287

sanctions. *See* damages
selection of disputes. *See* dispute
 selection
self-determination, ODR and, 67
settlements, 179
 civil litigation, Taiwan, and, 77–81,
 95, 99, 102–4
 civil litigation, U.S., and, 95, 99, 190
 debt collection and, 95
 patent infringement and, 10
 small claims cases and, 37
shrinkwraps (PNTLs), 207, 211–14
 citations and, 208–10
 Hill v. Gateway and, 211–14
 Klocek v. Gateway, Inc. and, 211–12
 out-of-circuit citations and, 214
 out-of-state citations and, 212–14
 ProCD v. Zeidenberg and, 211–14
small claims cases, 33–70. *See also*
 Franklin County Municipal
 Court Small Claims Division
 damages awarded in, 36
 enforcement of, 36
 factfinder and, 49
 jury trials and, 36
 litigation costs and, 34–69
 ODR and, 33–34, 40, 42–44, 46–47,
 67, 69
 settlements and, 37
small claims procedures, civil litigation,
 Taiwan, and, 77, 104
social science training of judges
 ex ante inefficiency and, 161
 Germany and, 161
 Japan and, 161
 Taiwan and, 161
 U.S. and, 161
social waste, ex post inefficiency and, 160
Sotomayor, Sonia, 215
Specht v. Netscape, 214–17
SPEs. *See* Supervisory Patent Examiners
standing, prevailing-party appeals, U.S.,
 and, 182, 186–89
state courts, U.S.
 Civil Justice Survey of State Courts
 and, 183–85
 prevailing-party appeals in,
 183–201

substantive efficiency, 1–2, 163–64
 procedural efficiency versus, 163
summary judgments
 civil litigation, Taiwan, and, 77–78,
 80–86, 97, 99, 109
 civil litigation, U.S., and, 76, 82–86,
 97–99
summary procedures, civil litigation,
 Taiwan, and, 77, 103–4
Supervisory Patent Examiners (SPEs),
 in Patent Office, 13–14. *See also*
 patent examination
Supreme Court, Japan, 135, 157
 consumer law and, 141–43
 corporate law and, 146–53, 155
 NOVA case and, 144–46
suspect classes, insurance
 antidiscrimination law, U.S.,
 and, 224

Taiwan, 76. *See also* civil litigation,
 Taiwan; judges, Taiwan;
 property law, Taiwan
Taiwan Civil Code, 162
Taiwan Supreme Court, 89–93
Tax Court of Canada, 3
 employees versus independent
 contractors in, 110–30
 intention of parties considered by,
 110–30
 judicial fact discretion in, 128–29
 predicting outcomes of,
 123–28, 130
 Royal Winnipeg impact on, 110–12,
 114–33
 Wiebe Door impact on, 113–14,
 116–20
Tecmo/Koei case, 155–56
Terms of Service. *See* browsewraps
torts damages, Japan and, 163
tournament winners, 205–6, 210, 212,
 220
traffic fatalities, 224–27, 231–32
 costs of, 226
 credit score discrimination and,
 224–26, 232–39
trespass, Taiwan, 170–75
 compensation for, 170–74

Lightning Source UK Ltd.
Milton Keynes UK
UKHW020229250223
417635UK00023B/257